Rohan Lloyd is a historian who specialises in North Queensland and Australian environmental history. He has published histories on the Great Barrier Reef, North Queensland and Australian environmentalism. Rohan works as an English teacher at Ignatius Park College in Townsville and is an adjunct lecturer at James Cook University. This is his first book.

SAVING
the
REEF

Rohan Lloyd

UQP

First published 2022 by University of Queensland Press
PO Box 6042, St Lucia, Queensland 4067 Australia

University of Queensland Press (UQP) acknowledges the Traditional Owners and
their custodianship of the lands on which UQP operates. We pay our respects to their
Ancestors and their descendants, who continue cultural and spiritual connections to
Country. We recognise their valuable contributions to Australian and global society.

uqp.com.au
reception@uqp.com.au

Cover design by Christabella Designs
Cover illustrations: Sea turtle: Elnara.G/Shutterstock; Coral: Anastasia Lembrik/
Shutterstock
Author photograph by Brook Elaine Photography
Map of the Great Barrier Reef by MAPgraphics
Typeset in 12/16 pt Adobe Garamond Pro by Post Pre-press Group, Brisbane
Printed in Australia by McPherson's Printing Group

 Queensland University of Queensland Press is supported by the
Government Queensland Government through Arts Queensland.

 Australia University of Queensland Press is assisted by the
Council Australian Government through the Australia
for the Arts Council, its arts funding and advisory body.

A catalogue record for this book is available from the National Library of Australia.

ISBN 978 0 7022 6575 4 (pbk)
ISBN 978 0 7022 6720 8 (epdf)
ISBN 978 0 7022 6721 5 (epub)

University of Queensland Press uses papers that are natural, renewable and recyclable
products made from wood grown in well-managed forests and other controlled sources.
The logging and manufacturing processes conform to the environmental regulations of
the country of origin.

For all my teachers, beginning with Mum and Dad

Contents

Author's Note   ix
Introduction   xi
Map of the Great Barrier Reef   xxii
List of Abbreviations   xxiii

1: European Arrival and Settlement   1
2: Exploitation and Enjoyment   17
Knowledge   42
3: Emerging Concern   49
4: Towards Saving the Reef   65
Catchment   80
5: The Save the Reef Campaign: Ellison Reef   86
6: We Must Appear to Be Well Informed   93
7: The Save the Reef Campaign: Oil Drilling   109
Seeing   123
8: The Black Ban   131
9: Towards a Reef Commission   148
Science   161
10: Royal Commission   169
11: The Great Barrier Reef Marine Park Authority   190
Change   200

Epilogue   208
Acknowledgements   213
Notes   216
Index   243

Author's Note

This book was written on unceded Wulgurukaba Country, where I live. I also travel daily across Bindal Country. Throughout this book I have sought to recognise the Indigenous names of the Reef's islands. Where I have been able to locate the Indigenous name, I have put this first followed by the settler name in parentheses. The exception to this is in cases where the settler names for islands have been used in quotations from source material. In these instances, I have not added the Indigenous name.

This book includes references in the form of notes. For a more comprehensive bibliography of additional material, I refer readers to my PhD thesis, *Fathoming the Reef: A History of European Perspectives on the Great Barrier Reef from Cook to GBRMPA* (James Cook University, 2016).

Aboriginal and Torres Strait Islander readers are respectfully cautioned that this publication contains mentions of people who have passed away.

Introduction

I began thinking about the Great Barrier Reef's place within Australia's national consciousness when I was a student living in Townsville. I was not an aspiring marine scientist but a historian with an interest in my region's history, particularly in how the landscape and seascape had shaped the narrative of modern Australia. Back then, around 2013, issues that have come to shape Australia's and Queensland's environmental politics – Adani, coal and port expansion – were the skirmishes within a broader 'climate war'. I remember walking past students distributing literature on port expansion, coalmining and the threats to the Reef and wondering if this kind of activism had happened before.

Had people who lived alongside the Reef ever been motivated to protect it? Was it only recently that the Australian community had shown such interest in the Reef's protection? I began to wonder what the earliest settlers thought about the Great Barrier Reef, or if they thought about it at all. So I started researching the Reef's history – looking into the journals of explorers, settlers and travellers, scrutinising historical newspapers, reading tourist guides and brochures, and reaching into the government archives – to understand how the Reef had been encountered after European settlers arrived.

The Great Barrier Reef is beautiful, interesting, enormous – and controversial. For centuries, maritime explorers and scientists have come from across the globe to better understand its origins, ecology and health. Similarly, travellers and pleasure seekers, drawn by lyrical descriptions and vivid imagery, have arrived from all over to experience its grandeur. The Reef has always stood as a wonder: a collage of corals and islands. A raging, humming, churning fairyland where life exists on a precipice between art and violence. Its densely wooded islands and scattered reefs, standing like parapets against the raging Pacific and hosting a diversity of life, fostered admiration from explorers and the early settlers. The goal of many has been to ensure the protection of these wonders, but also to locate some economic use. In the nineteenth and early twentieth centuries, at least according to scientists, politicians and nature writers of the time, too little was being done with the Reef's possible products – fish, lime, shell – for exploitation. From settlement through to the post-war period, governments, scientists and naturalists were actively searching for ways to develop the Reef for economic pursuits as a way of demonstrating the 'usefulness' and importance of the Reef. In the post-war period, technology allowed for both the expansion of Reef tourism as well as the possibility of developing the Reef's geological resources, and the competing demands on the Reef became more acute as the stakes and consequences grew.

Of course, the Reef, as it exists today, emerged several millennia after the arrival of humans to the landmass that became Australia. The Reef is traditional Country for more than seventy Aboriginal and Torres Strait Islander traditional owner groups. Their ancestors witnessed the rise of water following the last glacial period, which submerged their Country and formed the islands and cays that now decorate Queensland's east coast. They witnessed the origins of the Reef, and formed stories, songs and dances to carry the significance of that moment into the future. All interactions between the earliest explorers and the First Australians reminded the former that the Reef was already a utilised and valued environment. After settlement, Aboriginal and Torres Strait Islander peoples often guided settlers to sources worthy of commercial pursuit, or were exploited as labourers in Reef industries. But Indigenous people's interactions with the Reef also inspired some settlers to develop and promote a more sympathetic relationship with it.

As I researched the Reef's history, one story came to dominate – one that historian Iain McCalman has described as the greatest Reef story: the 'Save the Reef' campaign. In 1967, a Cairns cane grower lodged an application to mine a coral reef east of Innisfail for limestone. Immediately, objections to the application were raised by conservationists, who were worried that mining one reef would open the door to the entire Great Barrier Reef being developed for mining. While this battle raged in North Queensland, the Queensland government revealed that most of the Reef had already been carved into petroleum reserves, and permits for oil exploration had been approved by both the Queensland and Commonwealth governments. What had begun as a local mining issue had morphed into a much broader concern. Between 1967 and 1975, one of the most protracted environmental campaigns in Australia took place. It involved a popular campaign, issues of constitutional law, a trade union black ban, a royal commission, the establishment of the Great Barrier Reef Marine Park Authority (GBRMPA), and ultimately the Reef's protection from oil and mineral exploitation.

The Save the Reef campaign is the best known story of the Reef's history. That campaign remains a source of hope and heritage for modern Reef conservationists, and has been remembered as a 'David versus Goliath' story: a classic narrative of a small, ragtag group of activists fighting governments and the oil industry for the good of the Reef, and winning. But the more I read about this period, the more I came to see this characterisation of the campaign as a powerful example of how our understanding of past events is so rooted in public memory.

In the first lines of her book about the fight to protect the Great Barrier Reef, *The Coral Battleground*, poet and conservationist Judith Wright avowed:

> I have chosen to tell the story of the Great Barrier Reef from the point of view of those actually involved in the battle to prevent the Reef from oil-drilling and limestone mining. Obviously, I have not had access to a number of sources which could have presented the story from the other side.[1]

I designed to fill these gaps. I wanted to look at the 'other side' of the campaign. I wanted to understand how the Queensland and Commonwealth governments could reach the decision to drill the Reef for oil, and how the rest of the country reacted to the possibility of the Reef's mineral and petroleum exploitation. I also wanted to test the accuracy of Wright's accounts, and, like any good historian, to see if this historical event had a tail.

In 2008, the celebrated coral reef scientist Charlie Veron declared at the beginning of *A Reef in Time: The Great Barrier Reef from Beginning to End* that had he written his book in the 1970s, he would only have devoted one or two pages to conservation issues, and would have ended it with this 'heartwarming bromide: "And now we can rest assured that future generations will treasure this great wilderness area for all time."'[2] The Reef, he claimed, 'seemed more than big enough to look after itself, and what few issues there were seemed to fall easily within the scope of the newly constituted marine park authority'. But for Veron, and for many others, the notion of protecting the Reef became omnipresent. 'Saving the Reef' frames every discussion.

Historians Drew Hutton and Libby Connors have asserted that environmentalism, despite memorialising past campaigns, lacks 'a sense of its own history' and suffers from 'historical amnesia'.[3] The Save the Reef campaign has come to represent the beginning of Reef conservationism: it introduced a radically new way of seeing the Reef, distinct from the period of its mass exploitation. It is understandable why this is the case. The earliest forms of Reef conservationism, or protection, were local and species-specific. People understood and talked about the Reef as a single entity, but there was no broad vision, imagining or desire for a bureaucratic mechanism that could protect the entire system. Nonetheless, decades before the prospect of oil drilling on the Reef was being considered, its birds, turtles, shells, fish and lime deposits came under the protection of a variety of legislation and government departments. Islands themselves became local reserves and sanctuaries, and local Reef communities began to assert their valuing of the Reef by denying its destruction for the sake of commercial gain.

Coral reef science's emergence as a discipline in the second half of the twentieth century only adds to the idea of Reef protection as a modern phenomenon. While coral reef science is today one of the most significant forms of marine science within Australia, prior to the 1960s it was comparatively devoid of institutional and government support. Researching the Great Barrier Reef was heavily restricted by technology and the logistical barriers of undertaking longitudinal studies on isolated islands in the northern tropics. It was not until the advent of scuba diving and a global concern for oceans in the 1960s that coral reef science in Australia gained serious momentum. Further, the Save the Reef campaign was the first time marine scientists became public figures within the Reef's protection and management. Their ideas and research not only revealed unknown elements of the Reef's nature, but also showed how little was known about it. Their greatest contribution within the campaign was not asserting that drilling the Reef for oil could not be done effectively, but revealing that what might happen to the Reef if it were allowed was totally unknown. Doubt and uncertainty were tangible forces within the scientific community, among conservationists and inside governments.

One consequence of the emergence of Reef activism alongside modern coral reef science has been the increased politicisation of Reef science and the perception of reef scientists as acting in concert with conservationists. An overwhelming amount of literature has revealed the increasingly clear impacts of direct and indirect human disturbances on the Reef system. Reef scientists themselves have been able to leverage public fascination, and the desire of governments to at least appear to be protecting the Reef, to secure significant amounts of funding for further coral reef research. Reef scientists have therefore often been accused by climate change deniers of taking part in a broader 'climate conspiracy'. Some scientists have publicly criticised Reef science – and particularly research attached to significant public funds and expectations – for at best contributing to a climate change zeitgeist and at worst deliberately misleading the academy. Of course, there are scientists who are explicitly activist in the way they engage with the public. Yet most of the Reef science community refrain from engaging in the politics of Reef science. Their practice, however, is increasingly a political one, and the development of Reef science, and its politics, is a major theme of this book.

Central to this theme is what I term 'a language of the Reef'. Historically, the Reef existed as a distant, imagined reality for most Australians, such that the language of the Reef was often abstract and prospective. Descriptions of the Reef's economic importance, scientific value and beauty were used to arouse action. Few publications about the Reef failed to mention its astounding aesthetics, the intrigue surrounding its many life forms and formations, and its likely but latent potential as a site for economic development. These ambitious and entangled, but nonetheless distinctive, threads of discourse sought to clarify and establish the value of the Reef. For those who had not visited the Reef, these words created a sense of what it looked like, how it functioned and how it could be used. Even after the 1890s, when photographs of the Reef began to be published, it was language – the framing of the Reef's economic, scientific and aesthetic contingencies – that shaped the way people interacted with and imagined it. To speak of the Reef prior to the Save the Reef campaign required an ability to explain its value in those terms. And it was an almost unified chorus.

Clear links can be established between the history of this language and twenty-first-century Reef politics. What is most novel about present-day discussions of the Reef is the way in which governments, scientists, environmentalists and industry figures use the long-established 'Reef language' in distinct ways to assuage or aggravate our fears, stoke the flames of our imaginations, and mobilise us towards their political ends. For example, the economic value and function of the Reef, often listed in dollars contributed by the tourism industry, can underpin the signalling of the Reef's good health and contribution to the Queensland economy, a rationale for increased scientific research funding, or an indicator of what could be lost if too little action on climate change is taken. Accord has most often been found, at least in the past, in the expression of the Reef's value in economic, scientific and aesthetic terms and the need to 'save' the Reef. Divisions exist today about the degree to which it requires saving, if it does at all.

In recent years, the damage caused by increased ocean temperatures and acidification has meant that the Reef is synonymous with climate change. In 2014, the president of the United States of America, Barack Obama, urged Australians to do more to protect the Reef so he could visit with his daughters, and they with their children, and so on. Three years later, when images of bleached reefs in the northern waters off Queensland's Cape York were published, the scientists involved were just as likely to brief members of the United Nations and the British royal family as Australia's governments.

The Great Barrier Reef has come to symbolise the natural heritage at stake in an international effort to address climate change. This internationalisation has consequences for how the Reef exists within the identity and imaginations of Australians. Knowing the Reef in the twenty-first century is an entanglement of scientific and political perspectives fed by cultural and government institutions. While in the past Australians wrestled with what the Reef is, today they are struggling to reconcile what it will be.

This book tells two big stories about the Reef. First, it gives voice to the Reef's history prior to the 1960s, when governments and the public raised their concerns and acted to prevent its destruction. Understanding that the Reef has held a central place in the identity of settler Australians, particularly in Queensland, is an important element often forgotten in present-day debates about Reef use and management. Fascination with the Reef did not just emerge in the post-war period or with the advent of scuba technology. Rather, what I term 'Reef environmentalism' built on decades of shifting and dynamic attitudes towards the Reef, dating all the way back to Cook's *Endeavour* voyage.

Viewed this way, the Save the Reef campaign does not exist as an aberration within the Reef's history. Rather, it is a climax in which Australians were forced to deliberate on how various uses and valuations of the Reef could co-exist; it was a coming-to-terms with how Australians could manage the Reef in a modern world. This book explains how the nation reconciled this dilemma through the Save the Reef campaign, and explores how the campaign led to the establishment of the Great Barrier Reef Marine Park Authority (GBRMPA), as well as to a dramatic shift in the paradigm of Reef science and politics.

The second story follows, in five interweaving essays, the years since the campaign ended to examine the more potent elements of modern Reef politics. The present crisis has its own set of complexities, but central to this is understanding destroyers of the Reef: both human-caused and naturally occurring. From 1975 to the present day, the Reef has been zoned for specific user groups and agendas. Reef scientists pursue their investigations in marine research stations from Jiigurru (Lizard Island) to One Tree Island, and on research vessels that ply the Reef's roughly 2300-kilometre length. Notably, the GBRMPA, and the steady stream of scientific inquiry into the Reef that followed its implementation, has given legitimacy to a perpetual debate about the state of the Reef and whether it needs saving.

The title of this book plays on this debate. It questions the assumed novelty of this idea by tracing the history of 'saving' the Reef but also addresses a question thrown up by anthropogenic climate change: can the Reef be saved in a warming world? The original Save the Reef campaign succeeded in creating the GBRMPA and achieved World Heritage Listing for the Reef, but these events preceded the dire discoveries associated with climate change, particularly coral bleaching.

Although it is predominantly concerned with settler perceptions of the Reef, this book does not ignore the role of Aboriginal and Torres Strait Islander peoples within the Reef's story. But the history of Indigenous perspectives of the Reef, while intersecting at times with this narrative, has its own distinct trajectory. Consequently, the primary concern of this book is to consider how settler Australians, who as a group form a major ecological agent in Australia's recent environmental history, have come to be saving the Reef.

In the 1960s and 1970s, the Reef's future hung in the balance; the same is true of our present moment. With hindsight, establishing the GBRMPA seems an obvious and necessary step towards the Reef's protection. Today, however, the GBRMPA's role in managing the Reef into the future is less clear. Coral reefs are particularly vulnerable to a 1.5 degree Celsius increase, and Reef scientists can only proclaim the need to reach zero emissions by 2050. Marine park managers can neither halt climate change nor influence Australia's energy consumption or fossil-fuel policy. Instead, marine scientists are forced – by both climatic realities and funding priorities within the sciences – to research scalable and cost-effective interventions to assist Reef sites that hold economic, ecological and social value to adapt and respond to climate change.

Climate change – the environmental shifts and associated politics – has increased the public's unease about the Reef's use and future. If the Reef's corals are the climate's canaries, then its politics are equally warning. The diversity of stakeholders and values attached to the Reef demands a breadth of understanding that extends beyond its ecology. Saving the Reef requires us to confront the breadth and depth of our relationship with this treasured environment to locate a contemporary consensus on how to live with it into the future. To do this, we need to understand the Reef's intertwining human story.

Map of the Great Barrier Reef

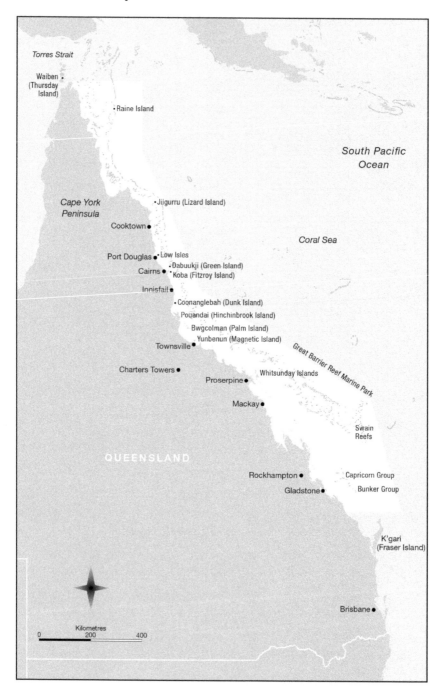

Torres Strait

Waiben (Thursday Island)

• Raine Island

South Pacific Ocean

Cape York Peninsula

• Jiigurru (Lizard Island)

Cooktown •

Coral Sea

Port Douglas • Low Isles
• Dabuukji (Green Island)
Cairns • Koba (Fitzroy Island)

Innisfail •

• Coonanglebah (Dunk Island)
Pouandai (Hinchinbrook Island)
Bwgcolman (Palm Island)
Yunbenun (Magnetic Island)
Townsville •

Great Barrier Reef Marine Park

Charters Towers •
Proserpine •   Whitsunday Islands

Mackay •

Swain Reefs

QUEENSLAND

Rockhampton •   Capricorn Group
Gladstone •   Bunker Group

K'gari (Fraser Island)

Brisbane •

Kilometres
0   200   400

List of Abbreviations

AAS	Australian Academy of Science
ACF	Australian Conservation Foundation
AIMS	Australian Institute of Marine Science
ALP	Australian Labor Party
AMPTO	Association of Marine Park Tourism Operators
ANTA	Australian National Travel Association
APEA	Australian Petroleum Exploration Association
ATC	Australian Tourist Commission
GBRC	Great Barrier Reef Committee
GBRF	Great Barrier Reef Foundation
GBRMPA	Great Barrier Reef Marine Park Authority
GBRRAC	Great Barrier Reef Resources Advisory Committee
JCU	James Cook University
NOAA	National Oceanic and Atmospheric Administration
NPAQ	National Parks Association of Queensland
QGITB	Queensland Government Intelligence and Tourist Bureau
QGTB	Queensland Government Tourist Bureau
QLS	Queensland Littoral Society
QTDB	Queensland Tourist Development Board
RAOU	Royal Australian Ornithological Union
RRAP	Reef Restoration and Adaptation Program
STRC	Save the Reef Committee
UNESCO	United Nations Educational, Scientific and Cultural Organization
UQ	The University of Queensland
WPSQ	Wildlife Preservation Society of Queensland

1

European Arrival and Settlement

The Reef has always formed an important part of Australia's natural identity. From the moment Cook smashed the *Endeavour* upon its eponymously named reef in North Queensland, settler Australia began interrogating the role and value of the long chain of reefs and islands. For them, the Reef held immense value in practical, economic and more romantic forms. The Reef offered up fish, whales and sharks, but also pearl shells, bêche-de-mer and trochus. Islands provided land for plantations. Corals could be collected and sold as ornaments or ground up for building materials. And the Reef, once charted, provided a safe seaway for mercantile and passenger vessels cruising north to the markets of South-East Asia and beyond.

The potential and actual economic function of the Reef was an important part of how it was perceived, and sat comfortably alongside similarly positive evocations of the Reef's natural grandeur. Explorers, scientists, travellers, politicians and settlers were all struck by the Reef's distinct beauty and curiosity. They sought to understand its origins and its animal inhabitants, and to indulge in its diverse scenery and tranquillity.

This entangled, and seemingly contradictory, valuing of the Reef was fostered over a century and a half of engagement. Those who drew attention to the apparently endless economic possibilities of the Reef simultaneously sentimentalised its environmental splendour. Within this view, for instance, some islands could be sites of pastoral and fishery development, while others, perhaps less suitable for development, could be set aside for tourism as nature reserves. The Reef, therefore, existed both as a wonderful showcase of Australian nature and as a source of wealth that should carefully, and under scientific guidance, be exploited.

Maritime explorers and early settlers feared the Reef – or at least that is the existing trope. Shipwrecks were common along Australia's north-eastern coastline. Within the Reef, that is to say between the Great Barrier Reef's outer wall and the mainland, there were the unmarked reefs and rocks that seemed to shoot up at ships suddenly from the water. Outside the Reef, in the deep Pacific, there were fewer obstacles, but ships seeking to enter the Torres Strait had to contend with making a westerly course without any knowledge of when it was safe to do so. In both settings, ships were also exposed to strong winds, storms and cyclones. The Reef was littered with obstacles, while on the mainland, as the literature of the day described it, hostile 'Aborigines' awaited those who managed not to drown. Within this narrative, explorers are brave and cunning navigators exercising guile and wit to 'tame' the Reef and render it safe. Their achievements, apart from forming part of the grand narrative of Australia's exploration, accompanied sensationalised accounts of shipwrecks on the Reef in the nineteenth century: of the *Endeavour*, the *Charles Eaton*, the *Stirling Castle* and others. The stories of these wrecks, widely publicised at the time, played into popular fears of a 'savage' north. Shipwrecks on the Reef were traumatic – a cause of death and financial loss – but they were experienced frequently enough to become a routine reality of Reef voyages in the early nineteenth century. They were not universally reported with hysteria, and many stories of shipwrecks reported in the media assumed a sense of banality.[1]

While James Cook's crash looms large in understandings of the Reef as a hazardous environment, his subsequent escape from and re-entry into the Reef offered an important alternative conception of the Reef: that of a tranquil and secure sea route. For settler Australians, this was the first example of the Reef being positioned as a valued resource for human development.

On 13 August 1770, after locating a channel through the Reef from atop the peak of Jiigurru (Lizard Island), Cook threaded the *Endeavour* out of the Reef and into the unfathomable Pacific Ocean. In the account edited by John Hawkesworth and published for the public following the *Endeavour*'s voyage, Cook experienced great relief once he made it beyond the Reef's outer wall, and reflected on the joy of his crew once they were past the danger: 'in open sea, with deep water [they] enjoyed a flow of spirits'.[2]

The surf of the Pacific, however, threatened to drive the ship back towards the outer coral wall. Unable to find secure anchorage, Cook elected to re-enter the Reef. After several anxious hours, the *Endeavour* threaded back through the Reef at Providential Channel (60 kilometres east of Lockhart River). With the *Endeavour* anchored within the Reef, Cook reflected: 'And now, such is the vicissitude of life, we thought ourselves happy in having regained a situation, which but two days before it was the utmost object of our hope to quit.' Cook continued to sail northwards within the Reef, keeping 'the main land on board [...] whatever the consequence might be'.[3]

These two competing conceptions of the Reef, one as frustrating and the other of it as a bastion, motivated the subsequent decades of exploration. Vessels intending to use the Torres Strait passage either sailed along the coastline within the Reef and entered the strait by rounding Cape York (as Cook had done), or attempted to enter it north of the cape after sailing along the Reef's outer edge. Both routes, with Reef charting in its infancy, were dangerous. Yet the Reef's inner route, despite its hazards, was perceived to be the safer and preferred sea lane.

Indeed, Matthew Flinders, following his own shipwreck

experience on Wreck Reef in the Coral Sea, made clear that, given a choice, he would thread the inner route. The 'extensive Barrier Reefs', he wrote, were 'mostly dry at low water' with high breakers on the outside, but inside it provided 'smooth and secure navigation'.[4] For Flinders, the Reef was only an obstacle for those wishing to enter the Torres Strait from the Coral Sea. His naming of the Great Barrier Reef – to replace Cook's more fearful label of 'labyrinth' – highlighted the importance of the sea lane for emerging trade interests – and, perhaps, for a future northern settlement of Australia's east coast.

After Cook and Flinders had provided a skeleton chart of the Reef, maritime explorers sought to fill in the gaps. Phillip Parker King made three voyages through the Reef between 1819 and 1821, and became a strong advocate for the usefulness of the Reef's inner route. In 1834, more than a decade after the completion of his voyages, King was still publicly defending the virtues of the route he had established from Breaksea Spit (a passage north of K'gari [Fraser Island]) to Cape York within the Reef. While King believed the route was safe, he also saw it as a way of extending the reach of the empire.[5] The Reef and the Torres Strait were crucial pathways. Increasingly, the links between the Australian colonies and the markets of South-East Asia and beyond depended on a safe and reliable passage to and through the Strait.

While the inner route was largely favoured, some merchant vessels opted to take the outer route 'to avoid the frequent anchorage necessary in the in-shore passage'.[6] The outer route, however, was endangered by the uncharted Coral Sea reefs and by the difficulties experienced by vessels attempting to enter the Reef on a 'casual' and 'often incorrect' observation of latitude. It was for this reason that the British Admiralty charged Francis Blackwood with taking the *Fly* and establishing a safe passage for those wishing to use the outer route. King had laid a pathway for the inner route; now Blackwood would locate accessible channels through the Reef and 'devise some practical means of marking them'.[7] In 1844, at Raine Island, a 64-foot (19.5-metre) beacon and store, largely composed of locally acquired phosphate sandstone and lime, and painted with red and black stripes, was erected.[8] However, the perception of the Raine Island entrance as a safe, government-sanctioned seaway created a 'ship trap'; shipwrecks on the island's surrounding reefs increased from five between 1840 and 1849 to nineteen between 1850 and 1859.[9]

By 1845, the Torres Strait was being touted as the 'most direct line of communication' between the Australian colonies and the trading stations of Singapore, China and Hong Kong.[10] The speaker of the New South Wales Legislative Council argued that the Barrier Reef, and specifically its inner passage, seemed 'placed by nature to interpose a shelter for steam vessels against the prevailing winds and waves'. Additionally, with the establishment of a penal settlement at Port Curtis in 1847, and the likelihood of further settlement north of Moreton Bay, establishing frequent steam traffic along the northern coast seemed a necessity for colonial expansion.[11]

With this in mind, in 1846 Owen Stanley, captain of the *Rattlesnake*, was charged with the task of making 'the approach to the Strait' via the outer route 'more secure and certain', by providing the choice of an alternative entrance further north than Raine Island.[12] Further to these orders, Francis Beaufort, the Royal Navy's hydrographer, issued the additional task of sounding and charting 'either side of the tracks' of the inner route to allow for continuous sailing at night.[13] Beaufort signalled the importance of improving the safety of the inner route for all those 'vessels who prefer its tranquility and security', and for the eventual introduction of steam traffic.[14]

Three years after the *Rattlesnake* completed its voyages, Henry Denham was commissioned to captain the *Herald* in undertaking an extensive survey of the Coral Sea, including further charting of the outer edge of the Reef. He completed this task, to little fanfare, in 1860.[15] Hardly a place of anxious navigation, the Reef evoked in chart and consciousness a sense of pleasure cruising. In 1864, George Henry Richards, the Admiralty's hydrographer, claimed the inner route of the Reef was 'as easy to navigate as the English Channel'.[16]

Along with demonstrating and advocating for the usefulness of the Reef as a sea route, these navigators were also alive to the economic opportunities that the Reef might offer settlers. Their comments on its climate, resources and scenery coloured their journals, fostering what Iain McCalman called a country of the heart and mind.[17]

Instead of being considered an impediment to settlement, the Reef was viewed as guarding the coastline, particularly the areas south of Cairns, providing sites of safe anchorage and potential harbours. Similarly, the Reef was envisioned as place for future industry. Of the Bunker Group islands and reefs at the southern end of the Reef, King commented: '[T]hey abound with turtle and bêche-de-mer, the latter of which, if not both, will at some future time become of considerable importance to the coasting trade of New South Wales.'[18] Whalers, while their exploits in the Reef are difficult to quantify, were undoubtedly frequenting the inner and outer passages. Whales, as King described, could often be found within the Reef, and the *Fly* passed wrecks of whaling vessels along islands and cays.[19] Both the *Beagle* (1837–1844) and the *Rattlesnake* also noted features of the early sandalwood trade along the Reef. The *Rattlesnake* encountered a cutter around Koba (Fitzroy Island, near Cairns), and John MacGillivray, the *Rattlesnake*'s naturalist, wrote that the vessel had been in search of sandalwood.[20]

While the resources of the Reef and its potential to sustain settlement were of immediate concern to those exploring the region, the beauty of the Reef itself was a source of immense interest too. At times, the reaction to a confrontation with the Reef was one of astonishment. The shoals and rocks, partly concealed along the coast, would, Cook described, 'rise abruptly like a pyramid from the bottom'.[21] Flinders, unable to forget Cook's experiences, initially considered the reefs as dangers, and provided indifferent descriptions of their appearance. Reefs, he wrote, 'were so much alike as to be of no use in distinguishing one reef from another'.[22] Flinders's first walk upon a dry reef, however, somewhere in the vicinity of the Percy Islands, provided a telling moment, with curiosity and astonishment subverting his fear:

> In the afternoon, I went upon the reef with a party of gentlemen; and the water being very clear around the edges, a new creation, as it was to us, but imitative of the old, was there presented to our view. We had wheat sheaves, mushrooms, stags horns, cabbage leaves, and a variety of other forms, glowing under water with vivid tints of every shade betwixt green, purple, brown, and white; equalling in beauty and excelling in grandeur the most favourite *parterre* of the curious florist. These were different species of coral and fungus, growing as it were, out of the solid rock, and each had its peculiar form and shade of colouring; but whilst contemplating the richness of the scene, we could not long forget with what destruction it was pregnant.[23]

The change in attitudes was further apparent when, days later, Flinders described a coral reef off the coast of Mackay as 'a beautiful piece of marine scenery'.[24] While corals were not the subject of natural history interest in Flinders's journal, they were considered beautiful to behold.[25]

The Reef's beauty and charms subsequently became a feature of the explorers' Reef descriptions. John Lort Stokes, the explorer, hydrographer, and commander of the *Beagle*, wrote of Yunbenun (Magnetic Island, near Townsville) that its dense tree cover, amid which 'a few straggling pines reared their lofty and angular shaped heads', gave 'a picturesque appearance to the scene'.[26] Stokes devoted most of his Reef commentary to theories of its geological origins. In the years between King's and Stokes's voyages, scientists paid increased attention to the geological origins of coral reefs. Stokes was given orders to test Charles Darwin's subsidence theory of reef formation. Additionally, when the *Fly* departed in March 1844, with the geologist Joseph Beete Jukes aboard as naturalist, a Sydney newspaper declared that it looked 'forward with much anxiety' to his assessment of 'whether Mr. Darwin's account be actually consistent with observation'.[27] Jukes portrayed the Reef as a great diverse collage of geological formations, formed over centuries, shaped by winds and tides, and colonised by the small coral polyp.[28] Jukes concluded that Darwin had produced a theory 'of much apparent weight [...] arranged with almost unexampled industry, and reasoned on with equal clearness and sagacity'.[29] If the Reef were drained of its water, Jukes wrote, 'This great Barrier would be found to have a considerable resemblance to a gigantic and irregular fortification, a steep glacis crowned with a broken parapet wall, and carried from one rising ground to another. The tower-like bastions, of projecting and detached reefs, would increase this resemblance.'[30] Jukes's descriptions had an important local effect. His commentary on reef formation, printed in newspapers, ultimately heightened public interest in the Reef, not as a sea lane or as a cluster of resources, but as a place of immense scientific interest.[31]

Scientific interest and appreciation of the Reef's beauty was a theme of Jukes's prose. Coloured with shades of romanticism, Jukes's descriptions of Reef life and scenery heightened the appeal of the Reef as a picturesque, tranquil and interesting environment. Coral reefs, Jukes wrote, while lacking in variety, produced 'considerable beauty', especially 'when viewed from a ship's masthead at a short distance in clear weather'.[32] Likewise, the roar of the ocean as it thundered against the Reef's outer wall was a scene of 'simple grandeur and [a] display of power and beauty [...] that rose even to sublimity'. He re-envisioned the outer wall, once a scene of Cook's torment, as a powerful display of nature's wonder:

> Both the sound and the sight were such as to impress the mind of the spectator in the presence of an overwhelming majesty and power, while his senses were delighted by the contrast of beautiful colours afforded by the deep blue of the ocean, the dazzling white of the surf, and the bright green of the shoal water on the reef.[33]

Despite the difficulty of viewing the underwater world with clarity, Jukes was able to make close observations. Consistent with the interest within oceanography in the mid-nineteenth century, he became fascinated with the variety and diversity of life that existed in the submarine world. After bringing a 'block of coral rock' up with a fishhook during anchorage, Jukes wrote a vivid description of 'the vast variety and abundance of animal life' it supported. The 'block', Jukes wrote, glaring with 'beauty from the many brightly and variously coloured animals and plants [...] was a perfect museum'. His descriptions always entangled aesthetics and science:

> It was a mere worn dead fragment, but its surface was covered with brown, crimson, and yellow nulliporae, many small actiniae, and soft branching corallines, sheets of flustra and eschara, and delicate reteporae, looking like beautiful lacework carved in ivory [...] What an inconceivable amount of animal life must be here scattered over the bottom of the sea, to say nothing of that moving through its waters, and this through spaces of hundreds of miles. Every corner and crevice, every point occupied by living beings, which, as they become more minute, increase in tenfold abundance.[34]

*

The emerging appreciation among scientists of coral's ornamental qualities was telling. While anchored in continental islands known as the Frankland Group, just south of Cairns, 'about one-half' of the *Rattlesnake*'s crew was out collecting shells and coral; they 'reaped a rich harvest of cowries, cones, and spider shells'.[35] MacGillivray added that, in his opinion, the Reef was 'the greatest assemblage of "pretty" shells' he had ever encountered.[36]

By 1860, along with its resources, virtues for settlement, scientific interest and beauty, the Reef had taken on a form of heritage. Explorers who followed Cook could not pass through the Reef without mention of his endeavours. King, who climbed Jiigurru's (Lizard Island's) summit twice, reflected on his second ascension: 'The island, from its connexion with Captain Cook's misfortunes during his perilous navigation within the reefs, will always be an interesting feature in the history of the discovery and examination of this coast, and deserves a more appropriate appellation.'[37] Stokes, too, remarked on the feeling of following 'in the footsteps of the immortal navigator':

> There is an inexpressible charm in thus treading in the track of the mighty dead, and my feelings on attaining the summit of the peak, where the foot of the white man, had perhaps but once before rested, will easily be understood. Below to the eastward stretched a vast expanse of water, broken at the distance of about eight miles [12.9 kilometres], by a long narrow line of detached reefs, on which there ran a white crest of foaming breakers, marking the outer edge of the Great Barrier, a name which few seamen could hear with indifference when in its vicinity. If I felt emotions of delight, on first perceiving the extent of a danger so justly dreaded, how much stronger must have been the feelings of Captain Cook, when from the same spot years before, he saw by a gap in the line of broken water, there was a chance of his once more gaining the open sea.[38]

Endeavour River was also considered 'classic ground', and Jukes, while on Jiigurru (Lizard Island), reflected: 'How little could he [Cook] have foreseen that in no short time a British empire would be founded on the shores he had first discovered, and that this reef-environed coast, dangerous though it be, should be in the daily track of vessels!'[39] Perhaps more profoundly, by the 1860s natural historians were asserting that they 'do not know of any physical feature in all Australia which interests one so much'.[40]

'The Taming of the Reef'[41] was truly a grand task, intimately connected with the ambitions of empire. While coastline settlers were interested in safe navigation, they were also concerned with the benefits the Reef held for them immediately. With the onset of steam navigation, those living in the coastal eastern tropics began to appreciate the efficiency of a Reef trip. When a Melbourne shipping firm Howard Smith and Sons began sending vessels to Townsville, a Charters Towers newspaper informed its readers that, with their 'fastest and finest' vessels, the firm could make the run between Brisbane and Townsville in sixty-six hours, 'quite as long as passengers care to be at sea on such a voyage'.[42]

Travelling along, or within, the Reef was part of the everyday life of early Reef settlers, and they revelled in its scenery. As early as the 1870s, Townsville and Cairns residents were visiting Yunbenun (Magnetic Island) and Dabuukji (Green Island) as holiday retreats. A correspondent to the *Queenslander* noted that 'four picnic parties left Ross Creek for Magnetic Island' on Easter Monday 1879.[43] In 1877, the *Queenslander* included correspondence from a Cairns contributor detailing the activities likely to occur during the festive season, and predicted shell collecting, pigeon shooting and picnics on Dabuukji (Green Island).[44] Charles Eden, a public servant and writer who spent time at Cardwell (about 170 kilometres north of Townsville) as police magistrate and sub-collector of customs, wrote that he preferred to frequent the neighbouring Family Islands to shoot nutmeg pigeons because it was possible to 'get as many as you pleased', while birds on the mainland, once shot, fell into the thick scrub and became impossible to find.[45] Further south, the Capricorn and Bunker groups were also visited. An article from the *Capricornian* in December 1884 instructed readers on how to enjoy 'turtle catching, fishing, shooting and oystering' during the holiday season.[46] Unsurprisingly, people from the coastal towns were quick to explore the possibilities of their neighbouring environment.

Descriptions of the Reef began to speak to a culture of 'cruising the Reef', and often evoked the romantic lyricism of Jukes's prose. The French writer Élisée Reclus described the ease with which the reefs could be navigated, 'aided by the clear atmosphere and the extreme limpidity of the water', 'their greenish tints' providing a pleasing contrast 'with the blue of the neighbouring abysses'.[47] Eden described Pouandai (Hinchinbrook Island) as 'a scene of beauty unequalled in Australia', and was similarly entranced by the submerged corals. He recalled that during a trip from Rockingham Bay (Cardwell) to Bowen:

> We passed through the Palm Islands – a most beautiful group – anchoring for a short time to collect specimens of the coral, with which the place abounds. It was a most lovely sight; allowing the boat to drift gently along and peering down over the bows at the beds of coral, seeming so close in the clear water that you felt inclined to stretch out your hand and reach it, although in reality two or three fathoms beneath the surface.[48]

Extracts of the explorer John Strachan's journey to the Torres Strait in the *Alice Maud* appeared in various Australian newspapers under the title 'A Cruise along the Great Barrier Reef'. In one excerpt, he described Bird Island (25 kilometres north-west of Cape Grenville), from which he operated a guano mining facility, as 'one of the loveliest tropical islands in these seas'. A coral reef, he wrote, 'presents a view of such magnificence and grandeur as defies description – every colour and hue of the rainbow is represented there, miniature forests teeming with life, and fairy bowers, where the mermaids might dwell'.[49] Such romantic appreciations of the Reef's natural qualities permeated the newspapers and literature of the late nineteenth century as increasing numbers of people frequented its waterways.

Steaming through the Reef increasingly became yoked to a growing curiosity for and leisurely enjoyment of its natural splendour. The Whitsunday Passage was beginning to earn a reputation for serene vistas and placid waters. A *Brisbane Courier* reporter who accompanied the premier's delegation to North Queensland in 1885 said that the Whitsunday Passage 'was a pleasure excursion of the most enjoyable character'.[50] A correspondent for *The Sydney Morning Herald* was also charmed:

> What is Whitsunday Passage like? It is a quiet sea between walls of verdure on one side and bold hills on the other, Seaward island after island rises; now a pretty beach comes white-banded towards you, or a score of channels glide into one another as if seeking a way into the mighty main again. A solitary hut with a solitary light flickering from the hillside, a tall palm outlined against the sky, a rugged spur in its passive menace to the toilers of the sea, a thousand quiet nooks, numberless surprises of the water and of the land – this is what one counts when Whitsunday Passage is passed, and yet it is not those things that impress one; but the general outlines, the general impression, the long contour of beauty.[51]

In 1895, another ministerial delegation travelled northward, and again the cruise through the Whitsunday Passage received attention. The article lamented that while the passage 'must rival if not surpass many of the world-famed beauty spots of the globe [...] comparatively few of those who have travelled up and down [Queensland's coast] had the opportunity to enjoy the full beauty of the scene'. Steamers, the article explained, usually made the passage at night, so the Reef's beauty was being poorly appreciated.

By 1900, however, early tourism operators were beginning to take advantage of the allure of the Reef's islands. In 1900, competing Yunbenun (Magnetic Island) hotel proprietors Richard Butler and Robert Hayles advertised in a Charters Towers newspaper their daily services, hotels and the merits of the railway link between Townsville and Charters Towers.[52]

While trips to the Reef's islands were becoming increasingly common, scientific understandings of the environment were also developing and changing. The origin of the Reef continued to intrigue the scientific community.[53] Despite Jukes's extolling of Darwin's theory of subsidence, the theory found challengers who asserted that volcanic upheaval had contributed to reef formation; subsidence, it was argued, was not the universal cause.[54] Yet Darwin's theory continued to find supporters. Discussions of the Reef's biology and geology in newspapers constitute some of the first examples of earnest attempts at popular natural histories of the Reef. A long article, written by an author adopting the pseudonym 'Sea Urchin', began with the assertion: 'Most people are familiar with the name of the great Reef without knowing much about it.'[55] Writers educated readers on the geological and biological forces that had formed the Reef's structure, and about the curious marine animals – beginning with coral itself – that lived within it.[56] Popular interest in the Reef provoked some to proclaim that it should 'be considered one of the wonders of the world'.[57]

Accompanying this increased interest in the Reef's scientific and aesthetic benefits was a surge of attention towards its various resources. The Queensland government was eager to locate and control the potential industries that the Reef provided. Guano and coral lime deposits along the Reef were important in the establishment of coastal settlements. For instance, an initial virtue of the site of the settlement of Somerset was the lime on neighbouring Pabaju (Albany Island).[58] Other coastal settlements also utilised their proximity to the abundance of coral-lime. Apart from shooting pigeons, public servant Charles Eden recalled that his visits to the Family Islands also included the collection of 'coral to burn for lime'. He described Cardwell's beach as 'one mass of dead coral', lying loose and easily collected in minutes.[59]

Another Reef resource of early interest to both the colonial government and settlers was dugong. Dugongs had been fished in the Moreton Bay and Wide Bay area by Europeans since 1847.[60] By 1860, it was apparent that while the dugong could be found in the waters off South East Queensland, their numbers were more prolific in the Reef's northern waters.[61] The utilities of dugong were deemed to be its edible flesh and its apparent medicinal qualities.[62] The naturalist George Bennett suggested that fresh dugong flesh resembled beef, and when salted had 'the flavour of excellent bacon', while its oil held various benefits for 'those afflicted with strenuous disease'.[63] The potential of a dugong industry in the north was abundantly clear to Eden, who saw a worthwhile opportunity 'for a man with the proper coppers, a good boat and crew'.[64] The writer Ebenezer Thorne considered that the 'flocks of dugong' along the coast of Queensland were more extensive and valuable than any of the Reef's other resources.[65]

In 1873, a resident of Cardwell gave a sense of the perceived potential of the fishery when he wrote to the *Queenslander* inquiring as to the 'mode of curing dugong hide'. He added:

In Rockingham Bay [Cardwell] there are swarms of dugong, one man alone having caught with his net one, two, three, and even seven fish at a haul. Attention is being directed to this important fishery at the present time, and it is proposed to convert every part of the fish to some use.[66]

From the moment European settlers encountered the Reef, they viewed it as a natural resource that could be conquered and exploited, that needed to be charted, with its flora and fauna classified according to the designs of colonial politics and science. However, as settlers engaged with the Reef more closely and regularly, they saw both its economic possibilities and its potential as a recreational playground. This led to its value exceeding its utility as a maritime highway; it was a lifeline that offered sustenance, commercial opportunities and leisurely indulgence.

2

Exploitation and Enjoyment

As the settlers began to identify potential sources of wealth from the Reef, the most valued industries that emerged were the pearl shell and bêche-de-mer fisheries.[1] Early accounts of the fisheries celebrated them as a source of profit in a wild northern frontier. By the late 1870s, bêche-de-mer fishermen were venturing further afield to find stocks, and reports of conflict between fishermen and northern Indigenous peoples were common. Yet despite the violence and hostilities, fishermen showed little inclination to restrain their expansion. Many believed that depleted beds along the coast meant it was necessary 'to push northward, and towards the coast of New Guinea' to allow the beds to replenish. The pearl shell fishery held a similar reputation. Early 'shellers' were celebrated as 'bold men', risking shipwreck and engaging in a 'fight for life against the ferocious and cannibal natives of the mainland, or the islands'. The reward for their 'daring' was 'a rich gold reef, a veritable "jeweler's shop"'.[2]

With no oversight by the state, policing and determining the fisheries' stocks and revenue was difficult. The Queensland colonial government was unaware of the industries' accounts. The only revenue the government received from pearl shell, for instance, was the minimal amounts paid into the Waiben (Thursday Island) customs office. 'The greater part of the capital,' colonial secretary Arthur Palmer proclaimed, 'belonged to New South Wales' – where most of the fishermen and shellers were from. Eventually, the notion that Queensland's waters had a wealth in pearl shell and bêche-de-mer pushed the colonial government to introduce legislation that aimed mainly at collecting revenue: the *Pearl Shell and Bêche-de-Mer Fishery Act 1881*. The legislation initiated a more thorough recording of the fisheries' make-up and revenue, providing a rationale for the first foray into preservation efforts of the Barrier Reef.

Both the pearl shell and bêche-de-mer fisheries proved to be prone to resource depletion. The pearl shell fishery saw yearly decreases in revenue, and by 1888, despite high global demand, the total value of the fishery had halved. This depletion prompted innovation. Full-dress deep-diving equipment was adopted as the shallow beds were depleted, and then schooner-based fleets or 'floating stations' – fleets accompanied by a large ship for provisions and storage – were introduced. These stations originated in the Torres Strait in the mid-1880s, but as the beds were depleted, they migrated to north-west Australia. By the time the fleets returned at the end of the 1880s, the Queensland government had appointed an oyster expert, William Saville-Kent, as commissioner of fisheries.

Saville-Kent immediately raised concerns for both fisheries. He believed the bêche-de-mer fishery required better policing to protect the largely Indigenous labour force, as well as better resource management, but his own limited understanding of the bêche-de-mer slug precluded him from making specific recommendations. Saville-Kent was better acquainted with the pearl shell fishery. It was, he asserted, suffering from extensive depletion caused by the 'indiscriminate collection' of young shells and the 'considerable depletion' of fishing grounds.[3] Saville-Kent stated that he had consulted with 'members of the trade' at Waiben (Thursday Island), whom he described as 'leading boat owners'. It was in these meetings that Saville-Kent claimed to have achieved consensus on recommendations to introduce an internal size limit of 6 inches (15 centimetres) and, possibly, the closing of grounds, as well as provisions to encourage cultivation, such as granting exemption to cultivators from the size restrictions. Many of Saville-Kent's recommendations were incorporated into the *Pearl Shell and Bêche-de-Mer Fishery Act*.

The legislation was not welcomed by the industry. Fishers blamed their low yields on the new size limits. They denied that Saville-Kent had been as consultative as he asserted, and called it 'legislation in the dark'. Resentment from the fishers grew, who saw their folk understandings marginalised by an outsider-scientist. It broadened the divide within the fishery between small, shore-based fishers and the larger fleet operators, who were capable of securing leases for 'cultivation' and could be exempt from the size restrictions.[4] For many of the smaller fishers, the legislation was perceived as an intrusion that threatened to further denude the beds and destroy the identity of the fishery. The larger fleet operators claimed, unsurprisingly, that the new legislation around cultivation was an important part of the industry's growth, and to remove their leases would be to 'roll back the wheel of progress'.[5] Nonetheless, in 1896, the Queensland government reduced the size limit and removed the exemption for cultivators; it also announced it would hold an inquiry into the fisheries the following year.

By 1897, Saville-Kent had left his post as commissioner of fisheries and didn't defend his recommendations at the inquiry. The inquiry heard cautionary evidence from the sub-collector at Waiben (Thursday Island) and Queensland's inspector of fisheries, George Bennett, that reducing the size limit would cause problems for the fishery. He was unequivocal that overfishing threatened to reduce the fishery to ruin within five years. However, this lone voice was drowned out by the fishers, who, while accepting that the fisheries needed better management, rejected the role of scientists and requested the appointment of a floating inspector equipped with a 'hardy vessel, a practical knowledge of the industry and a reputation that commands confidence'.[6]

Saville-Kent's dalliance with the Reef did not end here. In 1895, he published *The Great Barrier Reef: Its Products and Potentialities*. The book's colourful illustrations and photographs allowed for a new appreciation of the Reef's aesthetics. Yet accompanying the vivid descriptions was a promotion of the 'harvest-field, rich from both a commercial and a scientific standpoint, that this Queensland possession constitutes'.[7] The book's final chapters evoked notions of abundance, which, in time, proved a resilient idea among promoters of the Reef. Reef fish, Saville-Kent declared, presented 'almost unlimited possibilities of profitable development'. Sharks, rays and skates were 'almost unlimited', and the Reef possessed 'literally a mine of wealth' of coral for lime and ornamental purposes. He stated that the pearl shell fishery was 'capable of unlimited development', especially if cultivation methods were adopted.[8] Saville-Kent believed the establishment of a marine biological station could aid the Reef's economic development: the Reef's development would progress, hand in hand, with Reef science.

The debates around the pearl shell fishery were widely publicised in Queensland newspapers, as threats to the viability of the Reef's most identifiable and profitable industry were perceived as eroding the broader value of the Reef. In the late nineteenth and early twentieth centuries, the value of the environment was perceived and discussed in terms of its 'usefulness', both in Australia and abroad. Consequently, Australian science became linked with locating and advising governments on the best ways to develop the nation's dormant natural resources.

The pearl shell and bêche-de-mer fisheries struggled for the next decade or so. In 1908, a second commission was held, which, in the end, essentially drove the largest of the shelling companies out of the Torres Strait to 'liberate' it for the smaller fishers. However, this failed to bring the industry any real stability. Consequently, in 1913 another royal commission was held, but this one focused primarily upon the issue of labour. By this time, the market price of pearl shell came under attack from a new product: trochus, the shell of which could be substituted for Torres Strait pearl shell in button manufacturing, and which was considerably cheaper.

The trochus fishery, despite the lower quality of the shell, expanded rapidly in the inter-war period, with grounds along the Reef and into the Torres Strait. Additionally, the trochus fishery, along with the bêche-de-mer and pearl shell industries, were dominated by Japanese and Chinese labour. The prevalence of Japanese divers within the pearl-shelling fishery was a particularly vexing issue for the Commonwealth government, which was eager to keep these industries and the related profits in the hands of settler Australians. Apart from that, the fact that foreign nationals were pressing ahead with the exploitation of the Reef signalled a neglect of the Reef's value and the potential profits to be gleaned from it.

Despite the controversies surrounding its ailing fisheries, the Great Barrier Reef continued to draw the interest of both the public and the emerging Australian scientific community. In the early twentieth century, along with probing the Reef's economic potential, scientists began to investigate the Reef's other features; they were slowly piecing together its biological jigsaw.

Before technology allowed for routine underwater investigations, it was the animals that could be seen from the surface or that habituated on islands that drew the scrutiny of naturalists. Ornithologists, both professional and hobbyist, were the most ubiquitous scientists on the Reef in the early twentieth century, and birds became the Reef's first clearly identifiable 'wonder' worthy of protection. A community of birders from across the country made frequent visits to the Reef's islands and cays to document and survey their birdlife. Their appraisals appeared in newspapers and ornithological journals, and carried both standardised counts of birds as well as the occasional lyrical description of the atmosphere birds created. Accounts of birds as like 'bees about the hive' or of the mayhem of a shower of guano were common.[9]

Accompanying the descriptions of the Reef's birdlife were pleas from birders seeking to curb the shooting on these islands and cays. The Royal Australian Ornithological Union (RAOU), whose members had made two expeditions along the Reef in 1910, was already active in lobbying governments to take greater action in protecting the nation's birds. On the Reef, the RAOU identified the nutmeg pigeon as a particularly vulnerable bird. William MacGillivray, a prominent ornithologist who accompanied the 1910 expeditions, commented that the nutmeg pigeon is 'good eating, and [is] shot for the table all along the coast but with little appreciable effect on their numbers'.[10] Despite occasional such lapses of their preservationist agenda, ornithologists generally maintained their promotion of bird protection. This advocacy formed a principal part of ornithologists' role in informing the Australian public of the nation's birds at this time.[11] More importantly, they were able to articulate the importance of birds to the Reef's social worth.

Perhaps the most prominent defender of the Reef's birdlife was 'the Beachcomber of Dunk Island', Edmund Banfield. After departing the hustle of Townsville life and entering (with his wife, Bertha) into voluntary exile, Banfield became a Thoreauvian recluse, writing books that were informed by a 'sentimental regard for the welfare of bird and plant life' and a curiosity about the 'destructive instinct which prevails in mankind'.[12] His expressive prose – with flurries of romantic passion – brought the Reef to life. Banfield did not, however, restrict his descriptions to the picturesque and serene. To him, coral reefs were battlefields, where beauty lay in the 'perpetual conflict required' for they and their inhabitants to exist. His writings from Coonanglebah (Dunk Island) spoke to anxieties within Western societies about the degenerative effects of urban life. He wrote metaphors into the lives of coral critters. While he, like other Australian natural history writers of his time, applied some quantitative elements, his prose mostly emphasised observation, environmental knowledge, aesthetics and appreciation of the environment.[13]

An important aspect of Banfield's legacy was his criticism of the killing of nutmeg pigeons, which mated and nested on Coonanglebah (Dunk Island). The pigeon, Banfield wrote, congregated 'in large numbers on the islands to nest – and only to nest', and so offered 'quite charming sport to men with guns. They are the easiest of all shooting. Big and white, and given to grouping themselves on favourable trees.'[14] He lamented that 'a single expedition during the breeding season to one of the islands may cause immense destruction and unprofitable loss of life'.[15]

In his love and advocacy for birds, Banfield found solidarity with the newly established RAOU. A Cairns resident named E.M. Cornwall in 1903 congratulated the RAOU on their initiatives to protect the pigeon along the North Queensland coast. Cornwall explained that the birds could be shot, with little damage to their population, in September, October and early November, because their numbers were generally fewer. Shooting in the latter half of November and through December, however, was 'quite a different matter':

> The birds are then breeding in countless thousands on these very limited areas; every bush and tree bear their burden of nests, and many eggs are laid on rocks or even on the bare ground. Then there are hundreds of birds on the islands all day long. Eggs and young birds are destroyed wantonly, and thousands of birds shot which are never used, simply because they go bad before they reach the pot. Some years ago Green Island, which lies a few miles outside Cairns, was a favourite haunt of the Pigeons, but the shooters were too much for them, and now only a few pairs visit it during the season.[16]

The RAOU announced its suggestions to the Queensland government to reserve 'certain islands [...] with the view of protecting the Nutmeg or Torres Strait Pigeon from destruction'.[17] The bird was already protected during its nesting season from 1 November to 30 April, yet shooting continued to take place during the closure. Following reports that birds were arriving earlier than November and so became vulnerable in that period, the RAOU desired to extend the closed season by starting it from 1 October each year.[18]

Their agitations proved successful. In 1905, the government amended the *Native Bird Protection Act* to extend the prohibition on shooting nutmeg pigeons in various regions along the Reef coast.[19] Importantly, they listed Coonanglebah (Dunk Island), Kumboola Island, Purtaboi (Mound Island), the Family Islands and the Brook Islands as sanctuaries, and listed Banfield as the honorary ranger.[20] Banfield celebrated the news by announcing the achievement in the *Emu*, the journal of the RAOU.[21] Banfield also nailed notices, twenty-five of which had been sent to him, to trees on the protected islands to alert visitors to the prevailing law. Banfield and his fellow bird enthusiasts proved an influential lobby group, and bird preservation became one of the earliest forms of government-enforced conservation on the Reef, with many of its islands proclaimed sanctuaries in the early twentieth century.[22]

Upon Banfield's death on 2 June 1923, fellow nature writers Charles Barrett and Alec Chisholm, both of whom had visited him on Coonanglebah (Dunk Island), reflected on his passion for bird and wildlife protection. Barrett wrote in an obituary that had he 'been a mammal or bird collector, "The Beachcomber" would never have given me freedom of his isle'.[23] Chisholm, who had been in consistent communication with Banfield on the subject of bird and animal protection, paid homage to his selfless spirit and described him as 'jealous to passion of the rights and welfare of his friends in isolation – men, birds, dugongs, what-not – he would rush to the relief at even a whisper of need'.[24] To his contemporaries, Banfield's virtues were undoubtedly connected with his zeal for nature protection.

Yet even Banfield was a man of his time. Informed by a utilitarian outlook, he believed 'useful' land not only could but should be developed. In the case of the islands surrounding Pouandai (Hinchinbrook Island), Banfield suggested that because they were not endowed with features that served 'large practical purposes', they could form part of a 'national park'. Reflecting a kind of 'useless land' argument, similar to the one that emerged when Yellowstone was dedicated as a national park in the United States, Banfield said of Coonanglebah (Dunk Island) that while 'it is too small and dainty a spot to be devoted to large practical purposes, its exceptional gift of beauty need not necessarily be fatal'.[25] Banfield was a voice for careful engagement with the environment, but he was also a keen advocate for northern development and believed that the Reef held dormant opportunities for economic progress. He criticised the government's permissiveness towards Chinese and Japanese domination of the Reef's fisheries, agitated for greater development of tourism facilities on Dabuukji (Green Island) and Yunbenun (Magnetic Island), and consistently promoted the idea of establishing a permanent research station on the coast, not only to better understand the Reef's natural elements, but also to expose and better manage its economic resources.

Established in 1907, the Queensland Government Intelligence and Tourist Bureau ([QGITB], referred to as the Queensland Government Tourist Bureau [QGTB] from 1929) was also alive to the possibilities the Reef offered as a tourist destination well before the 1920s. In 1915, it began promoting the virtues of a Whitsunday Passage cruise.[26] In the absence of a completed Queensland coastal rail link before 1927, travel was still largely conducted by ship. Most travellers sailed through the passage en route to other northern destinations, forgoing a 'close study of the idyllic places'.

Nonetheless, the bureau maintained that the passage had become well known as Australia's 'grandest cruising ground'.[27]

Much as Banfield had, the bureau's promotion of the Reef linked the intangible beauty of the region with its prospective economic opportunities. The islands, in addition to bathing and camping in what were described as 'delightful tourist resort and beauty' spots, offered opportunities for those interested in pastoral, forestry or agricultural leases, had ample grounds for fishing and bird hunting, and possessed a rich supply of oysters. A 1923 bureau pamphlet tightened the links between the environmental and economic allures of the Reef by summarising a passenger's aesthetic response to seeing 'the wonderful shapes and colours reeled off beneath him' while sailing over a coral garden, and adding that 'the Barrier Reef has other attractions; it is the scene of several important industries which may under good management attain to larger dimensions'.[28]

Additionally, since Saville-Kent's popular book, momentum built behind the notion that the Reef held vast, hitherto neglected economic products. The Queensland branch of the Royal Geographical Society of Australasia was particularly active in promoting the Reef's scientific and economic importance. The *Queensland Geographical Journal* published an article written by the politician and journalist Randolph Bedford, who defined heaven as 'North-east Australia between May and September' and positioned the Reef as its most significant natural feature. He encouraged southern Australians to make the trip along the coast to behold environments that had 'been stolen direct out of paradise'. Bedford's essay, however, also framed the Reef's value in economic terms, asserting that on this matter it had been poorly utilised:

> The Barrier itself is practically unknown; yet its value economically, apart from its value in beauty, makes it one of the great assets of Australia – neglected though it be at this moment. It produces a hundred thousand pounds a year or so to Queensland trade,

and it has the potentialities of a million. The area inside the Reef in Queensland waters is 80,000 square miles [207,000 square kilometres]; it is full of raw wealth: pearl-shell and corals, fish and bêche-de-mer.[29]

Bedford's claim reflected principles that would become central to the Geographical Society's relationship with the Reef. Constrained by the paradigms of early Reef science, and driven by a desire for commercial and industrial relevancy in the Australian nation, early twentieth-century reef scientists reinforced dreams of the Reef's economic potential.

The most significant contribution the Geographical Society made to advancing awareness of the Reef was the establishment of the Great Barrier Reef Committee (GBRC). Until the establishment of the GBRMPA, the GBRC was Australia's peak Reef research body, consisting of marine biologists and geologists drawn largely from Australian universities.

The geologist Henry Caselli Richards gave an address to the society on 15 April 1922, in which he outlined the necessity of several investigations into the Reef. Ambitiously, and echoing the calls of Saville-Kent, he suggested that the Reef be completely recharted every decade, and advocated the establishment of a marine biological station. The final component of Richards's proposal was a 'general survey of the economic resources, especially in respect to trochus, bêche-de-mer, pearl-shell, sponges, and turtle-shell'.[30]

Support for a marine biology research station had been simmering along since Saville-Kent recommended it.[31] Banfield, when ideas were being entertained of a 'marine museum' at Cooktown, championed the prospect 'of an institution designed to demonstrate how best the riches of the Great Barrier Reef might be exploited'.[32] Underpinning those calls was a consistent national and economic imperative, which Richards affirmed:

For defence purposes it is obvious that the fullest knowledge of the fearful complex of coral reefs should be available. It happens that these areas are rich in pearl-shell, bêche-de-mer, trochus, sponges, turtle-shell, and other valuable articles of commerce [...] Not only are we not using these sources of wealth, but we are allowing others to use them in an unlicensed and uncontrolled manner.[33]

Richards concluded his address with an alarmed declaration of the economic opportunities lost to Australia through a lack of scientific initiative and the Geographical Society's responsibility to counter this trend: 'The exploitation of the economic wealth of the Great Barrier Reef by foreigners has gone on and we stand idly by [...] Surely this Royal Geographical Society is capable of making some definite move to point out our proper path!'[34]

On 12 September 1922, the GBRC held its first meeting in Brisbane and elected the president of the Queensland branch of the Royal Geographical Society, Sir Matthew Nathan, as chairman. Progressing Reef research became the GBRC's primary goal. In his 1923 address, Nathan emphasised the committee's role in discovering the economic resources of the Reef. He asserted that scientific and economic studies of the Reef's products, their associated industries and their markets were imperative and formed an essential agenda of the society.[35]

At the Pan-Pacific Science Congress held in Melbourne in August 1923, Richards brought attention to the paucity of research hitherto carried out on the Reef, and voiced his disappointment that, considering the Reef's size, 'and its interest both scientific and economic, it is remarkable how little real scientific investigation has been carried out'.[36] He recommended a marine biological station somewhere along the Reef to carry out zoological research, both 'economic' and 'pure'.[37] The pure research would fulfil the survey of the Reef's flora and fauna, while the economic research would assist in the identification of Reef life of commercial interest, and methods of managing their populations. In his 1924 address to the Queensland branch of the Royal Geographical Society of Australasia, Nathan was hopeful for progress on the study of 'the value of the reef'.[38]

The GBRC secured the Reef firmly within the Queensland scientific agenda. Furthermore, its advocacy for the Reef fed into the appeal that early nature writers and tourism providers had established. And yet, the GBRC still framed the Reef's value, nebulous as it was, in economic terms.

It is perhaps unsurprising, at a time when Reef science found its first eponymous committee and Queensland's newly established tourist body began actively promoting the Reef, that Reef science and tourism became yoked together. In 1925, E.F. Pollock, an active member of the RAOU and the Royal Zoological Society of New South Wales, launched his first tourist expedition to the Capricorn Group. Pollock's expeditions were advertised as 'Naturalists' Expeditions', where participants could complete their own nature surveys of the islands' wildlife.[39] They were forerunners to twenty-first-century citizen–scientist initiatives. By 1927, this scientific agenda was accompanied by the promise of 'excitement among big game fishes'.[40]

In 1928, two types of Reef expeditions were launched – one for tourists and the other with a specific scientific agenda. The first was Monty Embury's Reef Expedition to Yara-kimba (Lindeman Island), which was inspired by Embury's experience on Pollock's 1927 expedition. In 1929, Embury's expeditions began to utilise the turtle canning facilities on North West Island (75 kilometres north-east of Gladstone). Then, in 1932, Embury secured a lease on Hayman Island and established accommodation, dining and recreation hall facilities.[41] On Hayman, Embury also built research facilities, and his expeditions were accompanied by scientists who gave nightly lectures on marine life. Embury's quest to have scientists accompany his tours was aided by the concessions given to them by the Queensland Rail service, which had assumed responsibility of the QGITB from 1929.[42] Eventually, Embury himself, who later wrote a natural history of the Reef, began claiming 'scientist' concessions on Queensland's regional trains.

Like Pollock's, Embury's expeditions were advertised as 'scientific'. The images, anecdotes and articles describing the expeditions suggest, however, that 'science' was only one component of sophisticated Reef recreation. Participants were encouraged to enjoy bathing, fishing and collecting, as well as new forms of entertainment. Hilda Marks, who took part in the expedition in 1932–33, detailed the activities open to the tourists:

> A clearing at the back of the camp provided a rough golf course, and tennis courts had also been made where the young folk let off some of their surplus energy. With boating, fishing, reefing and picnic parties to the adjoining islands, there was no dearth of amusement and occupation, and it really took some resolution to stick to one's ideal of an idle, restful holiday.[43]

Hayman Island, like other Reef islands, had been populated with goats to provide food for shipwreck survivors fortunate enough to reach them. Luckily for the goats, few did – and now the goats became one of the islands' 'natural' attractions. Advertisements for Embury's tours promoted the goats, as well as Indian antelopes, as part of the island's rich environmental tapestry.[44]

Both Pollock's and Embury's tours intensified the Reef's appeal.[45] They, like local initiatives, commercialised the Reef's tourist charm, but they managed and altered the Reef to accommodate expectations. Additionally, the employment of scientists, and the establishment of makeshift 'research facilities' – the Great Barrier Reef and Whitsunday Passage Biological Station – helped highlight the scientific curiosities along the Reef. Consequently, their expeditions further popularised the Reef's natural wonders.

The expeditions also provided the rationale for declaring of the Molle Islands, Hayman Island and Double Cone Island as animal and bird sanctuaries in 1932, with Embury, Pollock and William MacGillivray as honorary rangers.[46]

The scientific expedition in 1928 was the research expedition to the Low Isles (15 kilometres north-east of Port Douglas). Jointly funded by the British and Australian governments, scientific societies (primarily the GBRC in Australia) and businesses, this expedition comprised ten British marine biologists along with some permanent and visiting Australian scientists. The agenda was to settle a range of problems that dominated the paradigms of marine biological and reef sciences in the 1920s.[47] The entire expedition was an overwhelming success, judging by scientific output: a total of sixty-two reports were written and published as a result of its investigations.

In addition to the 'pure' scientific agenda, the Queensland and Commonwealth governments invested in the expedition, hopeful that the elements of the Reef's commercial potential would be revealed. The Queensland government funded a marine biologist from The University of Queensland (UQ), Frank Moorhouse, who was also a member of the GBRC, to attend and investigate the bêche-de-mer, trochus, pearl shell and sponge fisheries for this purpose. Charles Maurice Yonge, a marine biologist from the Plymouth Marine Biological Laboratory and the expedition's leader, said in an interview with *The Brisbane Courier* that he hoped to 'throw light on the many economic problems' and asserted that the Reef was 'a region of great potential wealth'.[48] There were not, as James and Margarita Bowen, the Reef's first historians, suggested, 'genuflectory gestures to the main funding bodies'.[49]

Yonge would continue to publicise the economic value of the Reef. In his book published after the expedition, he suggested that the Reef offered 'a continuous supply of wealth'.[50] The promotion of the Reef's economic importance had been a significant part of Reef science's agenda since Saville-Kent. Reef scientists, especially those endowed with government money, were complicit in the broader pursuit of developing and informing Australia's primary industries. 'Economic' and 'pure' avenues of research were not considered to be competing agendas, and both revealed important elements of the Reef to the nation. Yonge's enthusiastic promotion of the Reef in economic terms reinforced this idea in the public consciousness.

These expeditions increased interest in, and consequently visitations to, the Reef. A reflection of this growth was the surge in books and articles written about the Reef (including by Embury and Yonge) between 1928 and the beginning of World War II, which typically fused scientific appraisal with romanticism.

Sydney Elliott Napier, a journalist who had participated in Pollock's 1927–28 expedition, marvelled at the coral polyp, whose work he described as 'infinitely greater and more lasting' than the pyramid builders of Egypt.[51] Similarly, in *Wonders of the Great Barrier Reef*, Theodore Roughley, the superintendent of New South Wales Fisheries, described the polyps as tiny architects 'responsible for the construction of these beautiful corals with a sculpture almost infinite in its variety'.[52] Embury also dramatised the Reef's outer wall as the 'rampart against which the great blue combers of the Pacific beat in vain', and said, 'Were it not for these reefs this east coast of Australia would be among the most dangerous in the world.'[53]

Yet, like Banfield, these writers also drew attention to the hostility of this underwater world and the thriving life therein, despite the vulnerability of coral reefs. Yonge exclaimed:

> Coral reefs are the site of a continuous struggle between the processes of growth and consolidation and those of destruction [...] The greatest cause of destruction is the sea itself, driven before the steady force of the trade winds or the occasional terrific fury of a cyclonic blow, to whose power the great boulders [...] which line the margins of the reefs bear striking testimony.[54]

In addition to the sea itself, other known destroyers of reefs at the time were lowered water temperatures, increased exposure to the sun through tidal activity or rising of the land level, and the contamination of water from natural silt, and fresh water.[55]

Despite the presence of coral and guano mining industries in North Queensland in the 1920s, none of the scientific or travel writers acknowledged its impact on reefs. Coral mining, however, was becoming an issue of concern for locals along the Reef coast, principally because of the associated impact on birds.

In 1922, Cairns man Edward Saunders applied for a series of mining leases on Reef cays and reefs for the purposes of obtaining coral lime for fertiliser. In February, he applied for leases on Upolu Reef and Oyster Cay, and in June he applied for a mining lease for Dabuukji (Green Island); all three applications faced local objection.[56] Saunders claimed his actions would not interfere with public use of Dabuukji (Green Island), largely because, he believed, the island was only used once or twice a year. He suggested that the 'Aquatic and Motor Boat Clubs' did not have suitable boats to reach Dabuukji (Green Island), and while he considered it 'a very pretty place', it was not 'one of the beauty spots of Cairns'.[57] The mining warden recommended that Saunders's application be refused for Dabuukji (Green Island), but endorsed the other two.

The Cairns City Council, however, wrote to the minister for mines, listing its objections to all three applications, and cited the sites' importance for birds and scientists.[58] Saunders, frustrated with the council's 'back door tactics', wrote to *The Cairns Post* asserting that his operations had the support of cane farmers and, in relation to the birds, they could 'migrate to another bank and there are many such banks along the Great Barrier Reef'.[59] The council continued to oppose Saunders's application, sending letters to the Royal Geographical Society and the Society for the Prevention of Cruelty to Animals, the latter of which also recruited the RAOU. The council, which believed lime could be obtained more cheaply from deposits on the mainland, considered the issue to be clear-cut. One alderman called the application a 'dastardly proposal'. *The Cairns Post* reported his sentiments:

> One of the greatest attractions to those islands was the bird life, and people who went there had to pick their feet for fear of stepping on eggs. To think that this scene should be devastated and destroyed because some one [sic] wanted to get coral lime from those islands was dastardly.[60]

Their protests, however, were to no avail. In November 1923, the minister approved Saunders's lease, and he began his work on Dabuukji (Green Island) in early 1924, placing 'the rich tropical growth of this fine picnic reserve' in jeopardy, according to the Cairns City Council.[61] The amount of mining Saunders actually accomplished on Dabuukji (Green Island) is uncertain. He encountered difficulties in securing a method of transporting the 'grit' from the island to the mainland, and applied for exemptions on his lease. The council seized upon the opportunity and claimed Saunders's operations were not 'bona fide'.[62] Adding to the complexity of the issue was another application for a lease on Dabuukji (Green Island) for the purposes of building a resort.[63]

The entire episode threw into relief the control the council had over Dabuukji (Green Island). Consequently, it began to pressure the Queensland government both to refuse Saunders's application for an exemption and to give control of the island and its lease arrangements back to the council. It was on this matter that the council had success.[64]

While the popular Reef writers seemed oblivious to the issues of coral mining, they were well aware of birdlife as an inherent element of the Reef's natural appeal. Echoing the calls of bird enthusiasts, Embury maintained that the 'sea-birds of the Great Barrier Reef are one of its greatest attractions, and therefore one of our assets. They are one of the wonders of the world of nature, and as such should be afforded the utmost protection.'[65] In particular, he demanded their protection from feral cats and sportsmen.

Superintendent of New South Wales Fisheries, Theodore Roughley, framed his opposition to the shooting of Reef birds in racial terms, displaying the white supremacy of the time:

> The slaughter by the aborigines can be excused; amongst a people who knew not even the rudiments of tilling the soil, whose weapons were for food, for their very sustenance. What be said of the slaying by white people? Perhaps the less the better; but indignation cannot help being felt at the thought of such ruthless, such senseless, slaughter, for much of this wholesale shooting was indulged in out of a perverted sense of 'sport' – or rather, should we say, a primitive lust to kill?[66]

Journalist Sydney Elliott Napier's position on bird protection was less dogmatic. Recounting his frustration at being kept awake by muttonbirds while camping on Musgrave Island, he lamented that he was denied the 'small satisfaction' of a shotgun.[67]

Despite Napier's one unpleasant evening, the birds of the Reef were generally regarded, including by Napier, as worthy of admiration and protection. Upolu and Oyster Cay, which continued to be mined for coral lime despite being listed as sanctuaries in 1926, and despite continued protests over the operations, finally received protection after the revocation of the mining leases in 1934.[68]

Attitudes towards turtles were more complicated. Tourists were exposed to turtles when they visited the canning facilities on North West and Heron islands, or when they witnessed the butchering of nesting females on coastal beaches. The process of the slaughter was laid out in bare terms in the *Australian Museum Magazine*:

> Turtle-hunters patrol the beaches of the islet nightly, turning over
> all the turtles they find *en route*, and leaving them out of reach
> of the tide. There they are helpless and lie on their backs, their
> flippers scooping up the sand with great force, until exhausted.
> They are often left in this position for a whole day or more, in the
> heat of the tropical sun, and their plight as they lie with drooping
> heads, often gasping for breath, is one which cannot fail to excite
> one's pity [...] the turtles are killed by decapitation, and later
> butchered.[69]

Their meat was used to make soup, their flippers dried and sold as
culinary products, and their fat extracted to be used in cooking and
as a lubricant, while their shells, occasionally sold for decorative
purposes, were usually crushed with their bones to make fertiliser.

While many writers affirmed the fine taste of turtle flesh and
recognised the importance of viable commercial industries on the
Reef, they considered the turtle too special to be threatened with
extinction and treated so callously. Roughley asked:

> Is it desirable that the turtle be exploited at all? Certainly the
> products, both soup and meat, are very palatable, but the industry
> is accompanied by much unavoidable cruelty to the animals. If
> we must have a turtle industry, however, at least let us so regulate
> it that the animals are not reduced to the very extinction as
> has happened to so many creatures man has exploited for his
> personal gain.[70]

Yonge suggested that 'if some measures were taken to protect the
young turtles in this early stage of their existence their numbers,
and so the potentialities of the fishery, would be greatly increased'.[71]
In 1932, the Queensland government issued an amendment to the
Fish and Oyster Act to 'absolutely prohibit the taking between
the first day of October and thirtieth day of November' of green

turtles and their eggs in the waters south of latitude 17°S.[72] The amendment corresponded with recommendations suggested by the GBRC scientist Frank Moorhouse, and represented a significant win for preservationists on the Reef.[73]

As concerned as these writers were with the possible extinction of the turtles, none raised any objection to the sport of turtle riding, which was displayed vividly on the cover of the December 1936 issue of *Walkabout*. The magazine depicted a young woman, sporting a large smile and dipping her eyes from the sun, dressed in bathing suit and cap, kneeling on the back of a bridled green turtle; the turtle's head is being pulled above the shallows. Napier, who lambasted the turtle-canning industry as inhumane, recalled the thrill of riding turtles like 'festive steeds', adding that 'I have not heard from the turtles; but, as they raised no verbal objection, it is to be presumed that they had none'.[74] As the anthropologist Celmara Pocock attests, turtle-riding wasn't only a tourist endeavour; scientists were just as likely to do it. Like birds, turtles were an easily identifiable, and popular, feature of the Reef. 'Turtle-riding', Pocock argues, was 'therefore a complex outcome of the confluence of time and space that gave rise to tourism at the Reef'.[75]

Even into the 1950s, riding turtles was a popular element of Reef tourism. What's more, the pastime never really seemed to gain any major opposition. Possibly, once the underwater world became more accessible – first via glass structures and glass-bottomed vessels, and then by means of snorkelling and scuba diving – viewing rather than riding turtles provided enough satisfaction to tourists. Perhaps, too, the post-war ecological sentiment meant that tourists felt less willing to participate in the 'sport'. Unlike the early-twentieth-century fascination with birds, there was no concerted attempt to redirect engagement with turtles from interaction to observation. The only clear objections focused on protecting them from exploitation for their meat.

*

Of all the industries along the Reef, pearl shelling, bêche-de-mer and trochus received the most romanticised appraisals. The bêche-de-mer and pearl shell fisheries received a post–World War I bump, following the forced closure of the fisheries during the conflict, but by the 1930s clear trends in their vulnerability were evident once more.[76] The industries continued to attract commentary over resource depletion and the racial mix of their labour force, but they had taken on a somewhat less alarming tenor.

Writers such as the popular novelist, poet and travel writer Vance Palmer suggested the abuse of Aboriginal and Torres Strait Islander workers had effectively been removed from the industry under 'the watchful eye of authority'.[77] Yonge claimed that, since World War I, the pearling industry had settled into 'an orderly collection from the bed of the sea of an important raw material of commerce'.[78] He wrote with particular admiration of the company boat scheme and its 'liberating' impact on Torres Strait Islanders. 'Nothing that I saw elsewhere', he said, gave him more respect for the Queensland government than this 'successful policy'. He stated that the Islanders had finally been enabled 'to live their own lives in their own way, and on islands which are more than ever assuredly their own, and to work out, with the most tactful of guidance, their own destinies'.[79]

Few considered the complex and restricting aspects of the industry upon the private lives of its labour.[80] Generally, the likelihood of resource depletion was of greater concern. Embury believed the industry would revive through artificial cultivation and asserted that 'scientists will lead the way to something of value commercially'.[81] Despite conceding that the industry had lost some of the romance and excitement of its 'old-time', a feeling that the industry would produce good yearly harvests prevailed.[82] The perceived value of the industries was, as Palmer asserted, much more 'than their figure-value'.[83] Their success and development was linked to settlement and explicitly the Reef's broader worth, and the notion that the Reef was commercially under-utilised prevailed. In a chapter titled 'Wealth of the Reef' in his book *Wonders of the Great Barrier Reef*, Roughley expressed particular enthusiasm at the prospect of a shark-fishing industry, and believed the industry's likely commercial success would be compounded by the removal of a 'shy, repulsive, cowardly' animal whose suffering would not induce 'the slightest sympathy'.[84] Napier accused governments of wrapping the Reef 'in a napkin', and considered the reason the Reef had yet to be properly exploited was because the 'islands and reefs have no population, and therefore no votes; but surely there are things which, even to a politician, may be greater than votes'.[85]

In comparison to commercial industry, tourism on the Reef was making serious strides in development. An increase in tourism advertisements from the early 1930s to 1939 accompanied the Reef writers' publications. The Australian National Travel Association (ANTA) and the QGTB advertised in popular magazines, including ANTA's own *Walkabout*.[86] The QGTB also commissioned a number of artists to design a suite of tourism posters: a number featured generalised depictions of the Reef, while others advertised specific islands. Further, the Queensland government decided to distribute copies of Roughley's book to 'tourist publicity offices and public libraries in America and England'.[87]

The increased awareness of and travel to the Reef was felt within local communities. In Cairns, the North Queensland Naturalists Club made guided tours of Dabuukji (Green Island) one of its earliest activities, fearing the destruction crowds of tourists would bring if they were free to trample across the island's fringing reefs.[88] An increase in transportation infrastructure to Dabuukji (Green Island) had led to its transition away from a place utilised by transient fishermen and towards day picnics and the like, and the club considered it imperative to provide travellers with informed guidance about its environmental features. In the Townsville monthly magazine *Cummins & Campbell's*, articles celebrated the

Reef as both a tourist pleasure ground and a commercial drawcard, and praised the development of hotels, roads and jetties on Yunbenun (Magnetic Island).[89]

By 1939, Reef tourism was increasingly popular, but a lack of infrastructure prevented it from becoming widely accessible. Signs that tourists were having a destructive effect, however, were evident. In 1933, the National Parks Association of Queensland was established, and many of its members were also members of the GBRC. The two organisations became entwined and began agitating for more islands to become national parks, and for management policies concerning resort development, resource stripping and foreign vessel intrusion.[90] The increasing awareness of the issues surrounding tourism was exemplified by a request to the Queensland government to provide travellers to Heron Island with iron hooks in order to protect their hands when they turned coral or picked up animals. The government sought advice from H.C. Richards, who told them not to encourage the activity because it would 'expose the marine life, which consequently dies'.[91]

In the same year, *Cummins & Campbell's* published a poem that alluded to the vandalism that tourism to the Reef brought:

Here tourists come from far away;
With clacking tongues and prying eyes
They stare through water-glasses on
The seagods' private paradise.

And on its flanks hang fishermen,
A hardy, dour and weathered band
That dangle hooks in opal lanes
And, chewing, spit in fairyland.[92]

As World War II erupted, the Reef was perceived as a place of unrealised economic potential, and it became increasingly clear that tourism would form the greatest source of the commercial wealth to be extracted from it.

Nature and travel writers who frequented the Reef's coral pools and islands were as likely to draw the reader's attention to its commercial products as to describe a beautiful or awe-inspiring scene. Travellers to the Reef were encouraged to consider it a recreational park where, in beautiful and unique natural settings, opportunities for industry might be found. Scientists, too, celebrated the Reef's economic possibilities, and considered it their duty to reveal its worth and assist in its exploitation. The Reef was perceived as a crucial part of the Australian environment, and it held heritage for settler Australia. Its seascapes and coral pools were an important part of the nation's environmental identity, and its birds, corals, turtles and other features were understood as vulnerable to human interference.

Yet despite the occasional opposition to the Reef's exploitation and development, there was no sustained Reef conservation movement prior to World War II. Attitudes towards the Reef's protection continued to be bound up in utilitarian ideals. While the Reef was beautiful, aesthetics alone would not provide wealth. Reef scientists openly discussed the Reef's economic value, but were forced to talk in terms of potential. They couldn't point to billions in tourism revenue so, instead, they stoked imaginations by conjuring up seemingly endless opportunities to develop the Reef. All they required was government investment and improved technology.

After World War II, when governments were keen to unlock and develop Australia's north, and had the technology to do so, these ambitions became a reality. Consequently, and in concert, ecological awareness of the Reef sharpened as the impacts of development became increasingly clear.

Knowledge

When David Attenborough's *Great Barrier Reef* aired on Australian television in April 2016, it inspired a rethink of the Reef's human story. The first episode focused on the formation of the Reef, animated through digital mapping of the ocean's flooding of a previously dry landscape some 10,000 to 14,000 years ago. On a screen – powerfully pixelated and programmed – this ablative glacial event was rendered much more visible than through the line graphs and numbers that usually explain the processes of the last glacial maximum. Even so, the drowning of an entire coastline seemed safely placed in the past; it appeared a non-human event, detached from the contemporary realities of rising sea levels.

Attenborough then turned to the Gimuy-walubarra Yidi, traditional owners of Cairns and its surrounds, and their story of Gunyah and the sacred fish. This lore-story, like multiple stories held across the Australian continent by coastal First Nations peoples, tells through dance of the rising of the ocean, and in this case the creation of the Reef. This 'folk memory', in Attenborough's words, 'coincides with what scientists are now discovering'.

For Attenborough, and many who watched it, this was remarkable. Survival of memory across generations, millennia; the accuracy of cosmology against the hard evidence of science. The dance itself, however, helped audiences to reckon with the drama of the Reef's creation. It provided a more meaningful and human narrative. While the animated mapping was comfortably seated in the deep past, the Gimuy-walubarra Yidi provided insight into the phenomenal drama of the oceanic rush through Country, and its erasing of some memories and its birthing of potent new ones. We were forced to envision the Barrier Reef's creation as a lived human experience, as we now contemplate our role in its decline.

At the core of this vignette was a separation – uncomfortable at times, if not a patronising differentiation – of epistemologies. On the one side stood a bank of science, built up over centuries of interrogating Earth's geological chronicles. On the other, a cultural memory, passed down through rigorous and defined methods of storytelling through millennia. Their alignment is astonishing, but so too is the latter's existence. The endurance of these memories – and stories associated with the formation of the Reef's islands and waters are common to many coastal First Nations peoples – is profound. Their continuity after settlement even more so.

Much like the rest of Australia's history, the Reef's is one of invasion, displacement and dislocation, but also of survival. First Nations Australians were dispossessed of Country; exploited for their labour, both scientific and economic; and forcibly relocated to reserves such as Bwgcolman (Palm Island). The Reef's islands and catchment were also sites of frontier violence and massacre. Within this story of exclusion, however, there is an important thread in which settler Australia relied on the knowledge and hospitality of Indigenous Australians, and learnt from their environmental ethic. In important ways, settler attitudes towards the Reef – how it was used, thought about, studied and discussed – were shaped by the First Nations peoples.

Before white settlement spread along the Reef coast, there was a sense that the Reef was a wild place. It is difficult to generalise about the feelings and emotions of the earliest white Reef explorers, but there was, often, an eeriness in the way they described passing through the Reef. Alone, far from security, they would scan the coastal hills and islands, looking for safe anchorage. They had a sense they were being watched; their presence communicated to others. They could see smoke rising, and Indigenous peoples on beaches. They knew they were in foreign country.

Nonetheless, their charting allowed for fishers and other maritime merchant and transport ships to thread through the Reef, extending Australia's colonial frontier and the war that followed. The exploitation of Indigenous labour, as well as the massacres of both Indigenous peoples, white fishers and wreck survivors on various Reef islands and within the catchment, prompted the fishery legislation of the late nineteenth century. Reports of shipwreck survivors being slaughtered by coastal First Nations peoples fuelled northern coastal expansion. Settlement along the Reef likely would have come, but violence enacted upon settlers, and the perceived damage to the settler economy, gave the process further impetus.

There were exceptions to this pattern of violence, such as the fascinating stories of Barbara Thompson (wrecked in the Torres Strait in 1844), James Morrill (wrecked off Townsville in 1846) and Narcisse Pelletier (abandoned at fourteen years of age near Lockhart River in 1858). All three found refuge with First Nations peoples for many years, before rejoining settler society. Later, when settlement in northern coastal areas began to develop, some settlers moved to offshore coastal islands. On Yunbenun (Magnetic Island), off the coast of Townsville, early arrivals were dependent on the Wulgurukaba people for water and foodstuffs. These stories recast and reorientate the narrative, both in today's time and in the past, of Indigenous Australians being reliant on the sympathy and hospitality of benevolent settlers; rather, white Australians became the dependants. These stories also provide examples of the complex ways in which Indigenous Australians helped settler Australians to view the Reef as a place where human life could thrive.

Even those settlers who helped foster an early fascination in the Reef relied on the labour of Indigenous Australians to survive. When Edmund and Bertha Banfield arrived at Coonanglebah (Dunk Island) in 1897, they were greeted by 'one of the few survivors of the native population': a man they referred to as Tom, who lived with his wife, Nelly, his mother-in-law and his son, Jimmy. Tom and his family had arrived a week before, unpacked a boat full of the Banfields' property and, in Banfield's words, 'spread out tents and rugs for the weak mortal who had greatly dared, but who, thus early, was ready to faint from weariness and sickness'.[1] Life on Coonanglebah (Dunk Island) was dependent on Tom, his family and other Indigenous Australian workers. They cleared land, planted vegetables, tended to Banfield's bees, transported harvests to and from the mainland, cooked and cleaned, conveyed Banfield around the island, and provided Edmund and Bertha with a seemingly constant supply of food from the sea.

Banfield wrote affectionately of Tom, especially in his second book, *My Tropic Isle* (1911). Tom figures in a series of stories: he is bitten by a spider, damages his finger poking at a shovel-nosed ray, helps Banfield rear a horse called Christmas, assists him with hauling a shark ashore, and educates him about the island's wildlife. More tragically, Banfield covers the events that led to the death of Jimmy, and the subsequent mourning. Eventually, Tom himself died from a spear wound he received from his half-brother, Willie, during a fight. Banfield wrote that his friend was an 'Australian by the purest lineage of birth "a citizen impossible to replace"'. Tom's services to Banfield were more than just practical: he offered friendship and philosophical inspiration.

Banfield's prose, when it comes to discussions of Indigenous Australia, is of its time: condescending and reflective of contemporary racial theories and the idea of Indigenous Australians as a 'dying' race. Banfield, so he claimed, was from 'enlightened England', while Indigenous Australia clung to 'cute' and 'fantastic' theories about human relationships with each other and the environment.

However assured Banfield felt of his ideas about nature, and the role of humans within it, upon arrival to his new home, his attitudes sharpened after interactions with Tom and his family. He saw within First Nations people a level of care and attention to the environment, which he hoped white Australia could learn from. White Australians, especially those who hunted the nutmeg pigeon, engaged in reckless destruction, while First Nations peoples were stewards. Banfield felt 'civilisation' had become fixated on modern trappings and he expressed an anti-materialist ethic. He saw that the First Nations peoples accepted environmental limits of production 'without thought of inciting Nature to produce better or more abundantly'.

Through Tom, Banfield learnt the island's intricacies – its flora and fauna, caves and crevasses, culture and chronicles. He learnt about the ancient custodial relationships between place and memory, and the law associated with them. Banfield hoped that 'the public conscience of Australia might have been aroused' to their ways of understanding nature. Episodes like these were generally expressed with romantic flourishes, which, in the early twentieth century, did more to highlight Banfield's own philosophical prowess and empathy. Although he exoticised the ethic of Indigenous Australians, he also came to understand, appreciate and respect it, and it is difficult to imagine Banfield defining his environmental perspective, let alone surviving life on Coonanglebah (Dunk Island), without the assistance of local Indigenous knowledge.

Banfield's writing inspired his readers to visit the Reef, where they themselves became dependent upon the First Nations peoples. Even before his writing, passengers who cruised through the Reef would anchor over a coral reef and on occasion send down a 'black boy, who dived' and grabbed 'as much as we wanted'.[2] Those same vessels would also visit Bwgcolman (Palm Island), an Aboriginal reserve by 1914, to watch traditional dances or dramatisations of 'American Cowboys and Red Indians'. In the latter, tourism was accommodated by having Indigenous Australians play out the violence inflicted on American First Nations peoples.[3]

Anthropologist Celmara Pocock has laid bare the instrumental role Indigenous Australians played in establishing early Reef tourism. Government reserves like Bwgcolman (Palm Island) and missions such as Yarrabah (south of Cairns), Pocock claims, were curiosities, museums – 'cultural remnants of another time'.[4] First

Nations Australians became enmeshed within the 'natural' appeal of the Reef, helping travellers to locate an idyllic 'Pacific' on Australia's coast. Cultural dances continued to form part of the Reef's tourism landscape, but eventually tourist expectations ensured that the dances conformed to 'Pacific Islander' tropes of costume, music and choreography. Indigenous Australians continued to function as part of the tourism experience as cheap labour, but their cultural links to the Reef were replaced by a vision of the Pacific that followed settler interpretations.

The labour of Indigenous Australians and their knowledge were also used by early scientific expeditions. Like the Banfields, early Reef scientists were reliant upon the affordability of Indigenous Australians' labour for carrying out major research operations. Throughout the entirety of the 1928–29 expedition to the Low Isles, Indigenous Australian workers from Yarrabah Mission were employed as chefs, boat hands, launderers, labourers, maintenance staff and cleaners. The expedition's research output continued to be published into the 1960s, and, until the establishment of the Australian Institute of Marine Science (AIMS) and the GBRMPA in the 1970s, it provided the majority of Australian coral reef science's contribution to global reef studies. Indeed, Maurice Yonge's research from the Low Isles was cited as recently as 2019.[5] In the lead-up to and during the expedition of 1928–29, as well as in the subsequent publishing output, the workers were barely acknowledged by Yonge. It seems, especially by our contemporary standards of authorship or contribution, that those Indigenous Australian workers – Andy and Grace Dabah, Claude and Minnie Connolly, Harry Mossman, and Paul Sexton – should receive greater acknowledgement of their role in this expedition. At the very least, the importance of Indigenous peoples' labour and input into early Reef science should be more firmly understood.

Increasingly, cultural heritage, particularly that of the Reef's traditional owners, informs the management of the Reef. Contemporary Reef scientists and managers are required to engage with traditional owners in developing their research initiatives and implementing their regimes. Contemporary tourism is also informed by Indigenous heritage. While there are many hotels and resorts that are relics of previous attempts to 'Pacificise' the Reef's islands, contemporary tourism initiatives are generally more conscious of the importance of Indigenous links. In many ways, these understandings are motivated by the failures of the past. It was not until the 1990s that the values of First Nations people were considered in the management of the Reef; prior to that they were ignored as irrelevant.

However, the deep past also informs this work. Attenborough's linking of ancient oral traditions to scientifically derived chronologies of change helps build a sense of cultural continuity that informs the rights of First Nations peoples to greater control and management over Country. This is important but difficult work. Settler Australia's understanding and perception of the Reef came at the expense of longer cultural links. Recognising how contemporary Reef values have been informed, and those values that have been lost, is vital to how we understand the Reef today. As the Australian historians Alessandro Antonello and Ruth Morgan write, 'whatever is known or can be known about the reef is the product of entangled natural and human histories'.[6]

What we know about the Reef, how we think about it and how we come to that knowledge will be decisive in how we comprehend and navigate future issues.

3

Emerging Concern

If the Save the Reef campaign of the late 1960s and early 1970s represents a tipping point – the moment when Reef concern became activism, and when the politics of the environment collided with the science – then the years preceding it witnessed the sharpening of those politics.

In the decades following World War II, both the Commonwealth and Queensland governments sought to improve the Reef's tourism infrastructure, increase investment in Reef science, and unearth new Reef resources. With the assistance of the scientific community, new resources were identified: this time, geological. In the 1950s, the GBRC geologists began reporting to oil companies and publicly broadcasting the Reef's wealth in oil. This stark agenda sat uncomfortably with some members of the committee, particularly those from the biological sciences. As the paradigm of coral reef science shifted towards having a more biological and ecological focus, the political canyon within Australian reef science widened.

Likewise, as governments, geologists and the growing cadre of tourist providers continued to look for ways to squeeze wealth out of the Reef, a public chorus of unease raised issues over the impacts or potential consequences of their actions. Interestingly, it was the increased development of the Reef's resources – not necessarily the broadening of scientific understanding – that stirred public concern with the Reef's health.

This anxiety was first expressed by local parties, including tourist operators, scientists and local nature enthusiasts, who were witnessing changes in their immediate Reef environments. Some lodged protests with governments and in newspapers about the over-collection of shells and corals from popular tourism regions, as well as the slaughter of turtles. Yet, rather than standing in outright opposition, the voices for conservation acknowledged the economic importance of the Reef but called for better management to ensure its natural and economic values were maintained.

One benefit of World War II, at least from the Queensland government's perspective, was the huge contingent of United States military personnel stationed along its coast. The government was eager to keep 'the name of the Barrier Reef [...] before the American public in view of the prospective trade between America and Australia after the war'.[1] The government thought that 'the presence of so many United States servicemen in this country and their correspondence with their families and friends in the U.S.A. [would] provide a potential tourist traffic for the Barrier Reef which can be stimulated *now*'.[2]

The Commonwealth had also bought into this strategy. The Department of Information produced a colour film titled *The Great Barrier Reef*, of which Arthur Calwell, then minister of information, stated: 'Everyone who has seen this film has been enchanted by the wonderful colour sequences.'[3] The department had also funded a lecture tour across the United States by Theodore Roughley between October 1945 and January 1946: 'a total of 27 lectures [were] delivered, the audience aggregating about eight or nine thousand people'.[4] Roughley saw potential in the American tourist who, he claimed, typically would travel to Europe but, given its post-war devastation, could be swayed to visit Australian shores. Yet it was not just an American invasion; the Reef was also welcoming returning interstate visitors and Queensland travellers eager to enjoy the life of fun and frivolity they had tasted during the inter-war period.

Reef tourism found new energy in the post-war era, and shell collecting was its draw. Tourists fossicking for and collecting shells and corals on tidal reefs began to adorn Reef brochures and pamphlets. William Dakin, professor of zoology at the University of Sydney, began his chapter on shells in his book *Great Barrier Reef* by exclaiming:

> Now a man who makes a hobby of 'fossicking' or, say, shell collecting, can find lots of interesting specimens on the shores of South Australia or N.S.W., for example. But there is something quite different about a coral reef. Its beauties and its peculiarities advertise themselves for everyone. It's fun to go exploring![5]

In September 1947, *The Australian Women's Weekly* carried a story about Mr and Mrs Andrews of Heron Island, commercial shell collectors who had struck it rich by fashioning their loot into costume jewellery. The article celebrated the plucky couple, who had abandoned their beauty salon in Brisbane to live a life of 'plain hard work'.[6]

The glamorisation of shell and coral collecting on the Reef quickly attracted criticism. The National Parks Association of Queensland (NPAQ) believed that the article from *The Australian Women's Weekly*, and others, did 'untold damage [...] to the coral and shells of the Reef'. Of significant concern to the NPAQ was the idea that tourists were seemingly unaware of the regulations prohibiting collecting, and its ecological consequences. The association called upon Premier E.M. Hanlon to enforce immediate protection to ensure the government's objective 'of bringing many tourists to the Reef' would 'result in a continuous flow for generations to come'. Without quick and rigorously enforced protection, the NPAQ warned, 'the government's efforts to popularise the Reef will come to naught by the sheer denudation and selfish vandalism at present invited'. At the very least, the NPAQ requested, the government must enforce a recommendation from the 1947 Queensland Tourist Development Board (QTDB) report 'prohibiting the removal and/or sale of all corals and shells'.[7] The government felt such a prohibition would be difficult, since the protector, appointed under the *Fish and Oyster Act*, was 'unable to visit these areas except at long intervals'. It did concede, however, that if tourist island lessees continued to allow visitors to remove shells and corals, it would 'not be long before the resorts lose much of their interest'.[8]

The QTDB's report endorsed a large-scale development of tourism along the Reef and encouraged measures to preserve its flora and fauna. The report provided a review of the existing tourist facilities, and a blueprint for improving them. It praised the efforts of the tourist proprietors on various Whitsunday islands, who faced difficulties in transporting and landing people and goods at the islands, as well as shortages of water, isolation and poor business during the summer and wet seasons. It identified Reef islands such as Koba (Fitzroy Island, near Cairns), Whitsunday, Hook and Pouandai (Hinchinbrook Island), along with various coral cays such as North West and Heron islands, as prospects for further development.[9] It recommended that ninety-nine-year leases be granted on various Reef islands already under lease, while islands that had no lease arrangements or were considered prospective major destinations should be organised under similar arrangements. The report concluded that unless land tenure on Reef islands was changed, 'large expenditure or improvements' would not proceed.[10] It was important that the accommodation be designed to have 'good scenic views of sea and islands', be architecturally beautiful, comfortable and blend with the natural setting, have 'easy access to coral which it should be possible to see by day and night and in all weathers', have good bathing and sport facilities, and finally have 'adequate night entertainment'.[11]

Despite these obvious intrusions onto the Reef-scape, the report was alive to the idea of preserving the Reef. The QTDB had gleaned from departmental reports that the existing suite of legislation protecting flora and fauna in national parks (which many of the Reef islands were), along with the system of honorary protectors, was working. They had received, however, contradictory evidence from elsewhere. In some cases, witnesses suggested that 'honorary protectors themselves were often the worst offenders, particularly in the removal of shells and coral'. The report, as the NPAQ had asserted, expressed concern about the collection of coral and shells from Reef islands. It concluded:

> On several islands we observed that shells and coral were for sale, and in certain shops on the mainland a flourishing business apparently exists in the sale of treated shells and coral as souvenirs. On the other hand, many of the operators, both on the islands and on the mainland, are doing everything possible, both by precept and example, to discourage the despoliation of our heritage. We are not unmindful of the fact that most tourists, particularly those visiting Barrier Reef islands, desire to take away with them some memento of their stay, but we feel that this attitude should be discouraged, otherwise, with an influx of tourists, our islands and reefs will soon lose their natural attractiveness.[12]

Along with legislating the prohibition of the removal or sale of all corals and shells, the report suggested that tourists would 'be reasonable in the matter' if they were better informed 'of the ultimate effects of the plundering of natural resources'.[13]

No notable changes to legislation dealing with the Reef's preservation were made, but development of its tourism industry powered on. By 1950, a Catalina Flying Boat Service linked Brisbane with Heron Island and the islands in the Whitsunday Passage; in the peak periods an extra service to the Whitsundays was provided.[14] There was also a daily plane service between Brisbane and Mackay. Later, in 1961, Proserpine opened its own aerodrome, hoping to capitalise on its proximity to the Whitsunday Islands.[15] Airline companies were important components in the post-war Whitsunday tourist industry – the most notable contribution being Reginald Ansett's purchase of Daydream Island and Hayman Island, the latter of which became the site of a large luxury hotel.

As historian Todd Barr has stressed, however, the development of the tourist industry in the Whitsunday region, and the successes of the enterprises, did not follow a uniform pattern. Rather, its post-war development was characterised by diversity. Daydream, for instance, did not become the home of a lavish luxury hotel; instead Ansett managed the island in much the same way its previous owners had, with 'moderate accommodation at relatively affordable rates'.[16] But, in 1952, Daydream was closed, largely as a result of Ansett's mismanagement of the Hayman Island resort; it would remain dormant until 1968.[17]

The islands further north also experienced post-war tourism development. Yunbenun (Magnetic Island), which had been the site of military forts during the war and now hosted permanent settlements in many of its bays, continued to be serviced by regular ferries from Townsville. Coonanglebah (Dunk Island), the Banfields' former abode, was now frequently serviced by launches departing from the coastline near Tully, as were Goold, Richard, Pouandai (Hinchinbrook Island) and the islands in the Family and Barnard groups.

Dabuukji (Green Island), the 'last stronghold of romance', continued to hold a significant place in the Reef's tourism industry. In 1954, Dabuukji's (Green Island's) popularity increased dramatically with the construction and installation of a 25-foot-long, 7-foot-high and 8-foot-wide (7.6-metre-long, 2.1-metre-high, 2.4-metre-wide) underwater observatory. In its advertisements, the QGTB continued to promote and portray the Reef's visitors fossicking and scavenging the fringing reefs for coral and shells. They did, however, include a disclaimer: 'visitors to the islands are reminded that the removal or damage of flora and fauna, terrestrial and marine, is prohibited by Order-in-Council'.[18] But the issue continued to fester, particularly at Dabuukji (Green Island), as not all tourists paid attention to these warnings.[19]

The post-war boom in Reef tourist infrastructure did little to alleviate the concerns of the Queensland government about the industry's long-term viability. They lamented that Reef tourist facilities were poor and failed to accommodate visitors expecting comfort, let alone luxury. In 1955, the Country Party's member for Mirani, Ernie Evans, complained that the Reef, like other tourist spots in North Queensland, was hindered by a lack of infrastructure such as roads and suitable accommodation. He considered that if tourists were adequately catered for, they could fill 'a 400 lb [180 kilogram] icebox with fish' and catch hundreds of crabs in one trip, as he boasted he had.[20] Fellow Country Party politician and the member for Isis, Jack Pizzey, ridiculed the Labor government for failing to adopt recommendations in the 1947 report that would assist in the development of Reef tourism. In particular, Pizzey thought Queensland should adopt a tourist loan scheme similar to the one utilised in Tasmania to assist in the improvement of facilities.[21] Both parties, heading into an election in 1956, positioned themselves as capable of opening up the Reef's vast tourism resources.

The National Parks movement, however, was persistent. In January 1956, honorary ranger Douglas Jolly wrote to Premier Vince Gair to propose the establishment of a consolidated 'Barrier Reef National Park'. For Jolly, the park would extend eastwards to the Reef's outer barrier, northward to Hayman Island and southwards to include Keyser Island. He considered that since the islands of the Whitsunday Passage were 'rapidly becoming renowned as major tourist attractions', the consolidation of many national parks into a single 'Barrier Reef National Park or

Whitsunday National Park' would dramatically improve their administration and also bring about further recognition.[22]

Since the proposed park would encompass 'all islands, reefs and water especially the reefs to protect them from tourists', the *National Parks Act* would need to be amended. The government believed that the protection of the various islands' fringing reefs – at least, the ones exposed at low water – could be dealt with under the *Fish and Oyster Act*. Under the *Fauna Protection Act* of 1952, most of the Reef's islands were already listed as sanctuaries, and the more frequented tourist islands were national parks. In each case, fauna and flora were protected to the high-tide mark. But this legislation did not include restrictions on coral and shell collecting.

In 1957, the Queensland government finally prohibited the removal of coral and shell from the Reef unless it was done within a licensed area or by a licensee. The government was less amenable to consolidating national parks. Thomas Foley, the minister for lands and irrigation, reasoned that the Whitsunday islands had names that were 'well established in the public mind and to include them under the one name would subjugate their identity and take away from the distinctiveness of each particular island'.[23] Therefore, the Reef would only be protected through existing legislation, in which individual islands would serve as distinct national parks, with their names and natural attributes protected to facilitate their publicity in Australia and abroad.

As Reef historians James and Margarita Bowen laid bare, the aspirations of Australian marine scientists to establish a permanent marine research station on Australia's east coast was an enduring frustration into the post-war era. Even the facilities on the Low Isles had to be closed as a result of the Great Depression; they were then destroyed by a cyclone in March 1934. The progress of Australian marine science, especially biology, stalled. Within the GBRC, largely thanks to Richards's privileging of geological questions, marine biology languished. Moreover, Australian science remained colonial in its outlook: even the Low Isles expedition was led by a British scientist. Few Australian-educated scientists emerged in the 1920s and 1930s to staff, lead and progress marine science within the nation's universities.

The GBRC, however, remained obsessed with its inter-war goal of establishing itself and the disciplines of marine science as essential. In 1950, plans were underway for erecting a marine biology research station on Heron Island. In September 1950, the deputy chairman of the GBRC, W.H. Bryan, wrote to Premier Hanlon requesting the government's financial support in the endeavour.

The GBRC believed that the research station would allow Australian scientists to make contributions to the growing field of marine biology and the understanding of coral reefs. The GBRC suggested many of the scientists would be associated with UQ (one of the few Australian universities that provided a full course in marine biology at the time), so the facility would provide a training ground for aspiring marine biologists. Additionally, they proposed that the station would assist in revealing economic benefits of the Reef, as well as heightening its tourist appeal.[24] Australian scientists, unlike their counterparts in Europe and the United States, had not been able to convince the state or federal governments of the Reef's merits in the first half of the twentieth century. Furthermore, Australian marine research along the Reef continued to be yoked to government funding, and therefore 'economic' or 'industrial' research remained an imperative.

The government, always eager to broaden the Reef's economic and tourist value, believed the station would be of economic benefit:

> The Great Barrier Reef is, in its way, unique and is a constant source of interest to scientific workers all over the world. Large numbers of such workers come to Queensland from the south every year to conduct investigations at various locations on the

Reef. Apart from any direct benefits to be gained from the study of marine biology, the establishment of the station will […] bring some prestige to this State and must have the effect of increasing public interest in the Reef as a tourist attraction.[25]

The GBRC was provided with a 5-acre (2-hectare) lease on Heron Island, and half of both its construction (£3750) and its ongoing costs would be paid for by the Queensland government.[26] The GBRC members were jubilant, and the media celebrated the fact that 'the world's biggest single coral area will have its first permanent marine research station […] made of coral brick on the spot'.[27]

The work to be conducted on Heron Island was varied but included research both on fisheries and on less economically driven questions. There was also a hope, especially since several of the GBRC's prominent members were geologists, that geological research would occur. In 1947, the GBRC's chairman, E.O. Marks, had already made a request to the Queensland government to approach the Commonwealth on their behalf to request that the GBRC could make use of their 'greatly improved modern techniques of Geophysical Survey' to investigate the problems of the Reef. The GBRC members were excited by the preliminary findings emerging from geological surveys conducted at the Bikini atolls; these tests provided clarity regarding the formations of coral reefs and affirmed Darwin's theory of subsidence.[28] The Commonwealth, however, was not willing to immediately lend the team and its equipment to the GBRC. Prime Minister Ben Chifley explained to Premier Hanlon that while the Commonwealth's geophysical group 'might well be used to throw some light upon' problems of worldwide significance, like the formation of the Great Barrier Reef, '[t]his group has many pressing commitments in connection with the search for coal, oil, metals, radioactive minerals etc., and the more urgent of these will need to be dealt with before geophysicists and suitable instruments could be made available for the more scientific studies'.[29]

It was perhaps an indication for GBRC geologists interested in the Reef that their future research, no longer driven by the quest to solve the origins of the Reef, should be directed at determining its geological products.

In the 1950s, the geological resources of the Reef came under greater scrutiny. In 1956, UQ and GBRC geologist Dorothy Hill compiled a report for the mining industrialist Maurice Mawby titled *The Geology of the Great Barrier Reef in Relation to Oil Potential*. The report catalogued the known aspects relating to the geology of the Queensland-Papuan continental shelf, including detailed descriptions of theories relating to the formation of the Reef, and the origins of its continental islands, coral reefs and other submerged features. It also dealt with 'knowledge and theory that might help in deducing what lies under the continental shelf in areas covered by the Authorities to Prospect of the Australian Mining and Smelting Co'.[30] Hill's report was largely speculative, but suggested that determining the existence of oil within the Reef required exploratory borings. Hill recommended a number of sites along the Reef for wells to be dug, including: Raine Island, Sandbank No. 5 and No. 8 (two cays, about 50 kilometres apart, on the outer barrier north-west from Cape Melville), Sandbank No. 1 (due east of Cape Melville), Harrier Reef (60 kilometres north-east of Cooktown), the Broad Sound region (roughly the area between Long Island and Sarina), in the Bunker and Capricorn island groups (specifically North West Island), Hixson Cay (one of the Swain Reefs) and Bell Cay (about 155 kilometres north-east of Yeppoon).[31]

The Queensland government was eager to locate oil. In 1959, the Commonwealth government introduced a subsidy system to encourage oil exploration, of which Queensland, along with Western Australia, New South Wales and the Northern Territory, took advantage. The subsidy, combined with uncertainty surrounding access to Middle East oil reserves, provided the impetus for Queensland to explore for oil. In 1959, Premier Frank

Nicklin announced that 551,740 square miles (1,429,000 square kilometres) of Queensland were held under prospecting titles and a further 200,000 square miles (517,998 square kilometres) were under consideration. He added:

> These areas incorporate the potential oil-bearing fields – the Great Artesian, the Bowen Gulf, Laura and Maryborough basins and the Great Barrier Reef. Climatic conditions at this time of the year restrict actual geological work but recently underwater gravity surveys were undertaken in the Barrier Reef area. Drilling of deep prospect wells is expected to begin on Wreck Island on the Barrier Reef in March.[32]

The well at Wreck Island (near Rockhampton) was one of three drilled on the Reef between 1959 and 1967; others were also drilled in the Capricorn region. None produced oil or gas, and all were conducted with a Commonwealth government subsidy.[33] Between 1953 and 1967, thirty-seven authorities to prospect and exploration permits for petroleum had been granted by the Queensland government. Of those, twenty-three were granted in the Reef area.[34] The huge initial costs involved in exploration would be, Nicklin stated, 'justified by the wealth it will add to industry and to the national income'.[35]

Petroleum was not the only geological resource that the Reef potentially offered. Frank McNeill, an Australian marine zoologist with the Australian Museum, explained in 'Wealth in Coral Gravels' that the Reef held a particularly high-grade quality of calcium carbonate:

> Tests of a number of samples from [the Reef] have proved boundless commercial possibilities and great potential national wealth. The vast deposits awaiting collection are scattered for twelve hundred miles [1,931 kilometres] along the north-eastern coast of the

continent – the fine gravels as well as sands which are the wastage or debris (detritus) of coral banks. In hundreds of places they comprise the low mounds heaped above or near to the surface by the action of the waves and the wind. Many are tree-decked coral isles, while others carry either little or no vegetation.[36]

McNeill attested that the 'big discovery of the value of the coral gravels' of the Reef had been the product of work being conducted since 1937 to investigate the quality of the Reef's dead coral matter. For McNeill, the quality of the product was not its only virtue. He wrote that 'the source of supply is limitless, easy of access, economically approachable and needs no selection'. The product could be used as flux for glaze on metal refrigerators, baths and sinks, in pottery and wall tiles, as well as in the manufacturing of sugar, gelatine and leather. McNeill pointed to the existence of a milling firm in Moreton Bay that dredged coral material 'from a dead reef', but its final product was 'not nearly the quality of that from the Great Barrier Reef deposits'.[37] He ended his article by asserting:

The vast accumulations of detritus along the Great Barrier Reef have lain dormant and unnoticed for centuries. They can be processed into highly valuable commodities for half the present cost. It will be interesting to see how long a time will elapse before this source of national wealth is turned to account.[38]

In McNeill's article, the economic metaphors of previous Reef scientists came into play once more: 'vast accumulations' of 'dormant' resources. The Reef's perceived value, at least in economic terms, was always expressed in these abstract, nebulous qualities. The politics, however, was clear. The Reef needed to be 'turned to account' to generate more than scientific intrigue: it needed to produce revenue worthy of its status and size.

*

While the Reef's potential geological resources were being investigated, the scientific community's preservationist agenda focused on the protection of one prominent Reef resource: green turtles. In January 1950, a number of Queensland papers publicised the exportation of Barrier Reef turtles to Britain. *The Central Queensland Herald* reported that on 12 January, sixteen turtles were being exported, and 'another 25 to 30 turtles' were expected to arrive in Brisbane for exportation within the week. They added that 'at least two consignments' would be sent every week until the end of February.[39]

Later in May, *The Daily Mercury* reported that Professor P.D. Murray, of the Australian Museum, was urging controls be introduced to protect the turtle. Murray described a scene at Gladstone Harbour, where captured turtles had been turned on their backs and were 'in a pathetic state, lying in the open under a blazing sun in a temperature of 100 degrees. They were thoroughly exhausted and mucus was streaming from their eyes and nostrils.'[40] Water was poured, intermittently, on their bodies, which seemed only to add to their distress. 'They reacted by impotently thrashing the decking with their flippers and struggling generally in a forlorn way to escape their tormentors.' For Murray, the treatment of the turtles was cruel, and the number of turtles being slaughtered put the population at grave risk:

> Ill-considered and cruel exploitation of the Green Turtle of the Great Barrier Reef – a practice which will endanger the existence of one of our greatest tourist attractions [...] In the light of the new and ambitious State tourist development of the Barrier Reef islands there should surely be some rigid control or else complete cessation of the present practice of turtle trading.[41]

The exclusive slaughter of female turtles had also, reportedly, had a noticeable impact on turtle populations in the nearby islands of the Capricorn Group.

The incident was memorialised in an article for the *Australian Museum Magazine* in 1955. Frank McNeill, who claimed he 'was the main instigator of the campaign', recalled that at a GBRC meeting when the turtles were discussed, 'a healthy reflection voiced at the meeting was that the tourist trade was likely to outweigh the turtle trade by ten to one'.[42] The GBRC settled that, since the turtle industry was demonstrating signs of revitalisation, its development should be 'placed on a reliable and scientific basis before it increased'.[43] It recommended 'that an investigation into the ecological and economic status of the green turtle along the Great Barrier Reef should be undertaken', and that, until this was completed, the green turtle should be protected.

In September 1950, the Queensland government amended the *Fish and Oyster Act* to 'absolutely prohibit the taking' of green turtles, and their eggs, 'in Queensland waters or on or from the foreshores of or lands abutting on such waters'.[44] In the 1920s and 1930s, the need to protect the turtle had been expressed in terms of the cruelty to the animal and the harm that over-exploitation would have on the industry. In the 1950s, those views were again promulgated, but there was increasing acknowledgement that the turtle was an important attraction for the growing tourist industry. While the GBRC remained open to the notion of a turtle industry, McNeill suggested that its slaughter on an industrial scale, even with controls introduced, would bring about the turtle's decimation.[45]

The total prohibition, however, was short-lived. Between 1956 and 1958, Cairns-based brothers Snowy and Neil Whittaker lobbied the Queensland government to lift the prohibition in the northern regions of the Reef.[46] They argued that turtles, particularly at Raine Island, were so abundant that nesting turtles were unable to find places to deposit their eggs, creating a situation in which laid eggs were dug out and left to be eaten by birds. The population needed thinning out, they claimed. Oddly, they also argued that they would save more than they would kill by assisting any hatchlings they found to the water and protecting them from the birds.[47]

Despite the awkwardness of their argument, their lobbying was successful. In 1958, the Queensland government rescinded the 1950 Order in Council and stipulated that, while taking green turtle eggs continued to be absolutely prohibited along the Queensland coast, the removal of green turtles was only prohibited south of latitude 15°S.[48] A subsequent revival of the industry began in North Queensland, particularly out of Cairns, which again drew protests. The Townsville and District Natural History Society were concerned that the 'slaughtering of North Queensland turtles for their meat' would result in their extinction as far south as Mackay.[49] Others, however, who were usually inclined to protect native fauna, like the North Queensland Naturalists, felt that the situation was 'very far from alarming'.[50]

By the end of the 1950s, the issues that would coalesce as the points of tension in the Save the Reef campaign had emerged. The threats posed by increased tourism development were beginning to highlight the conservation issues surrounding the Reef, and, while few were aware of it, mineral and petroleum exploitation were forming as the next major Reef industry. Within Reef science, divides were beginning to emerge as marine biology found some credibility with the establishment of the research station on Heron Island and Reef geologists sought to aid government and industry in exploiting the Reef's minerals and petroleum.

In response to the increased likelihood of Reef development, the prospect of protecting large swathes of the Reef had been advanced for the first time in the Reef's history. But this suggestion gained little support beyond a small group of concerned conservationists. Awareness within the public surrounding the threats to the Reef was still relatively disorganised. Any government initiative towards widescale protection of the Reef would require a more vocal and unified movement.

4

Towards Saving the Reef

The Save the Reef campaign did not emerge out of nothing. In the 1960s, a more vocal and organised Reef conservation ethic emerged. Partly motivated by the damage to local reefs, its appearance also reflected the rise of the global environmental movement at the time. The environmental consequences of economic development had been made devastatingly clear by the science of ecology; Rachel Carson's 1962 book *Silent Spring* turned it into popular knowledge. *Earthrise*, the image of our planet rising beyond the Moon's horizon, created a sense of Earth's vulnerability. Atomic and nuclear weapons, meanwhile, showed how suddenly life could be extinguished. In the 1950s and 1960s, environmental angst was growing, and in Australia it found expression in a cadre of grassroots conservation organisations. Yet while there were increasing calls for better conservation and management of the Reef, an explicit Reef environmentalism had not yet surfaced.

In 1962, the poet and public intellectual Judith Wright helped establish the Wildlife Preservation Society of Queensland (WPSQ), which expanded to have several branches across the state. One branch that would have an important role in future Reef endeavours was established in 1966 at Innisfail, by the Bingil Bay artist John Büsst.[1] Büsst was a former member of Justus Jorgensen's artists' collective on the north-eastern outskirts of Melbourne at the chapel known as Montsalvat.

In 1941, Büsst purchased a lease on Bedarra Island – part of the Family Islands National Park – and lived there until 1957, when he moved to the mainland and settled at Bingil Bay, close to the holiday house of his old schoolfriend Harold Holt. Beginning at Bedarra and continuing at Bingil Bay, Büsst became friendly with scientists, particularly the ecologist Len Webb, who travelled to study the rainforests that surrounded Büsst's home.[2] Büsst understood the importance of the surrounding rainforests and explained to the journalist Patricia Clare: 'We're battling to preserve them for the botanists. They're unique.'[3]

Büsst saw the interconnectedness of the Reef with terrestrial environments. Büsst, Clare reported, said that the rainforests were felled for sugar, cattle and bananas, and explained how this affected the broader ecosystem: 'They cut in July, and they burn it in December. Then down comes the rain of the Wet season – and this is one of the wettest areas in the world – and there's no cover on the ground. I see rich red topsoil every season pouring into the ocean.'[4]

In Büsst the Reef had a unique human advocate. He was a rare amalgam in the Reef's history of settler engagement: he knew the science, the politics and the politicians, and was one of the few people who had faith in their collective imagination.

The WPSQ and its branches were not the only Reef advocates established in the mid-1960s. During Easter 1965, a group of students from UQ and members of the zoology department of CSIRO established the Queensland Littoral Society (QLS), which focused specifically on the protection and preservation of marine environments.[5] They were young scuba-diving researchers, the beneficiaries of renewed government investment in Australia's tertiary education and of the subsequent broadening and advancements of scientific education, whose environmental politics informed their passion for science. Then, in 1966, the Australian Conservation Foundation (ACF) held its first meeting.

These groups formed part of a 'second wave' of the Australian environmental movement, which found itself in opposition to the increasingly obvious impacts of economic growth and technological developments in the post-war period.[6] In her book *The Coral Battleground*, Wright recalled how a feeling of togetherness and strength was brewing within the conservation movement:

> All of us began to feel we were no longer lone operators. We had now met many other people working in our field, we were full of the euphoria that comes to small embattled groups when the idea they are working for begins to break through; in spite of some internal doubts and disagreements, the conservation movement began to feel itself a happy few, a band of brothers and sisters, but with achievements ahead.[7]

Importantly, the organisations were a mixture of local grassroots institutions like the branches of the WPSQ and larger government-funded groups like the ACF. Individuals were often members of several groups. John Büsst, for instance, was a member of the WPSQ, the QLS and the ACF; from 1968, he was also a member of the GBRC.

Many of the organisations' members and conveners were scientists from various universities and institutions, and their number included influential and celebrated Australians such as Wright, the zoologist Francis Ratcliffe and Sir Garfield Barwick, a former federal attorney-general and from 1964 the chief justice of the High Court. Despite characterisations to the contrary, they were not ragtag outsiders.[8] Indeed, their broad membership, including members of the social and cultural elite, would be a significant factor in the success of the Save the Reef campaign.

While conservationists would make significant contributions to the preservation of the Reef and Reef politics generally, they had little input into Reef matters prior to 1967. In *The Coral*

Battleground, Wright recalled that in 1962 the WPSQ members were aware of the damage being done at Dabuukji (Green Island) from coral and shell collection. They had received correspondence from island residents, and from underwater photographers Noel and Kitty Monkman.[9] Patricia Clare, whose book *Struggle for the Great Barrier Reef* captured the broad concerns for the Reef in the late 1960s, described Noel Monkman as 'the northern sentinel of the forces opposed to the exploitation of the Reef'.[10] Clare recorded a Monkman sermon on the impacts of tourists at Dabuukji (Green Island):

> To preserve anything at all [...] you have to fight so many people. I've been an honorary fisheries inspector for twenty-five years – I'm also a flora and fauna protector – and I've found that everyone who comes here thinks they're entitled to take something away. 'One little piece of coral' they'll say – over and over again you'll hear it – 'just one little piece. I only want this one little piece to take home and show the family.' I say to them, 'First of all it will be dead long before you get home. You'll only arrive with the skeleton. And also,' I say, 'there are tens of thousands of tourists come to this reef every year. That means tens of thousands of people take one little piece. Just look at the reef that's left. Besides, you're stealing. You're a thief. It doesn't belong to you, it [...] it doesn't belong to any living person. It doesn't belong to our unborn children. None of us own it. We're only privileged to see it. Not to take it away, not to sell it. We're caretakers, and that's all.'[11]

Monkman's correspondence with the WPSQ prompted it to investigate the 'idea of the Reef's becoming a great underwater park'. Wright asserted, however, that neither state nor federal governments were interested, and the zoologists and marine biologists believed the introduction of a marine park was unnecessary.[12]

Among those who felt the issue was perhaps overblown was the naturalist Vincent Serventy, who had spent time at Dabuukji (Green Island) in October 1965. He wrote that he felt the island had been largely left unspoiled, and that high density of tourists 'need not affect the wild life'. Serventy reasoned that 'the presence of tourists stops the kind of vandalism and illegal killing which still takes place in sanctuaries where there are no wardens'.[13]

In addition to growing concerns from environmentalist groups about human influence on the Reef, a natural threat emerged that inspired broad anxieties over the future of the Reef: the crown-of-thorns starfish (*Acanthaster planci*). Before the 1940s, despite awareness of the starfish among Torres Strait Islanders, especially those engaged in the trochus fishery, Australians were largely ignorant of it. For the Torres Strait Islanders, the starfish was well known for its capacity to sting.[14] Familiarity, or at least sightings, of the starfish among non-Indigenous Australians between the years 1942 and 1960 increased as access to the Reef improved, including the introduction of scuba diving, rather than growth in the starfish's population. Nonetheless, prior to the 1960s, there seemed to be little understanding, including among scientists, that the starfish killed coral.[15]

In 1960, things changed dramatically; the proprietor of Dabuukji's (Green Island's) underwater observatory, Vince Vlasoff, first noticed the arrival of large numbers of the starfish and its destruction of coral.[16] When Vlasoff raised concerns over the starfish's destructiveness, however, he was 'advised of the many reasons that coral could die from and none of these included the action of the starfish'.[17]

The starfish's population at Dabuukji (Green Island) increased, and the constellation progressed along its reef. Vlasoff recalled that the outbreak became so severe that 'we would have to police the reef about the Observatory several times weekly for a distance of 100 yds

[91 metres] and even this [sic] we had to destroy many that go to the corals about the Observatory and caused damage'.[18] The numbers of starfish encountered during the peak period of the outbreak (1960–66) at reefs varied, and claims were often imprecise, but most anecdotal and statistical evidence suggested that thousands of starfish could be sighted at impacted reefs.[19]

By the end of 1965, the reports of the damage caused to the reefs, particularly those around Dabuukji (Green Island), had raised sufficient alarm that the Fisheries Branch of the Queensland Department of Primary Industries sent fisheries biologists to survey the damage. At the same time, the Dabuukji (Green Island) resort management began to employ divers to physically remove starfish from the surrounding reefs. Fisheries biologist N.M. Haysom recommended to the Queensland government in 1965 that the plague warranted the investigation of control techniques other than removal by hand, and that a research program should be instigated.[20]

As the starfish spread, tourist operators became increasingly anxious and frustrated by the resources they had to devote to combating the plague. In February 1966, B.L. Hayles, the managing director of Hayles Magnetic Island Pty Ltd, a company that ran launch services between Cairns and Dabuukji (Green Island), wrote to the Queensland treasurer, Gordon Chalk, about the increasing damage caused by the starfish. Hayles expressed serious concern over the 'continued prevalence of this pest and our inability to completely cope with the large numbers with our limited resources' and said:

> To date we have removed and destroyed over 20,000 of these specimens. This has been achieved by means of a diver who has been permanently engaged during the past five months on an incentive basis 1/- per specimen, assisted by three members of the crew of our M.V. *Marena* during the daily trip to Green Island.[21]

He warned that unless immediate action was taken, 'the destruction of one of the foremost tourist attractions in this country' would continue.

The government, it turned out, had already begun its response. It had been advised, presumably by Haysom, that protective measures to 'preserve the glass bottom boat viewing areas' of Dabuukji (Green Island) needed to be improved and reorganised immediately. Additionally, a Cabinet submission stated that the 'annihilation of coral in the Green Island area is probable', and that the annihilation of the whole Reef was 'possible'.[22] Worryingly, the submission conceded that 'very little is known of this star-fish. There is little mention in world scientific literature of the fish and its habits and there is no scientific knowledge on which we could base a campaign for eradication.'[23]

The government decided to employ Robert Pearson, a research scientist from UQ, as a fisheries biologist within the Department of Harbours and Marine. Pearson would undertake a two-year research project under secondment to UQ, which would appoint a supervisor, the marine zoologist Robert Endean. The project would ascertain several aspects concerning the starfish: its distribution and abundance, spawning behaviour, growth rate, feeding habits, migration habits, biological or other controls influencing its behaviour and occurrence, and possible means of control.[24]

Two aspects characterised the crown-of-thorns outbreak from the outset, and would continue in the following years. First, the language surrounding its appearance was alarmist, and has since been characterised as such.[25] The fact that the starfish was first sighted in devastating numbers around one of the Reef's foremost tourist attractions was likely a factor. The impact upon tourism seemed to override, at least initially, concerns for the corals themselves. Additionally, the lack of information on the starfish was stark. Scientists who could only speculate on the likely limits of possible destruction were prone to exaggeration, and so provoked debate in the public sphere. The uncertainty allowed for media outlets to construct headlines like 'Starfish dines on the Barrier Reef' or 'Weird starfish eating miles of Barrier Reef'.[26]

Second, the starfish immediately became a symbol of an ecological imbalance in the Reef.[27] Although the cause of the imbalance was not readily apparent, scientists' hypotheses included the removal of an important predator, or environmental changes such as an increase in water temperatures. Its arrival brought with it the realisation of the ephemerality of coral reefs. While many considered its population explosion to be 'self-limiting', the notion that something that had 'taken years to grow can be destroyed overnight' gave a sense of urgency to understand and protect the Reef.[28]

Significantly, the crown-of-thorns became a focus for all the concerns that had been developing over the Reef's conservation since the end of World War II. *Walkabout* called the starfish the most urgent 'of all conservation problems that confront Australia'.[29] The crown-of-thorns, unlike other naturally occurring destroyers of coral reefs, would require a human solution.

The crown-of-thorns outbreak did not diminish existing concerns for the Reef's conservation. Shell collection, particularly by tourists and commercial collectors, continued to be proclaimed as a major threat to the Reef's future. In 1965, the GBRC's chairman, O.A. Jones, implored the public to direct their opinion 'against the ruining of one of Australia's big national assets'.[30] Jones and the GBRC wanted greater protection for coral and shells across the Reef. *The Courier Mail* erroneously reported that shells and marine species were only protected at Dabuukji (Green Island) and Heron Island. In 1965, however, removal of coral and shells from the Reef was illegal (except in distinct locations, which did not include Dabuukji [Green Island] and Heron Island), and the collection of coral and shells could only be conducted by those who held a licence. The impression Jones and *The Courier Mail* created was that tourists and commercial collectors were robbing the Reef, and that some reefs had been 'swept clean'. What was required, apart from broader protection, was an increased presence of fisheries rangers. As Jones stated, however, 'you can't have a ranger on every reef'. *The Courier Mail*'s editorial suggested that the Reef would be ruined unless protections were introduced. They called on 'those dependent on the Reef for their livelihood' to be the first to protect it, and demanded the apprehension and punishment of those who continued to rob it.[31]

The Queensland government called for 'some perspective' on the issue. The treasurer, Thomas Hiley, reasoned that most of the Reef 'has never been touched by human hand and probably never would be'.[32] The most alluring reefs, those that had 'the greatest potential as a tourist attraction' and were 'constantly covered with water', were great angling grounds, and provided opportunities to view the reef from a glass-bottomed boat. Hiley added that the corals and shells collected by licensed operators were spread throughout the world, 'quietly advertising the wonders of this unique attraction'.

Hiley accepted, however, that foot traffic on coral reefs, particularly at popular locations, had the potential to cause damage, and imagined that 'the time will come when, in the really dense areas, foot traffic on the reef will have to be prohibited as live coral is a delicate animal'.[33] These were comments indicative of a government, and a public, struggling to come to terms with the future of an environment as vast, isolated and scientifically unknown as the Reef.

Despite these concerns, a desire to fully uncover the economic potential of the Reef continued throughout the 1960s. The growing awareness of the impacts of exploitation failed to diminish the urge to draw revenue from the Reef. Queensland parliamentarians, particularly those from seats adjacent to the Reef, called on the government to assist in revealing the potentially limitless resources that had been long promised.

The Labor member for Cairns, Ray Jones, said that the 'glorious seemingly endless Great Barrier Reef' would leave any tourist either from abroad or the south breathless with 'its simple, unique and unspoilt beauty'. Earlier, though, he had claimed: 'The harvest of the Great Barrier Reef waters and the Coral Sea, particularly the yellow-fin tuna, could make the establishment of a fish cannery at Cairns a worth-while and attractive proposition.'[34] The Labor member for Townsville North, Perc Tucker, lamented the paucity of the Reef's fish being exploited by the Queensland fisheries. Tucker asserted, rather simplistically, that only 30 per cent of the Reef's fish were being harvested, leaving 70 per cent unharvested. As if failing to harvest all possible fish was not worrying enough, Tucker then exclaimed that the fish 'have been left to [the] Japanese, and now possibly the Russians'.[35]

History's echo could be heard in Tucker's and Jones's exclamations: the Reef holds profitable quantities of unlimited resources and the government was neglecting an economic resource while others plundered it at will. For these men, saving the Reef meant protecting its economic resources for Australia alone.

The appetite for petroleum exploration had moved along since the 1950s. In early 1967, the Commonwealth and state governments finalised the joint offshore petroleum legislation that had been under consideration since 1962. The legalities of offshore oil exploitation had become increasingly relevant in Australia following BHP-Esso's discovery of oil reserves in the Bass Strait in 1965.[36] Most of the states had hitherto granted offshore concessions for petroleum leases, and Queensland had been granting offshore concessions since 1953.[37] Queensland's minister for mines, Ron Camm, signalled in 1965 to the Legislative Assembly that legislation was imminent and offered this reminder: 'Over the past few years there has been considerable activity in off-shore petroleum exploration in Australian waters, and, in particular, adjacent to Queensland's coastline. As Minister for Mines, I have granted a number of off-shore authorities to prospect for petroleum.'[38]

By the end of January 1967, the Queensland government considered it a matter of urgency to complete the drafting of the legislation, in order to empower companies to begin further exploration of the Reef's oil deposits.[39]

Tourism, too, continued to be an industry in which governments were eager to invest, and the Reef was considered essential to both Queensland's and Australia's future tourism economies. In his 1967 address to the Commonwealth government, Governor-General Richard Casey announced the government's intention to establish an Australian Tourist Commission (ATC), the purpose of which would be to advertise and publicise Australia as a tourist destination.[40] The commission's advocates in the Commonwealth parliament imagined it would make Reef tourism – especially in the coastal cities, where sugar and pastoralism were still the dominant industries – the number-one 'drawcard from an international point of view'.[41] Its critics were concerned that advertising tourist attractions overseas might mislead travellers, who would inevitably find lacklustre tourist facilities. The Labor member for Dawson, Rex Patterson, commented on the scenario this would create for travellers who had been promised paradise:

> They will go to Mackay, the gateway to the Barrier Reef, from where they will visit the islands along the Barrier Reef. But first they will land at the Brisbane airport. We know what that is like. There they will board planes for Mackay on which they will get good treatment. I have seen in literature overseas Mackay advertised as the gateway to the Barrier Reef. On landing at Mackay, if it is raining there, as it is tonight, they will run like rabbits for about 215 yards, in some instances less. There are

no umbrellas at the airport. They then come to two sheds. This is at the gateway to the Barrier Reef! After having been feted on an aircraft from Brisbane passengers might want to use the conveniences, but if it is raining they will need an umbrella as these facilities are across the road.[42]

Patterson's assertion – that what was needed was investment in Reef tourism infrastructure to accompany this vast advertising campaign – was shared by many within the federal parliament. The Liberal member for Mackellar, Bill Wentworth, queried: 'I know that we have some outposts on the Barrier Reef but are they sufficiently accessible and sufficiently commodious and do they have the necessary facilities?'[43] A fellow Liberal, Harry Turner, imagined that a future traveller to Australia would report: 'Don't go to that country, the accommodation is atrocious […] I wanted to see the Barrier Reef but the way I saw it I don't advise my friends to go and look at it.'[44]

Despite the lack of publicised complaints about expansion of Reef exploitation in the mid-1960s, the public, government, scientists and conservationists accepted that the Reef was about to enter a period of significant development and that intervention was required. In December 1966, *Australian Natural History* published a special Reef edition. The papers in that edition pointed to the lack of scientific research conducted on the Reef since the Low Isles expedition, and identified issues of pressing concern in marine biology and geology. The publication perfectly embodied the well-established tradition in Reef sciences of celebrating the naturally valuable and interesting aspects of the Reef, while also signalling its possible economic resources.

For instance, articles from J.C. Yaldwyn, A.B. Cribb and Howard Choat surveyed various 'striking inhabitants' of the Reef, seaweed and the parrotfish. Articles from Joseph Rosewater, on giant clams, and O.A. Jones, on the Reef's geology, both concluded with an assessment of their subjects' possible economic contributions. Rosewater said of giant clams that their size and ease of capture made them a popular food source within South-East Asia and Polynesia. Their most 'commercially important use', however, was 'as curiosities which ornament homes and business places the world over'.[45] Jones emphasised that there had been considerable interest 'taken in the oil possibilities of the reef area and extensive geophysical work' had been carried out. He asserted that the Wreck Island well had created interest among oil companies.[46]

In previous scientific publications about the Reef, the tension between the natural and economic values of the Reef was left to be inferred. In this publication, however, the tensions between the Reef's development and exploitation and the maintenance of the environment were addressed explicitly. An article by John Barnes on the crown-of-thorns starfish hinted at the possibility of a human factor in the imbalance of the Reef's ecosystem. Donald McMichael, who at the time was curator of molluscs at the Australian Museum, contributed an article titled 'The Future of the Reef', which addressed the ongoing damage being done to the Reef from a variety of human causes. He wrote: 'Most people have regarded the Reef as something completely permanent, of great age and with a future stretching ahead just as long as its past. They would probably agree that nothing we could do would conceivably affect the future of this enormous complex of coral reefs.'[47] McMichael believed that the damage caused by the crown-of-thorns starfish brought attention to 'the need for serious thinking about the future of the Great Barrier Reef'. He praised the 'positive steps towards safeguarding the Reef's future' introduced in the preceding decades, and considered these to be important experiments in conservation.[48]

McMichael was eager, however, to bring attention to greater threats to the Reef caused by 'major alterations to the environment', and he believed that, rather than natural threats, the largest alterations were more likely to come from 'direct or indirect contamination of the marine environment' by humans.[49] He cautioned that pollution from oil (either from exploratory or production wells), from agricultural pesticides, and from sewage and industrial waste was going to increase with development and must be addressed. If the Reef was to be saved for posterity, he argued, then people would need to look upon it not as a dumping ground, but as one of the world's greatest natural assets.[50]

Absent from McMichael's outlook was any articulation of a plan for the Reef's ongoing protection. At most, McMichael signalled the need for a Reef management scheme. He welcomed tourism and industrial development of the Reef, and recognised their likely important contributions to the economy. Conversely, he was compelled to assert 'the point of view of the conservationist' and reiterate the Reef's existence as a 'natural phenomenon of great scientific interest and as a wonderful tourist attraction'.[51] The acknowledgement of these competing agendas was not novel in the Reef's history; the consideration of a future of unknown damage was.

In *The Coral Battleground*, Wright created an impression that, prior to 1967, there was little awareness, either among the public or within governments, of the need to halt the ongoing development of the Reef. This is accurate, but only to a point. By early 1967, the Australian and Queensland governments were moving ahead with plans to rapidly expand the Reef's tourism industry infrastructure and publicity, and to open the Reef up to oil exploration. To some extent, these moves were endorsed by a public and a scientific community eager to enjoy in the economic spoils of the Reef.

Yet by 1967, angst about human encroachment on the Reef had sparked a series of controversies, resulting in protections for birds, turtles and flora on many of the Reef's islands, industrial regulations in a number of fisheries, and prohibitions relating to the collection of corals and shells. The outbreak of the crown-of-thorns starfish at Dabuukji (Green Island) had also prompted grave concerns surrounding the Reef's future. So, by 1967, there was an increasing sense that the development of the Reef, or at least the politics that informed it, had to be challenged.

Catchment

What the Reef *is* has always been historically contingent. For example, Cook's map of the Labyrinth only included those sections of the Reef that gave him grief. His was a diminutive structure compared to the outline of the Barrier Reefs Flinders produced fewer than four decades later. Flinders had been relatively untroubled by the Reef's maze of corals and saw it as a single cartographical formation.

In the following decades and centuries, the Reef continued to shift in shape and dimensions to reflect changing scientific, cultural and political understandings and realities. Over the last half-century, insights into the connectivity between the happenings on Queensland's coastal mainland (both human and natural) and on the Reef have led to the inclusion of the entire Reef catchment area into contemporary management charts and policies. The Reef now constitutes – at least from a management perspective – an additional 424,000 square kilometres of Queensland's mainland. The combined management area of the Reef's marine park and catchment is more than twice the area of the states of Tasmania and Victoria combined.

As we have seen, the consequences for the Reef of terrestrial and island development were beginning to become apparent by the 1960s. However, the severity and scale of the effects that coastal development has had on the Reef – particularly the decline in water quality, which affects coral growth rates, increases in coral disease and frequency of crown-of-thorns outbreaks – has only recently surfaced. Since the 1980s, and more significantly since 2015, the Australian and Queensland governments have given greater attention and funding to remedying the Reef's declining water quality. Climate change is the most concerning and escalating threat to the Reef, but declining water quality is a major management issue that impacts the resilience of the Reef.

From a scientific perspective, these new insights into the connectivity between the Reef's catchment and the Reef itself have broadened opportunities for marine science research. For others, how this perceptual enlargement reaches into their personal lives, and links them with the decline of the Reef, has been more confronting. The public has been challenged to consider how their lives link to the decline of the Reef. In coastal areas within the catchment, city gutters remind pedestrians that their effluent water 'drains to the Great Barrier Reef'. Perhaps, once, people were comfortable dismissing the issues facing the Reef as a matter of nature. The Reef's size protected it from serious harm, we thought, and our individual and collective impact could only be negligible. However, these recent insights have brought the Reef closer. Social media, too, has made the Reef more visible to those who previously weren't able to envision their place within its existence. Something that existed in or beyond the imaginary is now part of the everyday lives of those who live within the catchment. The Reef was 'out there'; now, it is in my kitchen.

More significantly, the Reef's expansion has created novel schisms within its history. Urban land use constitutes less than 8 per cent of the Reef's catchment; approximately 79 per cent of the catchment is devoted to some form of farming or grazing. Therefore, farmers, particularly graziers and sugarcane farmers – or more specifically their practices – have come under scrutiny. Land management practices by graziers, and fertiliser run-off, have been significantly linked with increased sediment and nutrient loads in the Reef's water. In the case of graziers, soil erosion accelerated by land clearing or overstocking has led to increased loads of sediment entering the Reef. Similarly, excess fertilisers that have failed to be absorbed into the soil of sugarcane fields flow into the Reef and increase nutrient loads. Farmers, therefore, have become the Reef's closest 'enemy'.[1]

Scientists have known since the early twentieth century that coral reefs suffer when smothered with sediment. However, the plumes of silt that flowed into the Reef following flooding rains were not previously considered to be associated with unnatural loads of run-off. The source of the silt was not an issue to be solved by government management – it had come from the river as part of a cycle of water flow. In the wave of environmentalism that surged from the early 1960s onward, a greater awareness of the links between terrestrial development, land use and water ecologies emerged. John Büsst expressed his concern about the land-clearing practices in the Mission Beach area to Patricia Clare in 1971, and before the Save the Reef campaign began there were others who expressed concern about pollution created by tourism operators. Similarly, port expansion along the Reef coast began to be associated with coral reef decline in localised areas, although studies at the time often dismissed 'unsubstantiated' complaints by locals of declining coral cover in their nearby reefs.

For example, at Yunbenun (Magnetic Island), Townsville's port expansion had, according to locals, devastating impacts on the fringing reefs of Nelly and Cockle bays in the late 1960s. Reports into the history of dredging, conducted in the 1980s, dismissed the likelihood of dredge spoil as the culprit for these episodes of coral decline, and suggested diluted water from increased rains, increased ocean temperatures and coral bleaching were to blame. Emphasis was placed on the need to recognise that both natural and human elements influenced coral reef decline. Since the 1980s, however, it has become increasingly difficult to disentangle the human and the natural elements associated with reef decline. Coral bleaching is now firmly recognised as a major destroyer of coral reefs, and dredge spoil has been directly linked to coral disease and death. This new knowledge and way of thinking has brought contemporary farming practices under scrutiny.

History is riddled with examples of 'outsider' scientists or governments failing to convince farmers, fishers or foresters to adjust their practices. In managing the Reef, the Queensland government has employed catchment management policies, which have ebbed and flowed in the intensity of their regulatory oversight since 2009. For the most part, these regulations have included mandates on land clearing, the application of fertilisers and record-keeping standards, with fines applied for those who failed to comply. When they were first introduced, these regulations targeted specific landholders in 'high-risk' basins, or large, corporate land users. At the same time, farmers entered industry-led, voluntary Best Management Practices programs (BMPs) to build their skills and knowledges surrounding sustainable land use, to avoid compliance oversight and to gain access to incentivised funding and grants.[2]

In the last five years, however, government regulation of farming within the catchment has increased substantially. The slower-than-desired uptake and shifts across farming – both crop-based and grazing – coupled with marginal improvements in the Reef's overall water quality, resulted in more regulations being introduced within the farming industry in 2019. There are reasons for the slow uptake. Fear of short-term losses in farming productivity to facilitate and finance the transition towards meeting the required standards, coupled with the poor results in water-quality improvement within the Reef, could have deterred land use changes. There are also considerable challenges involved in providing location-specific assistance to farmers who are willing to volunteer. Many of these are logistical problems thrown up by the size of the catchment or the geography of the land and water flows. Additionally, these top-down approaches to land use changes are an important initiative in catchment management, but many scientists and social scientists have argued that they have the potential to alienate the very groups whose cooperation is needed.[3]

The politics of land and Reef management have been propelled and enveloped by the broader politics of climate change and its associated culture wars. Politicians, public intellectuals, media outlets and researchers have deepened existing political divides by criticising the lack of evidence for improvements in the Reef's water quality. Importantly, the criticisms of the science are largely coming from a small group of scientists; the vast majority of coral reef scientists accept the links between run-off and coral reef decline.

Nonetheless, at the centre of these dissenters' claims is the argument that the level of funding provided for both management and research, along with the initial financial costs passed on to farmers, has produced little evidence of improved water quality. Dissenters also claim that the associated science is not credible, and is symptomatic of a more significant quality assurance failure within twenty-first-century scientific research. Those who reject the notion of Reef decline and deny the science as fabrication have turned marine pollution – a transnational issue faced by every nation with a coastline – into a sideshow.[4] Of course, conservationists have also engaged in controversial public campaigns that seek to hold individual farmers accountable for illegal land-management practices. Both approaches only further foster the notion that there are 'savers' and 'destroyers' of the Reef.

A great deal of the tension on this issue arises out of a failure to communicate effectively across stakeholders. This is understandable, for several reasons. First, people expect results from intervention, but there are lag effects involved in shifting land-management practices. The changes in water quality take time to see. There are also complexities in the science that impact management, especially surrounding the changes in land use and its effects on run-off and diffusion.

From a perceptual perspective, however, there is more to contend with. It is completely reasonable for a person to view a seemingly thriving reef like the one that grows on the wreck of the *Yongala* (a popular dive site about 40 kilometres off the coast from the Burdekin cane-growing district) and feel confused about the Reef's broader decline. There is also room for empathy for those whose livelihoods come from farming, but who understand the Reef is in decline – who want to be and are assisting, but who don't want to be perceived as enemies or destroyers.

Since 2007, especially in Australia, there has been a tendency to amplify the moral contingencies of climate change, and to marginalise the other contingencies at play. The science and economics of confronting climate change has at times been usurped by our collective and individual emotions. Anger at those we see as saboteurs; anxiety for our futures; helplessness in the face of inaction. As many scientists and social scientists have argued, improving the Reef's water quality is a social problem, and cooperation and consensus are essential. If humans, and in this case farmers, are contributing to the decline of the Reef's water, then they must form part of the solution. This will be more difficult if they are cast as obstinate wreckers and their concerns minimised or dismissed.

The Great Barrier Reef is a big, complex place; it is difficult to hold it all in your head. For centuries we have tried to define its perimeters, but the more we learn, the more difficult it becomes to know it completely. Complicating things further is the understanding of how the Reef forms part of a larger Indo-Pacific oceanic system. It has become increasingly difficult, or perhaps more confronting, to reckon with how we live with the Reef. Understandably, many of us cling to a simple concept: a single place, image or memory. Others see it larger; they can envision it as a whole system linked to lands, seas and global currents of water, politics, cultures and economics; others can envision it as songlines or stories.

Everyone carves out their own image of what the Reef is. Common to most, if not all, is an appreciation of the Reef's beauty and importance. We do need to lean into the complexities, as historian Tom Griffiths has said, and not shirk from the hard truths that science offers up. But simple truths are important scaffolding towards agreement. Irrespective of how much of the Reef we can comprehend, we can all admire and care for it – whatever we imagine it to be.

5

The Save the Reef Campaign: Ellison Reef

On 23 August 1967, a notice appeared in *The Cairns Post*. Cane farmer Donald Forbes had applied for a lease to mine the 'The Ellison'. His application, along with any objections, would be heard on 29 September at the Innisfail Mining Warden's Court.[1] Ellison Reef, situated about 35 kilometres north-east of Coonanglebah (Dunk Island), was to be dredged for lime destined for the canefields of North Queensland. Here began the Save the Reef campaign.

It is likely that, in the past, Forbes's lease application would have gone unnoticed. Ellison Reef, unlike Dabuukji (Green Island), was neither frequently visited nor culturally or economically valuable to non-Indigenous North Queenslanders. In 1967, however, attitudes towards the environment and awareness of development's impacts on marine environments were primed. His lease activated the established networks of Australian conservationists. The Ellison Reef skirmish would eventually be enveloped by the broader issue of oil development on the Barrier Reef, but it was Ellison that highlighted the effectiveness of, and divisions within and between, the conservationists and scientific communities.

Donald Forbes's voice rarely appeared in the debate about his Ellison lease. Thankfully, he did rationalise his endeavours to the journalist Patricia Clare for her book *The Struggle for the Great Barrier Reef*. To her, he argued that 'the lime he wanted to take was not living coral': it 'had been beaten down into sand [...] that was lying all over the place out there, just waiting to be gathered up'.[2] He failed to grasp the reasons for the objections. He had consulted a geologist at a southern university and believed his lease could produce an important experiment on the viability of mining the Reef.[3]

Forbes's lease notice was broadcast on radio and caught the attention of Alison and John Büsst at Bingil Bay.[4] Five days later, John Büsst approached scientists from the University College of Townsville to lodge 'a strong protest' against the application.[5] With the assistance of local solicitors, Büsst began organising a case against the application and 'preparing to treat the matter as a vital test case – the setting of a legal precedent', warning that 'the commercial depredations of the Reef on a large scale could prove disastrous'.[6] Büsst wrote to the ACF, CSIRO and various connections in Canberra, seeking a 'full scientific objection to the granting of the lease'. To Judith Wright, he stressed that 'any press publicity, including letters to, say, the Courier Mail and The Australian, by yourself as soon as possible, before the case is heard would be invaluable'.[7]

Wright obliged, and the case quickly drew the attention of the media. The Courier Mail interviewed Wright and published elements of a letter she had sent to the Innisfail mining warden. In the article, Wright emphasised the issue of precedent and urged that 'some principle must be laid down to protect' the Reef.[8] The next day, The Courier Mail's editorial awarded 'full marks to Queensland Wildlife Preservation Society's Innisfail president for his prompt action on a Barrier Reef application'.[9] Signalling its support for the objection, The Courier Mail argued that granting the Ellison application would be 'the green light for a complete exploitation of this acknowledged wonder of the world'. The newspaper called on the government to refuse to sanction 'bulk destruction by dredging', warning that the damage caused by the crown-of-thorns starfish would be 'trifling compared with 84 acres [34 hectares] of what could only be called shameful vandalism soon to be considered by a mining warden'.

This 'fair amount of publicity' was the first time the campaign had entered into the media.[10]

Bingil Bay and Mission Beach residents also pressed forward with the campaign, and strategically targeted government tourist organisations. G.E. West of Mission Beach wrote to the ATC's general manager seeking a 'strongly worded protest' and publicity on the Ellison case. West stressed 'that any inroad made on our Barrier Reef' would lead to its 'complete despoliation and the wiping off of perhaps our greatest tourist attraction'.[11] Fellow Mission Beach resident and motel proprietor Jack Romano urged the QGTB to consider the situation: 'If permission is granted for the mining of our reef, it could be the precedent for future operations of this kind, which would certainly be the beginning of the end for our most precious National heritage.'[12] To the QGTB, Büsst asserted that 'the Reef is an important item in the development of Queensland's rich tourist potential'.[13] Initially, tourist organisations were, it seemed, favourably inclined towards the conservationists. The QGTB expressed its opposition to the destruction of the Reef, 'unless for exceptional circumstances'.[14]

Regardless of the potential profits to be gained from coral and limestone mining, if the Reef was despoiled, the profits of tourism – which were imagined as being superior to potential oil profits – would be jeopardised. The perceived importance of tourism was central to Büsst's initial letters to John Herbert (Queensland minister for labour and tourism) and Ron Camm (Queensland minister for mines and main roads). Büsst explained the grounds of his objection to both ministers: he feared the creation of a 'dangerous legal precedent for further granting of mineral leases' across the Reef, argued that adequate deposits of lime for agricultural purposes were readily available and accessible on the Queensland mainland, and debunked Forbes's claims of innocuousness, stating that 'there is no such thing as a "dead reef"'.[15] Finally, Büsst declared that the Reef's importance to science and tourism necessitated its protection through a marine park, and that his objection would be the initial phase of a campaign 'to bring this about'. Objections, he claimed, were being lodged by the University College of Townsville (now James Cook University), UQ, the University of Sydney, Johnstone Shire Council and Chamber of Commerce, the QLS, the GBRC and the Cairns Naturalists Society, and he was awaiting the support of the ACF and the World Wildlife Preservation Fund.[16] Immediately it was clear that the conservationists planned to identify tourism as the largest potential loser in this controversy, and to utilise networks and institutions across the country to place pressure on governments.

Büsst, however, had jumped the gun. He would not receive support from the GBRC. Robert Endean, the chairman of the GBRC, informed the WPSQ secretary, Arthur Fenton, of their intention 'not to oppose [...] the lease on Ellison Reef'.[17] The GBRC's reasons were varied. Endean had consulted with officers of the Department of Harbours and Marine, who contended that 'there is no living coral in the region over which a lease is sought', and that dredging 'dead coral rubble' would have a negligible effect on marine life. The Department of Harbours and Marine, Endean explained, intended to cooperate with the Department of Mines in the hope that they would refuse future leases in areas where mining 'could do a lot of damage to the fauna and flora'.

Endean, however, had also consulted with various members of the GBRC. He reminded Fenton that 'conservation of the fauna and flora of the reefs' was one of the principal objectives of the GBRC, which advocated for '*controlled* exploitation of Barrier Reef resources', and since the Reef is '80,000 square miles [207,199 square kilometres] [...] there should be room for manoeuvre'.[18] The GBRC's members were at the time giving consideration to an overall plan for the Reef's research, development and conservation. The significance of their plan had grown, they believed, because 'several oil companies' were preparing to drill the Reef. Consequently, Endean decided it was unwise for him personally, or the GBRC, to make public statements on the Ellison case, which might have prejudiced 'the good relations' between the GBRC and 'interested government departments'. Endean, however, encouraged the WPSQ to proceed with its opposition, since it would help the GBRC 'in subsequent negotiations with the Queensland government'.[19]

The GBRC's willingness to compromise on issues of the Reef's geological exploitation for overtly political reasons contrasted with its publicly professed apolitical agenda. Endean's letter, which was widely distributed to conservationists, was the source of a rift between them and the GBRC. The conservationists were left to press their case with limited scientific support.

Further hindering the conservationists' cause was the refusal by the mining warden to accept written submissions. Both the WPSQ and the QLS had planned to deliver written submissions, and only Büsst, Don McMichael (then director of the ACF) and another local would prosecute their objections in person. A joint decision was made by the WPSQ and the QLS that some of the latter's members would travel north to conduct a survey of Ellison themselves and present their evidence to the mining warden. If they were going to make it to Innisfail, however, they would need considerable assistance.[20]

Büsst organised everything. He targeted tourism companies, exploiting their concerns that the Reef, already under attack from the crown-of-thorns starfish, might disappear under a cloud of dredge spoil. Avis car rentals provided complimentary vehicles, Trans Australian Airlines provided complimentary flights, Kodak provided photography equipment, the Queensland Skin-Divers Association provided diving equipment, a local citizen provided a plane for aerial surveys, and some local cane farmers who enjoyed fishing in the area provided boats and pilotage.[21]

The QLS completed two sets of survey trips. On one trip, the divers were joined by journalist Barry Wain from *The Australian*. Wright and Büsst had approached Wain and convinced the young reporter that the Ellison case 'was going to be news, and big news'.[22] As the Queensland correspondent for the national broadsheet, Wain produced six articles on the Ellison case, drawing attention to evidence provided by the QLS as well as to McMichael's argument that no mining on the Reef should be allowed until a full investigation of its resources had been made.[23] The conservationists may not have had the support of the elite scientific community, but they were garnering advocates with a wider, popular audience.

Importantly, the survey constructed an image of Ellison that contrasted sharply with its proposed 'dead' status. It was home to various living hard corals, molluscs, fish and charismatic fauna, such as turtles. Its crevices, sand and rubble (the 'dead' parts) between the reef's exposed crest and its flat were covered with algae and home to several types of small herbivore. Ellison was characterised in the survey as a complex living community, challenging popularly held conceptions of what constituted a 'live' reef.

At Ellison, the highest density of live corals was found in the areas least exposed at low tide. Its crest and flat, both exposed at low tide, had little coral but high algal densities. Speaking specifically on these sections, the survey argued:

> It can be seen that there are relatively large areas of coral reef which to outward appearances are 'dead' because of the relative paucity of live coral growths. However, as noted above, those areas provide essential substrate for the algal growth upon which a high proportion of grazing animals are dependent. Therefore, any large-scale disturbance of these areas will have considerable repercussions in terms of the whole reef.[24]

On 8 December 1967, the mining warden declared he would recommend to Camm that the application be refused. While the recommendation did not speak specifically to impacts on tourism, the warden seemed convinced by the QLS survey. He announced that 'the term "dead reef" is a misnomer [...] the reef is in fact not "dead" but very much alive [it is] in the public interest and in the interest of the Great Barrier Reef that the application be refused'.[25]

For the conservationists, there were lessons to be learnt. First, the success of their opposition had largely depended upon the work of the Innisfail branch, and principally on work done by the Büssts.[26] Second, it was clear that the conservationists could not rely on the GBRC for support. Third, they formed the opinion that the Department of Harbours and Marine, those 'responsible for prosecuting the defence of the reef', were likely to act in consort with the Department of Mines rather than with those concerned with the Reef's conservation. Last, the members of the WPSQ enthusiastically believed that 'the Australian public does not wish to see the Great Barrier Reef destroyed'.[27]

In the immediate period following the warden's recommendation, the conservationists' attitude towards the campaign began to crystallise. As the WPSQ and the QLS focused their energies on the issue of oil drilling, they did so with scepticism towards the government and the GBRC, but with an understanding that protecting the Reef had broad support.

6

We Must Appear to Be Well Informed

A lesson the Queensland government likely should have learnt from their experience of the Ellison Reef battle was the importance of credible scientific information. There was a tendency within government and industry, and among scientists, to characterise conservationists as emotional and lacking in any sense of the reality of things. In the Ellison campaign, however, the conservationists had trumped attempts to mine the reef by utilising scientific expertise.

The prospect of oil exploration on the Reef had advanced considerably by the conclusion of the Ellison hearings. In late October 1967, minister for mines Ron Camm, along with all other Australian mines ministers, introduced the Petroleum (Submerged Lands) Bill. Opposition and government members immediately expressed concerns for the Reef.

Queensland's Labor leader, John Houston, criticised the introduction of the legislation without cross-party negotiations. 'No other State has a natural asset as valuable as is the Great Barrier Reef of Queensland,' he said.[1] And he enjoyed some cross-party support. The Liberal member for Chatsworth, Bill Hewitt, said Houston's remarks 'spoke for us all'. The Labor member for Salisbury, Doug Sherrington, demanded that no geological exploitation take place 'until a full appreciation is gained of its value'. Sherrington, acknowledging the diverse interests in the components of the Reef, suggested a joint government venture 'to ascertain just what this reef is and just how much of it must be preserved for posterity'.[2] The Liberal member for Wavell, Alexander Dewar, joined the chorus, advocating for the Reef's protection: '[N]o amount of royalty from oil taken from the sea-bed,' he said, 'would be worth the risk of having the Barrier Reef wiped out.'[3]

In response, Camm asserted that, as the member for Whitsunday, he was uniquely positioned to understand the importance of the Reef's natural heritage, and declared:

> The man who never made a mistake never made anything. There is always the possibility of an accident, but if everyone sat still and said, 'I won't do this because there might be an accident,' nothing would ever be done. I can assure hon. members that all precautions will be taken.[4]

Camm's remarks, in their starkness, overshadowed the initial bipartisan opposition to the Reef's geological exploitation.

Other issues emerged during the Ellison inquiry. The most alarming, from the Commonwealth's perspective, was the encroachment of Chinese fishing vessels into Reef waters in October and November 1967. In late October 1967, the Commonwealth introduced a bill to amend the *Fisheries Act 1952–1966* to extend the Commonwealth's sovereignty over fisheries from 3 to 12 miles (approximately 5 to 19 kilometres). The federal member for Leichhardt, William Fulton, however, was unconvinced that the prohibition, especially in the remote areas of the Reef, could be policed. 'I have seen as many as six foreign vessels fishing within the 3-mile limit north of Cairns to Charlotte Bay,' he said in parliament. 'But as soon as a boat comes into sight they are off. They have good diesel engines and they get away as quick as lightning.'[5]

The Queensland government shared Fulton's views, and believed it was incapable of policing its coasts against foreign intrusion. It held that the Commonwealth needed to take a more pragmatic approach. The stand-off inspired *The Courier Mail*'s cartoonist to caricature the governments as emus with their heads stuck in the sand, as foreign vessels plundered Reef waters.[6] 'Protecting the Reef', in government nomenclature, referred largely to the obstructing and policing of foreign vessels.

The Queensland government was under pressure, and in response to questions during parliament about intrusion of foreign vessels into Queensland waters, Gordon Chalk announced that it would 'take punitive action to enforce our rights'.[7] But it was not just the violation of Australia's sovereignty that was of concern. Links were made between the Chinese intrusions and the Reef's degradation. Fulton even suggested that foreign fishing interests – by plundering clam communities, trampling coral reefs and destroying birdlife – were doing more harm than the crown-of-thorns.[8]

Endean had completed his initial study into the crown-of-thorns starfish by early 1968, and concluded that the outbreak had been caused by a disturbance in the predator/prey relationship. He was resolute that the primary cause was the removal of the giant triton shell (*Charonia tritonis*). Decades of removal by shell collectors and sellers had caused a scarcity in the shell, he claimed. As a result, souvenir shops now rarely sold them, and most collectors, Endean asserted, regarded the shell as 'a somewhat rare mollusc in Barrier Reef waters'.[9] While other causes of the outbreak had been considered, particularly increased pesticide loads, Endean believed there was little evidence to support them.

Endean's report provoked immediate controversy. The Keppel Bay Shell Club considered the claims entirely baseless. 'The innocent Australian shell collectors', they proclaimed, should not bear the 'onus for this catastrophe'.[10] The QLS dismissed Endean's assertions and believed insecticides had caused the imbalance in the ecosystem. One of its members, Owen Kelly, wrote to Büsst and argued that proof of the pesticide theory would strike 'a useful blow for conservation generally', and may 'provoke a few of our legislators into getting off their arses and thinking a little more deeply about the effects of development and unplanned exploitation'.[11] As a bonus, Kelly thought, it would not hurt to make 'Endean feel a little foolish'.

Endean's pursuit of the crown-of-thorns issue in the media agitated the conservationists. Kathleen McArthur, co-founder of the WPSQ, quipped in a letter to Büsst that Endean must have had his own public relations agent, and she hoped, in jest, that the poisonous 'cone shell gets him'.[12] *The Courier Mail* had, reportedly, conceded to the QLS that it was 'embarrassed at the amount of publicity' it had given Endean, but felt he 'always had newsworthy items to throw at them'.[13]

The tourist operators were equally frustrated about Endean's publicity, and concerned that 'highly exaggerated' reports of Reef damage would hinder tourism in the region. The Cairns Chamber of Commerce requested that Don Chipp, then the Commonwealth minister in charge of tourist activities, take action to 'counter the effects of the bad publicity which filters through to overseas sources'.[14] They had been particularly agitated by a *Four Corners* program that had, in their estimation, 'not helped the situation'. In 1969, as Endean continued to prosecute his case, the manager of the Cairns office of the QGTB wrote to the director general expressing concern over the publicity given to remarks 'that something like 80% of the Reef in the vicinity of Green Island' had been destroyed. The manager also said:

> Whilst the infestation at Green Island in the last three years has been most noticeable, there has also been unexpected recovery. In fact, the rejuvenated Reef is nearly as good as it ever was and the

Glass-bottomed boat trip across the Reef at Green Island is of an exceptionally high standard. It is felt that the adverse publicity of the past few weeks could deter numbers of tourists visiting North Queensland during the coming winter season: therefore, it is suggested that you might care to give some publicity to the fact that the coral inspections in the glass-bottomed boat at Green Island and the visit to the Underwater Observatory still remain the premier attractions in Great Barrier Reef waters and, ostensibly, remain unaffected by the Crown of Thorns Starfish.[15]

The government felt, however, that 'the extent of coral regeneration appeared slight' and refused to publicly state anything to the contrary.[16]

That same year, the proprietor of the Dabuukji (Green Island) underwater observatory, Vince Vlasoff, wrote to the government in frustration asserting that it was wrong to present the image that 'all reefs' were '80% destroyed'. For Vlasoff, the rise of the starfish was a natural, cyclical event, and the claims that the starfish would destroy the Reef were panic-driven.[17] The Cairns Chamber of Commerce suggested to the minister for tourism that scientists be urged to 'use more discretion in making public statements'. Of particular concern were the ramifications for potential overseas tourists of estimations that the Reef would be destroyed 'inside two years'. What required publication, they argued, was the 'fact that the reef has been in existence for some two million years and doubtless has withstood many adverse conditions and effects over such period'.[18]

The Queensland government was alarmed, however, by the paucity of knowledge about the causes of the outbreak and appropriate control measures. The government believed that banning the collection of all molluscs on the Reef would ensure the protection of the giant triton shell. It wanted further evidence to support Endean's claim before it implemented a policy that would intrude on a popular tourist activity.[19] So, it commissioned further research, organised a joint government committee and cooperated with Japanese and American research teams that arrived in Australia to conduct their own investigations of the starfish.[20]

By the end of 1969, little clarity had been reached on the issue, and Endean was continuing to bring attention not only to the plague but also to the need for further government funding.[21] In August, Endean was invited to appear before the joint government committee, on which sat Robert Pearson, a fisheries biologist with the Department of Primary Industries – and Endean's research assistant. The committee recommended that Pearson, not Endean, be employed full-time to conduct ongoing research into the starfish. They added, damningly for Endean, that the 'information released to news media has been unnecessarily alarming [and] no irreversible damage is being done to the Reef'.[22] By October, Queensland Premier Joh Bjelke-Petersen was asserting that there was no plague on the Reef.[23]

Endean continued to campaign on the crown-of-thorns into the 1970s. In 1971, another joint government committee was appointed to investigate the starfish, which concluded that it did 'not constitute a threat'. The committee considered the plague to be localised between Cairns and Townsville, and while devastation had occurred, most reefs had experienced some recovery. Endean's triton theory, it asserted, was unsubstantiated, and any attempt to police collection of the shell was 'unwarranted at the present time'. Finally, the committee recommended continued monitoring of popular reefs with social and commercial importance, and the manual removal of the starfish, if required.[24]

Endean's marginalisation, and the perceived neglect of the issue, became sensationalised in two books, to which he contributed introductions.[25] Both criticised the government for failing to recognise the severity of the plague, and tourist operators for publicly undermining Endean's attempts to bring attention to its severity.

Endean never faced the same degree of government-led suppression and intimidation as John Sinclair during the campaign against sand mining on K'gari (Fraser Island). His daughter, however, recalled an evening when a police officer pulled their car over and smashed its headlights.[26]

This event aside, conflict with Endean seemed to emanate from within the scientific community. Marine biologist Patricia Mather, who succeeded Endean as the chairperson of the GBRC, remembered in a 2009 oral history interview that Endean was 'looking for a cause to make him famous', and said he 'lost his support' on the GBRC 'because he behaved very badly' and did 'some pretty dirty things'.[27] In a book about the global history of the crown-of-thorns starfish, Jan Sapp ascertained from the marine ecologist Donald Potts that 'Endean was influential, had a long memory, held grudges, and that people were afraid that he was in a position to hurt them if they spoke up against him'.[28]

A more generous reflection was offered by Isobel Bennett, a significant marine biologist in the 1960s and 1970s, who compared Endean to American marine biologist and conservationist Rachel Carson and declared that, despite his criticisms and the controversy he came to embody, the 'very, very great amount of research' on the Reef was due to the 'fuss' he made and the awakening of people 'to the realisation that something was happening'.[29]

Lyndon DeVantier, a former PhD student under Endean, remembered the scorn levelled at his supervisor and couldn't help but compare it with the politics of Reef science today:

He was of an earlier era to many of the newer generations of course, and did become ostracized by some for his outspoken views on reef management [...] and particularly the ensuing media attention. This was at a time when scientists weren't supposed to speak out – look how well that has worked![30]

Additionally, scientists have focused significant recent research into 'refining or validating' Endean's earliest work, and affirmed his 'exceptional insights' around things like migration habits. This has meant his work now sits comfortably and importantly as scaffolding for contemporary research into the crown-of-thorns starfish.[31]

What is most curious about the crown-of-thorns issue, especially in the context of the Save the Reef campaign, is that conservationists refused to engage with it. In *The Coral Battleground*, Wright claimed that they decided to stay out of the affair until the scientists had resolved the cause of the outbreak, but added: 'If those scientists who pointed to human interference as the probable cause of the starfish plague were right, further interference must surely be perilous.'[32] At the time, the two most ubiquitous theories, apart from those claiming that the event was part of a natural cycle, suggested human interference was a root cause. Surely it would have been in the conservationists' interests to have some strong evidence pointing to the consequences of human interference on the Reef?

Endean and the conservationists made similar demands for further research on the Reef's biology and ecology. D.W. Connell, president of the QLS, later wrote that the conservationists were at a 'disadvantage in deciding on an effective course of action [...] as most of the information' was with the government or Endean.[33] The record suggests, however, that a core reason they refused to lend their support was personal. Endean's refusal as chairman of the GBRC to object in the Ellison case and his preference for mutually beneficial relationships with the government permanently tarnished his image among the conservationists. Consequently, they refused to lend their energies to his support.

In late 1967, it was clear to the Queensland government that the conflict between the Reef's exploitation and conservation needed to be resolved. The scientific community was advocating that the government implement conservation strategies to allow exploitation 'without serious damage'.[34] On 13 December, Premier Frank Nicklin received a letter from the Australian Academy of Science

(AAS) expressing its desire to establish a committee 'to prepare a report on the scientific and other resources of the Reef'.[35]

The GBRC made a similar proposition, and in January 1968, following Nicklin's retirement, it provided the new premier, Jack Pizzey, with a report titled 'Proposals Relating to the Conservation and Controlled Exploitation of the Great Barrier Reefs'.[36] Importantly, 'controlled exploitation' included geological exploitation. The report, which emanated from the initiatives Endean had flagged with Fenton, conceded the inevitability of the Reef's exploitation.[37] Indeed, it revealed that the GBRC had held discussions with government geologists and oil companies concerning the Reef's geological exploitation.

The GBRC accepted that 'exploitation on a large scale' was imminent, and desired to manage the Reef for all the competing interests: scientists, tourism operators, potential oil companies, fisheries and recreational users. They believed, however, that competing valuations of the Reef were barely understood, and advised:

> Unless a plan for the controlled exploitation and conservation of the Great Barrier Reefs is formulated in the near future major clashes of interests among the various parties who wish to exploit the Reefs will occur [...] major clashes of interests will occur between the exploiters on one hand and conservationists and scientific organisations on the other [...] There is also a need for the establishment of a planning, co-ordinating and advisory body consisting of people with specialised knowledge of the Reefs and their resources. This body would have the task of formulating an overall plan and would make recommendations based on this plan to relevant government departments.[38]

Here, the GBRC dealt directly with the entangled approaches and valuing of the Reef. Its concessions on the Reef's geological exploitation, however, would become a source of tension with the conservationists.

Nonetheless, the GBRC found some sympathy within the Queensland government. Pizzey wrote to treasurer Gordon Chalk asserting the need for controlled exploitation, which would 'ensure that the potential of the reef is not reduced and that it is preserved for the future'.[39] Pizzey expressed regret that 'basic knowledge is completely lacking at the present time' to coordinate the breadth of work imagined by the GBRC, but agreed that some form of plan was necessary. Yet he recommended that any plan should be coordinated by a subcommittee of the AAS. Committee members would be drawn from various organisations, including the GBRC, the Department of Harbours and Marine, and the Department of Mines.[40] It appeared that the GBRC's interests in the biological sciences, and the political views of those scientists specifically, had attracted scepticism from the government, which consequently refused to cede control of the Reef's management to them.[41] Pizzey conceded, though, that it would be 'virtually impossible to consider planned development' of the Reef 'without substantially improved knowledge of all its resources. Whatever the source of the essential knowledge [...] exploitation of the resource should be controlled by the Queensland Government'.[42]

The Queensland government was determined to control the Reef's future. After meetings with the AAS, Pizzey rejected the GBRC's proposal but accepted the AAS's offer to complete a report of the Reef's scientific and 'other' resources.[43] The report, the AAS proposed, would be completed by a national body consisting of two AAS members, as chair and deputy chair, and members drawn from the AAS and Commonwealth departments, mostly from within Queensland.

The scheme prompted the establishment of a Cabinet subcommittee, which countered that a Great Barrier Reef Resources Advisory Committee (GBRRAC) be established, and be comprised of eleven members: one each from the AAS, the Commonwealth, the Queensland government, UQ and the GBRC, and six others selected by the Queensland government.[44] The majority would be Queenslanders 'selected from men of outstanding commercial experience'.[45] The emphasis here on Queensland members indicates the state government's clear desire to control the Reef. The government wanted not only to initiate an investigation of the Reef's resources but also to maintain its supervision.

While the government was pro-development, it did not ignore the Reef's environmental value. It was cognisant of the need for a program of exploitation that, in its opinion, would not undermine the Reef's natural attributes. A Cabinet report argued that the Reef was not 'just another series of reefs': it was 'unique', albeit with great potential in the fields of mining, fishing, tourism and scientific research.[46] Nonetheless, the report urged that 'interference to the Reefs must be approached scientifically and with caution', because '[i]n general the probability of a change in biological balance following interference to the Reefs is strong. Such a change may prove to be within tolerable limits but in certain circumstances it could prove dangerous to the Reefs and their potential.'[47]

The report suggested the completion of surveys of the Reef to determine a plan for its exploitation and the creation of specified zones for various uses, including mining.[48] The government, it seemed, was attempting to ensure that the Reef and its access by competing agendas could be maintained. After Cabinet endorsed the constitution of the GBRRAC, the state government invited the Commonwealth to participate.[49]

The Cabinet discussions surrounding the formation of the GBRRAC demonstrate, if nothing else, a concerted effort by government to come to terms with the Reef's future. Additionally, they helped the government to sharpen its attitudes towards the Reef's conservation.

The process proved beneficial when, in May 1968, the NPAQ submitted a proposal to divide the Reef into three separate marine national parks, as they feared the Reef would be destroyed by 'uncontrolled exploitation'.[50] Northern (Cape Melville to Cairns), central (east of Townsville) and southern (mainly Swains Reef) marine national parks would, in the NPAQ's estimation, ensure the Reef's protection and its use by scientists.

The government, while endorsing the need for the Reef's protection, believed the NPAQ's proposal was too exclusive and failed to account for 'other uses to which the Reef could be subjected', such as tourism and exploitation 'in other directions'.[51] The government began considering the establishment of a Reef marine park, but the process was compromised by the royal commission into petroleum drilling on the Reef.

The controversies surrounding the Reef inspired reflection by the Queensland government as its lack of knowledge of the Reef – specifically, its incapacity to determine what constituted 'tolerable interference to the Reefs' – had hindered its response to the Reef controversy.[52] In its own words, it had failed 'to silence or satisfy the vociferous objections of the absolute conservationists'.[53]

The government not only needed to be well informed on issues of the Reef's exploitation, but also had to *appear* to be well informed. One immediate solution was to employ an expert to compile a report 'on the exploitation and conservation of the mineral resources' of the Reef.[54] Mining minister Ron Camm, in particular, advocated for 'expert advice on the problems of exploitation and conservation, particularly having regard to the problems of mining, petroleum drilling, tourist fishing and tourism generally'.[55] Camm explained that Harry Ladd, a marine geologist and supervisor of the geological studies at Bikini Atoll and the Marshall Islands, had already been assigned by the United States Geological Survey to carry out the survey required by the government.

Meanwhile, the government was yet to formally resolve the Ellison issue. Camm had not made a decision following the mining warden's recommendation, and the conservationists feared that he would approve the lease. The Department of Mines had reportedly given a draft copy of its decision to staff at UQ.[56] The conservationists felt that Camm would receive the necessary scientific support from the GBRC or UQ staff to approve it: a suspicion that forced some scientists to reassure the conservationists that the GBRC was encouraging refusal of the lease.[57] In February 1968, the conservationists' distrust of the GBRC led to the Innisfail branch of the WPSQ to formally call for the GBRC's disbanding and reconstitution as a committee 'against commercial exploitation, not as a committee which at present is actively promoting the exploitation of the Great Barrier Reef'.[58]

Again, Endean was perceived as complicit in a potential endorsement by Camm of the lease. Media reports suggested that Camm's decision on Ellison was being delayed because a survey was being conducted by the Department of Harbours and Marine. Eddie Hegerl, a founding member of the QLS and a participant in the Ellison survey, suggested to Büsst that the survey would find anything 'they think they can get away with' in order to create a rationale for the lease's approval. And he believed Endean was involved: 'Endean's main motives seem pretty obvious. By saying exactly what the government wants to hear, he will find himself given personal control of the future of the Reef. Lots of power, lots of research money, maybe even more spending money.'[59]

Relationships between some conservationists and Endean were strained. Arthur Fenton had reportedly threatened to resign from his position as secretary of the WPSQ 'in a fit of temper at Endean'. Hegerl informed Büsst, who was living at Bingil Bay and was not privy to the day-to-day proceedings in Brisbane, that 'everyone is behaving very very irrationally about the whole thing, as feelings seem to be running rather strongish'.[60]

Fearing the government would not endorse the mining warden's recommendation, the QLS re-emphasised the need for 'a proper large-scale survey' of the Reef before further exploitation.[61] They were joined by several other objectors to the lease's approval. At the 1968 Country Party conference, a motion was moved that 'the needs of the Tourist Industry take precedence' over mining, and that priority be given 'to the preservation of all areas of scenic value'.[62] Others publicly queried what more the minister for mines needed to consider.[63]

Nonetheless, in May, Camm announced his decision to follow the mining warden's recommendation. He added the qualifier, however, that 'if the current objections to the proposal can be proved to be incorrect', he would reverse the decision.[64] The government regarded the Reef as a natural asset that they were eager to protect, but Camm also said:

> There are literally millions of tons of coral broken off the Reef and swept in towards the mainland by cyclonic storms and heavy seas. This dead coral could be used for the establishment of industries in North Queensland. The cement industry of south-east Queensland is, of course, based primarily on the support of dead coral from Moreton Bay.[65]

Camm concluded that no mining would occur until 'overwhelming evidence is produced to suggest that there could be some limited exploitation' without damaging the Reef.

Shortly after Camm's decision, American marine geologist Harry Ladd arrived. He conducted a 'rapid survey' between the Torres Strait and the Swain Reefs, and held meetings with members of the GBRC, the University College of Townsville, the AAS and various government departments.[66] Ladd's report endorsed the notion that the Reef's resources could be exploited while it was also protected from 'serious and widespread damage'.[67] Importantly, however,

Ladd suggested that before the Reef could be exploited, especially for geological resources, there was a need for a 'comprehensive survey that would make it possible to evaluate the dangers in present trends – notably in the rise of tourism and in attempts to exploit natural resources – and to determine what actions may be necessary to protect the reef'.[68]

Ladd's proposal took two years, and formed the basis of selection criteria for sites for geological exploitation, but he stressed that strict and rigid controls were needed. Immediately following the tabling of Ladd's report, the GBRC called for a moratorium on oil drilling on the Reef until 'a long-range and all-embracing policy on the future of the Reef was decided'.[69] It appeared, initially at least, that Ladd's report was further endorsement of the increasingly common view that a formal policy of Reef management and exploitation, following a large program of research and consultation, was required.

Instead, Ladd's report became a political tool utilised by the government to endorse the Reef's geological exploitation. The initial rationale of Ladd's visit was to provide some base knowledge for the government to assist them in making decisions regarding the Reef's management. It was not explicitly stipulated that Ladd's survey would form the basis of future government initiatives. Even Ladd believed his report would simply serve as a brief for the GBRRAC, the construction of which, by 1969, had hardly advanced since Prime Minister John Gorton was invited to participate in 1968.[70]

But, by the time Ladd's report was released in early September 1968, large political shifts had occurred in Queensland – the most significant being Joh Bjelke-Petersen's rise to the premiership. Camm, who retained his position as minister for mines, also became deputy premier. Queensland was now under the leadership of two men whose disposition towards the environment was far less nuanced than that of the previous leadership, and for whom geological exploitation of the Reef was far less problematic.

Bjelke-Petersen himself was a major shareholder in several mining and petroleum companies, and was dismissive of any conflict of interest accusations. Ladd's report provided the government's rationale for oil drilling. The government concluded that Ladd had expressed 'no major problems in connection with oil exploration', and ignored the qualifications throughout the report that diminished the accuracy of that claim.[71]

The conservationists were immediately critical of Ladd's report, and especially its perceived rationale for the Reef's geological exploitation. Fred Grassle, an American marine biologist visiting Australia on a Fulbright Scholarship, publicly criticised the report and questioned Ladd's competence to advise on Reef conservation.[72] An uncritical interpretation of Ladd's analysis regarding limestone deposits on the Reef, Grassle argued, suggested that three-quarters of it could be mined. Less dismissively, Townsville University College's Professor C. Burdon-Jones asserted there was 'no evidence that removal of so-called "dead" coral material' could be conducted without harming living corals, and called for the establishment of a 'Scientific Advisory Council' to 'secure the continued safety and well-being' of the Reef, as well as access to its resources.[73] To Burdon-Jones, Ladd's report indicated the 'necessity for a more intensive and functional approach to the assessment' of the Reef's wealth.

Nonetheless, for Büsst, and indeed for most of the conservationists, Ladd's report was tainted by its association with the Department of Mines. Büsst considered it wholly political, and not 'pure scientific' research.[74] Since the government had adopted Ladd's report as an endorsement of geological exploitation, the notion of 'controlled exploitation' – a term popularised by Ladd's report – became for the conservationists a euphemism for oil drilling. Consequently, issues relating to the exploitation of the Reef quickly became centralised around the issue of oil drilling.[75]

The Save the Reef Campaign: Oil Drilling

With the Ladd report's tacit endorsement of oil drilling in hand, the likelihood of the Reef being developed for petroleum became a more immediate concern. Despite their objections to its content and the way the government had interpreted it, the conservationists now had to reorganise their initiatives to ensure that drilling did not take place. This would require greater cohesion and consistency among the various groups, and a stronger, perhaps more interventionist, stance from the Commonwealth government.

Ladd's report supercharged the push for a moratorium on oil drilling. Büsst, the QLS and other members of the WPSQ had incorporated the idea of a moratorium, raised by the GBRC in response to Ladd's report, into their strategy since early 1968. Soon, other groups, including the People the North Committee, a North Queensland pro-development lobby group, began to lobby the government in support of the moratorium. In a letter to Camm, its chairman wrote:

> My Committee's views are that no further exploitation of our national heritage – in fact a world heritage that it is Australia's responsibility to preserve – should be permitted until extensive research has been carried out on the entire ecology of the Great Barrier Reef [...] I therefore strongly urge you to impose a

complete moratorium on any mining exploitation of our Great Barrier Reef until such time as a full research programme has been implemented.[1]

The ACF was preparing to put forth a motion to formally call for a moratorium.[2] While the WPSQ and QLS supported a moratorium, Wright feared a moratorium would provide an opportunity for the Queensland government to initiate a suite of experiments to test the effects of spilt oil on coral reefs.[3] The conservationists understood that research on the Reef was required, but were concerned that it would lead to exploitation and pollution. Adding to these concerns were doubts about the Queensland government's capacity and willingness to enforce a moratorium. The conservationists thus began to consider whether the Commonwealth could impose a moratorium itself.[4]

The Commonwealth had been a consistent advocate of preserving the Reef since the Ellison campaign. Büsst visited his friend Harold Holt in 1967, who personally assured Büsst 'that the federal government will take over the Barrier Reef'.[5] That promise – with its implications that the Commonwealth could take control of the Reef and, consequently, all decisions concerning its oil exploration – became an obsession for Büsst. Holt's successor as prime minister, John Gorton, maintained the Commonwealth's preservationist stance, but federal intervention was hindered by the issue of sovereignty. Any attempt by the Commonwealth to claim exclusive sovereignty of the offshore petroleum reserves might encroach upon the *Petroleum (Submerged Lands) Act 1967* and trigger a High Court challenge from the states. Indeed, this very issue had discouraged the Gorton Cabinet from introducing Reef-seizing legislation in favour of a cooperative approach to the Reef's management with the Queensland government.

The conservationists were circulating information on issues of Reef sovereignty and science among themselves and connecting with scientists and politicians to raise awareness to their cause. Büsst was particularly active. He wrote to Gorton demanding that the 'Commonwealth take full control of the area' and institute a moratorium.[6] By the end of 1968, he had met with Gorton at Coonanglebah (Dunk Island), and with the federal opposition leader, Gough Whitlam, in Cairns.[7]

From his house at Bingil Bay, John Büsst wrote reams of letters to gather support from politicians, lawyers, scientists, and business and union leaders, while the QLS and the WPSQ came up with innovative strategies for gathering broader public support. While the lobbying of politicians was vital, equally important was the continued role of the media.[8] Wright and Büsst had already convinced Barry Wain of the importance of the Ellison case. During 1968, Büsst maintained contact with Wain and sent him letters for publication. So close were Büsst and Wain that Büsst signed the journalist up to the QLS; it would be Wain, in 1971, who wrote Büsst's obituary, titled 'The Bingil Bay Bastard'.[9] *The Australian* and *The Courier Mail* newspapers both continued to publish the letters of Wright and Büsst throughout the campaign.

The QLS adopted equally innovative measures to spread the message. They distributed their Ellison survey widely, with the hope of attracting donations. Contributions, however, were not arriving at an adequate rate. A decision was reached in early 1968 to make and sell 'Save the Barrier Reef' car stickers to raise funds. The idea proved successful: by August 1968 nearly 8000 stickers had been distributed.[10] The stickers spread so far that Wright recalled arriving in Perth from an overseas trip and seeing cars sporting orange 'Save the Barrier Reef' stickers.[11]

The QLS and the WPSQ maintained close links throughout the campaign, and together helped circulate a petition that obtained 10,000 signatures against the Reef's geological exploitation.[12] While both groups considered other issues to be of concern, and had mentioned in their material anxieties around tourism development, shell collecting and the proper management of islands, it was clear that the priority for both organisations was preventing mineral exploitation.

The unity between the QLS and the WPSQ was unique. Their position on the Reef's conservation and exploitation diverged from that of the scientific community, and even, at times, from that of other conservationist bodies. Wright recalled that the GBRC's refusal to object to the mining of Ellison made the conservationists' position 'awkward'. Patricia Mather, who later became chairperson of the GBRC, reflected in an oral history interview:

> I don't think scientists get on all that well with conservationists except in certain ... conservationists will always go further than the scientists are prepared to go in what they say. And scientists always insist on being objective ... Judith's lack of objectivity about the Great Barrier Reef was trying. It was hard to work with.[13]

Iain McCalman considered that the 'elusive' nature of scientists provided a useful 'chink of division within the conservationists' cause, for Bjelke-Petersen to exploit'.[14] It is worth considering in detail how the divide between the conservationists and scientific community manifested, and the impact it had on the Reef's conservation and exploitation.

Following the Ellison campaign, the frustration of Büsst and the QLS with the GBRC was profound. Büsst directed his criticisms to those staff of UQ who held affiliations with the WPSQ, the QLS and the GBRC. Jiro Kikkawa, an ornithologist, tried to rationalise the GBRC's position for Büsst: 'The pressure of the mining groups is a strong one and GBRC is trying to solve the problem more sensibly without agitations. So please hold your horses. I can assure you, in spite of everything, that GBRC is not supporting the mining of the Reef.'[15]

Büsst remained sceptical. His own position on the Reef's geological exploitation was becoming more resolute. In a letter to Sir Garfield Barwick, Büsst argued that 'mining, no matter how expedient, is a wasting asset. The Reef, on the other hand, if preserved intact, is a continually increasing scientific and touristic asset.'[16] Büsst's position was increasingly shared by the QLS and the WPSQ, a fact that aggravated the tensions between those groups and the scientific organisations.

It was not, however, only the GBRC's inaction that frustrated the conservationists. The ACF, too, was reluctant to object outright to oil drilling on the Reef. Büsst targeted Francis Ratcliffe, the CSIRO ecologist and key figure within the ACF in the 1960s, to encourage the ACF to adopt a formal policy opposing oil drilling on the Reef, and to call upon the Commonwealth to seize sovereignty of the offshore petroleum reserves. Büsst achieved this in October 1968, when the ACF amended and passed his motion stipulating that the Commonwealth should 'lay claim internationally to all those parts of the Reef and the area it occupies which may not now be internationally recognised as under Australian control'.[17] The motion included the strict provision that the Reef should be under 'one control', which, through scientific investigation, it said would determine:

> What if any human interference in the course of industry or commerce could be allowed without harm to any part of the Reef or the area it occupies, and [...] the Commonwealth and State Governments should ensure that no industrial or commercial activity, other than fishing and tourism, takes place on the Reef or in the area it occupies.[18]

Wright recalled that she and Büsst were 'delighted and relieved' that the motion passed. Wright felt that finally the ACF and the

GBRC, which had also passed a similar declaration at their most recent meetings, were on their side and significant progress had been made. It was also arranged that the ACF would, in May 1969, hold a symposium on the future of the Reef. Wright was initially enthusiastic about this prospect.[19] She excitedly declared to Büsst that it was 'all because of you, this book has to be written!'[20]

In early 1969, however, the ACF dragged its feet on lobbying for its recommendations and instead focused on arranging the symposium. There were plenty of opportunities for action on the Reef that year. In February, six companies had been granted rights to explore for petroleum in the Reef area.[21] The announcement of these leases emerged at the same time as oil began to leak from a pipe off the coast of Santa Barbara, California. For the conservationists, the Santa Barbara disaster was 'the big break'. Wright wrote: 'Santa Barbara's tragedy was the Reef's good fortune. It made the best possible publicity for the possible fate of those coral reefs and beaches.'[22] The ACF could have made significant and important contributions to the Reef issue, but failed to muster any energy in that direction.

In the political sphere, Queensland was preparing for an election in May 1969, and the government's plans for 'controlled exploitation' received immediate criticism. Büsst wrote to *The Townsville Bulletin* to remind the public that 'oil exploration in California is also permitted *only* under the *strictest control*', and demanded the government take its 'Hands off the Great Barrier Reef'.[23] Patricia Mather wrote to the Senate Select Committee on Off-shore Petroleum Resources, which had been established following the introduction of the *Petroleum (Submerged Lands) Act*, and asserted that Santa Barbara made evident the necessity for the establishment of a single authority to govern the Reef's management.[24] Pressure was mounting on the Commonwealth to give assurances that it would refuse to ratify any leases issued by the Queensland government.[25] The Queensland government, however, was resolute that drilling would take place irrespective of the Commonwealth's actions.

Then, in early 1969, the Commonwealth intervened. It decided to not approve future applications, and began investigating how to broaden its authority over the Reef for the purposes of controlling and managing fisheries and the resources of the continental shelf.[26] Its decision made the Queensland government's options of issuing new leases legislatively impossible, since the *Petroleum (Submerged Lands) Act* required both governments to approve leases. In March 1969, Camm announced that the Queensland government would defer indefinitely the granting of new applications to prospect for oil and minerals in Reef waters. The pressure of the state election, the Commonwealth's stance and the conservationists' activism had seemingly forced the Queensland government into this announcement, and it pledged that the Reef would henceforth be protected.[27]

Despite this sense of momentum, when the ACF symposium was due to commence, Wright recalled having doubts over its value.[28] The symposium had been designed to allow varied views on the Reef to be heard, including those from government and mining companies. Büsst publicly accused the ACF of being apologists for controlled exploitation, which prompted Dick Piesse, the director of the ACF, to respond: 'I need hardly assure you that this Foundation has organised this Symposium with the main aim of generating light, not heat, on the conservation issues surrounding the Great Barrier Reef and its region.'[29] Organisers of the symposium had arranged for a discussion on the issue of Reef sovereignty. Additionally, they planned to recommend that the Commonwealth establish a committee to manage the Reef's development.[30] The symposium would provide the recommendation for the Commonwealth to act, as well as the legal argument with which to do so. The conservationists, however, considered these manoeuvrings insufficient to marginalise the concessions to exploiters.

For the QLS and the WPSQ, the symposium was a 'shambles'.[31] There was little time after presentations for questions and discussion, which left some of the 'controversial points raised by geologists and others in favour of the commercial exploitation' of the Reef unchallenged.[32] Additionally, the conservationists considered that too little time had been allowed for discussion of the Reef's biology and ecology. Even the symposium's resolutions, they believed, did not adequately encourage the protection of the Reef.[33]

The QLS and the WPSQ's Innisfail branch lodged protests with the ACF, which responded that the Reef's management was complicated by legislative realities.[34] In its formal recommendations to the Commonwealth, however, the ACF proposed a moratorium and the establishment of a commission to formulate an overall plan for the Reef's development and consider 'whether oil exploration should be encouraged or permitted in the Reef area'.[35] Yet despite these eventual concessions, the ACF was no longer considered a 'logical platform' from which the other organisations could advocate.[36]

The damage the symposium caused in the relationship among the conservationists has been noted by some historians. McCalman considered that the symposium demonstrated the naivety of the ACF's leaders, who, along with those of the GBRC, had continued to appease the Queensland government and oil companies. He added, as suggested by Wright, that the symposium demonstrated the divergence of views on the Reef held by geologists and biologists.[37] Frank Talbot, marine biologist and director of the Australian Museum at the time, had emphasised this divide at the completion of the symposium: 'The Reef is a biological-physical complex [...] It seems very necessary for biologists and geologists to get much closer to each other to understand the processes involved.'[38]

Curiously, as noted by the historians of Australian environmentalism Drew Hutton and Libby Connors,[39] James Bowen argued that the symposium 'was a conservation event of great national significance, and one of the most important contributions to conservation of the Reef'.[40] Despite this assertion, the symposium was and still is considered a disappointment by the non-ACF participants. Other issues surrounding the Reef's conservation and exploitation – namely, fishing and tourism development – were discussed; by 1969, however, the QLS and the WPSQ were not interested in considering them. Only geological exploitation drew their attention, and the symposium had conspicuously failed to reach an unequivocal stance on its prohibition.

The symposium did have some merit, however. One topic of discussion was the legal aspects of the Reef, which was presented by Percy Spender, the former Australian politician, minister and diplomat, who had recently retired from his position as president of the International Court of Justice. Spender's paper, which concerned the legalities of sovereignty over Australia's continental shelf and the natural resources of its seabed, revealed crucial misunderstandings. Spender concluded that, excluding internal waters (such as large bays), Queensland's territorial boundaries expired at the low-water mark, and that all the natural resources of the seabeds bordering Australia belonged to the Commonwealth, not the states. Vitally, Spender claimed that under international law, 'dominion over the sea bed and the natural resources of the whole of the Continental Shelf commencing at low water mark, and the right to explore and exploit these, or permit others to do so, is vested exclusively in the Commonwealth'.[41] Spender's argument was supported soon afterwards by the High Court decision in *Bonser v La Macchia* (1969), which affirmed that the states were not sovereign bodies, as recognised in international conventions. Spender threw into question the constitutional legality of the *Petroleum (Submerged Lands) Act 1967*, which maintained that the states were sovereign bodies with regard to international conventions on offshore oil reserves.

Nonetheless, the Commonwealth government maintained

a cooperative relationship with Queensland. In August, an interdepartmental committee report recommended to Cabinet that successfully ensuring the Reef was not 'despoiled' would be best achieved through 'joint action and co-operation between the Queensland Government and the Commonwealth Government'.[42] Additionally, the report, co-authored by the minister for primary industry, J.D. Anthony, the minister for national development, David Fairbairn, and the attorney-general, Nigel Bowen, concluded that the 'weight of evidence' supported a policy of 'mining under strict control rather than total prohibition'.[43] Reef geologists such as Harry Ladd, Dorothy Hill and William Maxwell had all endorsed this position, and their approval was the only evidence cited in the Cabinet submission. While the Commonwealth maintained a publicly cautious position and continued to reaffirm a Reef-positive message in the media, its Cabinet was unwilling and philosophically opposed to intervening in Queensland.

Days before the 1969 Queensland election, the Japanese petroleum exploration company JAPEX, which had entered into a farm-out agreement with the Australian petroleum company Ampol, signalled its intention to drill a well in Repulse Bay.[44] There was a pre-existing lease granted to Ampol in 1964, which had not been invalidated by the *Petroleum (Submerged Lands) Act*; consequently, the Commonwealth could not intervene in this lease. Additionally, the proposed well site was in Queensland's internal waters, so there was no doubting Queensland's sovereignty. An empowered Camm declared:

> This Government will not repudiate any agreement that it has entered into. Repudiation could cause a world-wide loss of confidence in the integrity of the Government of Queensland resulting in a drying-up of capital for investment in the State and a flight of capital from the State. In such a case it seems almost certain that the State would be called upon to pay

compensation [...] We can control drilling so that the risk is remote and it is my intention to do this.[45]

A drilling rig, the *Navigator*, was due to depart Texas in September 1969 and arrive in Australia in early 1970 for the Repulse Bay operations.[46] For the conservationists, protecting the Reef from oil drilling now became an immediate endeavour.

The Queensland government came under immense pressure to alter its stance. The conservationists maintained their presence in the media, and new organisations emerged: the Save the Reef Committee (STRC) and the Housewives Concerning the Protection of the Barrier Reef, among others.[47] The media not only continued to serve as an organ through which the conservationists could express their concerns, but was itself a voice for concern and conservation. *The Australian* argued in favour of delaying oil exploration on the Reef until further biological research had been conducted, and emphasised the importance of the biology of the Reef to tourism.[48] Prime Minister Gorton stated resolutely that 'anything which in any way would seem to endanger' the Reef, 'not only on the question of drilling for oil, is something which should not, as far as legal possibilities are concerned, take place'.[49]

The public were outraged too. On 18 September, the premier's department was inundated with telegrams from members of the public with various single-line messages including 'Please save the Barrier Reef', 'No drilling no more promises', 'Don't make our Barrier Reef one of the great blunders of the world' and 'No drilling Barrier Reef otherwise no vote'.[50] A Mrs B.A. Walton from Brisbane posed a question to Premier Bjelke-Petersen:

Why should we in Australia take a chance with this priceless gift to satisfy the greed of overseas oil interests or even some of our own who may also have a share in the oil industry[?] [...]

Agreements may be made. Agreements can also be suspended or even broken. There is no dishonour in this if it is to the national interest.[51]

L.J. Jones, also of Brisbane, appealed to the Queensland government to listen to the conservationists and experts, and to stop the 'cowardly' drilling from taking place.[52]

Objections came from interstate too. Ms Campbell from Victoria added her 'strong protest' and urged the establishment of an authority 'to protect this wonderful asset'.[53] Mrs White from New South Wales asked the premier to 'consider where your greatest obligation lies – to a business contract or to the preservation of the greatest coral reef in the world?'[54] The Bowen Shire Council, the Humanist Society of Queensland, the Zoological Society of Frankfurt, and the Townsville and District Tourist Development Association all lodged their objections to the Reef being drilled for oil.[55] The economic rationale for drilling the Reef was clearly not persuasive for the public. Most objections noted that tourism offered 'renewable' wealth from the Reef, while drilling the Reef placed that income in jeopardy.[56] Despite the protests, the government proclaimed the drilling would go ahead, under strict controls.

In response, the conservationists began to make inquiries with the trade unions. On 5 September 1969, Büsst wrote to Whitlam and asked if 'the appropriate unions would care to take strike action against Ampol – after all the Reef is the workers' playground!'[57] On 16 September, the Commonwealth secretary of the Amalgamated Engineering Union wrote to Bjelke-Petersen: 'If Ampol-Japex persists, in the face of public opinion and drills in Repulse Bay, a voluntary Australia-wide boycott on all Ampol-Japex products will be called for, and a similar boycott on any other oil or mining company endangering the future of the Great Barrier Reef.'[58] A month later, Bjelke-Petersen was urged by the Australian Primary Producers Union to make a 'clear statement of policy indicating that a conservation approach' towards the Reef would be adopted 'and that no exploitation would occur'.[59]

Despite the overwhelming antipathy it had attracted, the government refused to shift. On 31 December 1969, John Büsst refused to accept the likelihood of the Reef being drilled. He had that month met once more with Gorton, and on 31 December he issued a further plea for the federal government to intervene. He asserted to the prime minister that while Repulse Bay was in internal waters, and the Ampol-JAPEX lease had been issued under an earlier act of parliament, the current lease was constitutionally invalid.[60] Büsst was desperate. He imagined that drilling on the Reef would begin within the month, and then it would be 'very difficult to restrain the oil companies'.[61] He made a request to a Melbourne law firm to examine the *Petroleum (Submerged Lands) Act* to determine whether any flaw existed and might provide grounds for him to issue a writ against the Commonwealth and state governments.[62]

From August 1967 through to the final day of 1969, the issue of the Reef's conservation had blown out from a contested application to mine a reef for limestone to the prospect of union-enforced labour bans and constitutional challenges to prevent the Reef being drilled for oil. The crown-of-thorns starfish, which had initially directed attention to the possibility of the Reef's decline, was now considered a lesser issue. Throughout the campaign, agitation for the Reef's protection had come from scientists and conservationists. It would be erroneous, however, to neglect the significant support they enjoyed from the media, the public, the Commonwealth government and the unions. It would also be inaccurate to contend that the Queensland government maintained a consistently pro-development and anti-environment position on the Reef's geological exploitation.

Nonetheless, by the end of 1969 it appeared more than likely that the Reef would be drilled. The Queensland government was refusing to sever any existing contracts, while the Commonwealth was refusing to intervene and risk a High Court challenge. Frustratingly for Büsst and Wright, Australia's peak conservation and Reef science bodies had also refused to make vehement protests against the Reef's drilling.

These tensions between and among the conservationists and scientists embodied the divergent attitudes towards the Reef's preservation. The Save the Reef debate provoked a broader question: how should the Reef be managed into the future? And what principles of conservation should underpin its future use? Regardless of their attitudes towards oil development, all parties – including the Queensland government – were searching for a way to answer these questions.

Seeing

The city of Townsville's foreshore promenade, The Strand, provides a constant vista towards the Reef. At dawn, it is a hive of exercise: boot-campers, runners, walkers and swimmers find their space to win their mornings. Throughout the day and into the evening, the exercisers are joined by those who sit on The Strand's manicured grass eating fish and chips, or stroll its length sipping coffees and eating ice creams.

There is one figure, however, who stands constantly in the bay. Ocean Siren, modelled on a young Wulgurukaba girl, faces towards Yunbenun (Magnetic Island), her ancestral home, and lifts to the skies a bailer shell – a traditional Indigenous communications device. Her back glows brightly in the evening light, in tune with the changes in the Reef's water temperature. If the temperatures are normal, she glows blue; orange if temperatures are above average; and if temperatures are high and concerning, she will glow red. Ocean Siren is an interactive sculpture that blends science with art: it is an attempt to cut across the complexities of science and deliver a visible message about the Reef's health. It is a call for change, a symbol of optimism. It is also part of a sophisticated Reef tourism enterprise.

Since the 1930s, Reef tourism has become the most significant economic element of the Reef. It is a $6 billion a year industry that supports thousands of jobs both directly through on-water tours, and indirectly via hospitality and transport in coastal towns and cities. Reef tourism's significance to Queensland's economy, and particularly the economies of Queensland's coastal cities, was made clear by the nearly complete shutdown of the industry during the Covid-19 pandemic. Usually thriving tourist centres were brought to their knees by the cutting-off of international and interstate travel through

2020 and 2021. The sudden absence of international tourists, and the financial and psychological despair this brought operators, was a reminder of Reef tourism's importance to the Queensland economy.

Before 2020, however, tourist operators would not likely have imagined that it would be a pandemic that would bring Reef tourism to a halt. In the decade prior, tourist operators and scientists had been engaged in a loose dialogue about the Reef's decline and how vociferous the claims of its deterioration should be. If Reef tourism was going to come to an end, it would be, in the imaginations of the most alarmed, because the Reef itself had died.

This issue was sparked largely because of a series of mass bleaching events along the Reef (in 1998, 2002, 2016, 2017 and 2020). In 2016, the bleaching event was so severe that 95 per cent of the reefs between Cairns and Papua New Guinea, an area usually regarded as more resilient due to its distance from major urban centres, were affected by bleaching. This event was covered widely by the international news media. Aerial video footage of snow-white corals beneath crystal-clear waters was shown across the globe. Stories of the deathly smell emerged. Metaphors of bushfires were invoked. Even an obituary of the Reef was written.[1] Like the Ocean Siren's bright lights, this bleaching event signalled to the globe that the Reef's water temperatures were beyond dire. It was a tremendously damaging event. In 2017, the Reef bleached again, and scientists, shocked at the consecutive events, continued to argue that they were likely to increase in frequency and severity.

Reef tourist operators were faced with a complex and confronting challenge: the environment that they showcase to the world was badly damaged and in visible decline, a dying attraction, but they still needed to attract international tourists. In response, lead Reef tourist operators lashed out at the coral scientists who had broadcast the news of the bleaching. Terry Hughes, the former director of the ARC Centre of Excellence for Coral Reef Studies at James Cook University, was reportedly called 'a dick' by Col McKenzie, the CEO of the

Association of Marine Park Tourism Operators (AMPTO).[2] McKenzie had claimed that scientists were sending a misleading message that the Reef was a 'graveyard', throwing future tourism profits into relief. There was also an implied argument that since the funding for the research into the bleaching had come from the government, the scientists should have provided messaging that would be less damaging to the nation's economy. Hughes, however, criticised those who claimed the Reef was dead. The important thing, he continued to stress, was that the Reef was alive, but under serious threat.

Unsurprisingly, the issue was enveloped within Australia's broader climate wars. After the bleaching event in 2016, Pauline Hanson, leader of the far-right One Nation political party, threw her support behind tourist operators by orchestrating a media event at Woppaburra (Great Keppel Island). Importantly, the reef Hanson and her party visited that day had not been hit by the 2016 bleaching; they were around 1000 kilometres south of the epicentre of that event.[3] Nonetheless, Hanson and other members of One Nation claimed that climate change was not a concern, that Reef scientists were exaggerating their claims and damaging the economy, and that Australia was in danger of losing its sovereignty to international organisations such as the International Union for Conservation of Nature (IUCN). For their part, conservationists were bemused and angry that tourist operators would see scientists as responsible for damaging the economy, and not polluters.

The entire scenario bore some resemblances to, but did not entirely mirror, the conflict that emerged between science, tourism and conservationism in the 1960s following the first outbreak of crown-of-thorns starfish. In that scenario, potential alliances between the three groups deteriorated in the face of individual ambitions and competing agendas. Tourist operators accused Robert Endean, the lead crown-of-thorns starfish scientist, of exaggerating his claims of reef damage in order to secure media attention and additional funding. Conservationists felt Endean's media attention was detracting from the broader issues of the Save the Reef campaign and sought to undermine him. As we have seen, Endean's claims surrounding the crown-of-thorns – the origins of outbreaks and the severity of their impact – were also publicly criticised by scientists at the time.

In 2016 and 2018, to prove that the government was taking the issue of the Reef's decline seriously, Australia's federal government, then led by Prime Minister Malcolm Turnbull, provided considerable funding towards combating the crown-of-thorns starfish. The government argued at the time that the Reef's best opportunity to survive the threats posed by climate change was to help improve its resilience to manageable threats. One arm of this strategy was to fund projects to improve land management within the catchment; the other was to investigate opportunities to reduce the threats of crown-of-thorns. Since then, the government has spent over $100 million in programs for research and controlling the starfish. The level of funding directed to curbing the starfish has at times been denounced by conservationists, who are critical of the federal government's failure to be more proactive in response to climate change. Again, some conservative politicians have suggested that even the crown-of-thorns, which are natural inhabitants of the Reef, are part of the cycle of coral reef decline and growth.

In this instance, far-right politicians are not aligned with the tourist operators. AMPTO has become a key partner in a crown-of-thorns surveillance and control program by supplying the materials needed to carry out the raids on the carnivorous starfish. One of the more aggressive elements of the control program relies upon teams of divers using needles to inject individual starfish with chemicals. Since the 1960s, this has been the only reliable method of controlling the starfish. Given the intensity of the labour required, and the size and scale of outbreaks, the control program must target specific areas. A key priority of the control program is targeting reefs with high visitation rates and significant tourist appeal, so tourism has emerged as a crucial ally in the defence of the Reef against the crown-of-thorns.

In a world where coral reefs are in decline, and eco-tourism is on the rise, the alliance between tourism and science is a seemingly natural one, but the two have not always confronted crises in lockstep. In more recent years, however, Reef tourism operators have begun to cooperate with scientists and conservationists to place increased pressure on Australia's governments to do more to reduce the pace of climate change.

After being defensive about the state of the Reef following the mass bleaching event in 2016, AMPTO penned and signed a declaration in 2018 calling on Australia's government to protect the Reef, and its associated tourism jobs, from climate change. '[T]he Reef is still a dynamic, vibrant, awesome place,' McKenzie said in 2018, 'but it is under serious threat from climate change, and we need our leaders to put in place strong climate and energy policies to protect its future.'[4]

That same year, the Australian Marine Conservation Society's Reef campaign director, Imogen Zethoven, said that the tourist operators had found themselves 'in a state of shock' following the 2016 bleaching event.[5] This seems reasonable, given the extent of the damage caused to the Reef and the starkness of the images that emerged from the bleaching surveys. In 2021, Gabrielle Wong-Parodi and Irina Feygina, researchers from Stanford University, published a study that suggested that people are more likely to shift their attitudes on climate change if they experience an emotional response to the subject.[6] In the study, participants were asked to read texts explaining the impacts of Arctic warming on charismatic animals like polar bears and mythical figures such as Santa Claus. Their findings suggested that participants who experienced negative or unpleasant emotions were more likely to change their minds. A suppressed emotional response was expected from conservative participants; however, even those who view climate change sceptically were drawn to perceive the temporal and physical proximity of climate change's effects more closely, and encouraged to act and bring others to do the same.

Rather than read about the impacts of climate change, Reef tourism operators had to confront them firsthand. Experiencing the effects of climate change and facing the possibility of losing their environment and livelihoods, as Reef operators have over the last two decades, exaggerates the negative responses, but nonetheless provides the same impetus to change.

Since the 1950s, Reef tourism operators have been under increasing pressure to be more responsible users of the Reef. For decades, the Reef has been managed and protected from tourists 'loving' it to death. What tourists and fishers can take from the Reef, as well as what they leave in it, has been increasingly regulated since the end of World War II. Importantly, while visitor engagement with the Reef can be an extractive and destructive force, their impact is a drop in the ocean in comparison to the larger drivers of reef decline, such as climate change. Nonetheless, the industry has demonstrated a capacity to adapt and utilise changes in attitudes and technology to facilitate visitor experiences. Gone are the days of turtle-riding, fossicking reef-flats and large floating hotels. There are still audacious visitor experiences, like being flown by helicopter to isolated resorts, or the proposition of islands being cleared for golf courses and casinos, but visitor experiences to the Reef are usually centred around less intrusive forms of tourism.

An additional inescapable consequence and contradiction of Reef tourism are the climate-changing emissions created by tourists visiting the Reef who want to have a personal connection with the environment. Reef tourism has always been a significant factor in building awareness of the Reef's biology and, consequently, raising support for its conservation and sustainable development. Without Reef tourism, the Reef would largely only exist within the imagination of Australia's tourists. Quite apart from the economic argument for the Reef's tourism industry, it provides a gateway to understanding and appreciation.

Despite the Reef's declining health, it remains a major drawcard for both international and domestic tourists. A 2015 Tourism Australia report stated that 42 per cent of international tourists to Australia ranked the Reef as the most appealing attraction.[7] In 2019, before the pandemic, tourism to Australia was increasing, and so too were the number of permits for commercial tourism on the Reef.[8] It is possible that the Reef's poor health is a factor in these numbers. The Reef has become, according to some, a 'last chance destination'; it is a fading attraction. There are, however, tourism operators who are helping to rehabilitate coral reefs. On reefs from Cairns to the Whitsundays region, tourism operators, given their skills in diving and enthusiasm for their environment, have become important sources of labour in collaborative projects with scientists. Tourists themselves can also join research teams on fieldwork and assist in small-scale Reef restoration projects.

There are also more innovative forms of Reef tourism that capitalise on the ways in which art and science intersect. Beginning in 2018, marine sculptures, including Ocean Siren, have been installed along the Reef. Other examples are of a series of sculpted structures – made from concretes, aluminium and steel – at Langford Reef in the Whitsundays region and the 'Coral Greenhouse' at John Brewer Reef. All of these structures show the ways in which the Reef and humans are connected. There are statues of humans, fish and other marine life that have been submerged on the Reef floor awaiting diving tourists and, one day, the settlement of coral polyps.

Like tourism and science, art and science have also historically been entangled. The Reef inspires romanticism, and these installations are designed to foster a conservation ethic and a broader appreciation of Reef science. But they are not without controversy. Some critics claim that these structures exist purely to attract tourists, and will put greater pressure on thriving, protected reef ecosystems. Others have argued that the placement of some figures, and the depiction of Indigenous peoples, is culturally inappropriate. Although these sculptures are novel and earnest attempts at promoting a conservation ethic and appreciation of the Reef, they have dredged up old tensions between Western science, tourism and Indigenous cultural heritage.

Scientists often cite the economic importance of the Reef as a rationale for their research. They frame the Reef's huge monetary value as a reason for its protection. Tourism's existence helps Reef scientists locate relevance within a competitive field for funding. Conversely, science – or, more specifically, the knowledge it provides – has always given Reef tourism its narratives. Visitors can look at a coral reef, but without the context and understanding that science provides, it is possible to become overwhelmed by the life the Reef sustains.

The industries – science and tourism – have been entangled for over a century. Though frictions may emerge, they are bedfellows. In this sense, Ocean Siren represents tourism's and science's entwined pasts and necessary futures: a personification of the necessity of both knowing and seeing the Reef.

8

The Black Ban

On 5 January 1970, as the oil rig the *Navigator* approached Reef waters, Labor senator George Georges announced that the Transport Workers Union and affiliates would impose a black ban on any ship or rig intending to drill in Repulse Bay.[1] The Repulse Bay plans had been foiled.

The black ban was celebrated in the media. *The Australian* published Georges's telegram to JAPEX, Ampol and the owners of the *Navigator*, which warned: 'I intend to launch a campaign to declare the vessel black and to withhold service of labor [sic] and essential goods for its operation.'[2] Georges announced that 'militant action' was necessitated by the failure of both governments 'to take action to ban drilling'. According to Patricia Clare, 'people of all political opinions came together to cheer'.[3] Queensland Labor politician Doug Sherrington declared that 'anything that will save the reef will have my whole-hearted support, particularly if it comes from the trade union movement'.[4]

In its editorial about the ban, *The Australian* stated:

The obdurate refusal of the Queensland and Commonwealth governments to heed public demands for action to stop oil exploration on the Great Barrier Reef now looks like rebounding on them. The black ban proposed by Senator Georges to abort drilling plans will have an unprecedented measure of public support and will probably succeed. It deserves to.[5]

Heavy criticism was levelled against the Queensland government: *The Australian* accused it of prioritising foreign investor confidence over maintaining credibility with its constituents. In a letter to Bjelke-Petersen, Judith Wright gave her 'whole hearted support for Senator Georges' call for a black ban' and stressed that the Reef 'must be fully protected from all mining exploitation'.[6]

The black ban had major consequences. First, it forced Ampol to recommend to JAPEX that drilling be postponed.[7] Ampol also suggested and offered funds to the Commonwealth for a 'thorough investigation' by a joint government committee of inquiry to 'allay public concerns over the possible pollution of the Reef by drilling for oil', and a provision to investigate the crown-of-thorns starfish plague.[8] Unimpressed by Ampol's decision, Bjelke-Petersen wrote to Prime Minister Gorton, emphasising the precautions Queensland had taken to 'ensure that any possible risk of pollution' had been 'reduced to the absolute minimum' by the application of 'the most stringent conditions' to the Repulse Bay operation. Bjelke-Petersen also stressed his government's responsibility to undertake oil drilling to reveal the benefits for science, for the economy and for the state's self-sufficiency as quickly as possible. 'I am convinced that the drilling in Repulse Bay should go ahead and I am also convinced that it is quite safe for this to take place,' he declared.[9]

The black ban, however, provided the necessary political capital for the Commonwealth to intervene and leverage a general postponement of all oil drilling on the Reef. On 14 January, the day after Ampol's decision to postpone its operations, Gorton issued a press release praising Ampol's decision.[10] On 15 January, Gorton sent a telegram to Ampol congratulating it on its initiative, and expressed support for its attempt to persuade JAPEX, which was yet to reply to Ampol's decision.[11] Gorton refused the offer of funds from Ampol for an inquiry, to avoid the taint of partiality, and reaffirmed the commitment of both the federal and state governments to settle the side issue of the crown-of-thorns starfish. The Commonwealth was willing to have a joint government inquiry, but it was awaiting the Queensland government's cooperation.

The Queensland government, however, was still awaiting a response to its invitation – sent to the Commonwealth in June 1968 – to participate in the GBRRAC. An embattled Bjelke-Petersen claimed: 'The proposals then made and the supporting information given were and still are pertinent to the question of Reef drilling and therefore I see no reason why they should not appropriately provide the basis for any joint Commonwealth/State investigation now.'[12]

Gorton finally replied, dismissing the notion that the GBRRAC was a 'joint' initiative (it only allowed one Commonwealth representative on a committee of eleven), and rejecting it as not being 'specifically concerned with drilling for oil on the Reef'. In rebuffing the proposal, Gorton added:

> The proposal before us now is that drilling be suspended on or near the Reef pending a truly joint Commonwealth/State inquiry which will report to both our governments and which will make public its reports. The Commonwealth is prepared to endorse this specific proposal and I should be glad if you will let me know whether the Queensland Government is also prepared to do so.[13]

Whether Bjelke-Petersen or the Queensland government sincerely believed the GBRRAC was still a live issue is hard to determine. The GBRRAC was a holistic approach to the Reef's conservation and exploitation. In the aftermath of the black ban, however, Bjelke-Petersen's claims of Commonwealth inaction on the GBRRAC were perceived as obstructionist.[14] Nonetheless, a day after Gorton's response, the Queensland government capitulated and agreed to send a Cabinet delegation to Canberra to assist in formulating a joint inquiry.[15]

Bjelke-Petersen and his government gained little support from the public as a consequence of their pro-oil position. Mrs Raynes of Brisbane expressed her disappointment in the premier and his 'attitude to oil drilling on the Barrier Reef. For the first time in my life I voted Labor at the last election on this issue in particular,' she wrote. Mr Bootle of Sydney criticised Bjelke-Petersen for failing to utilise Ampol's decision as 'an opportunity for the Queensland government to bow out gracefully' from their 'ill-conceived move to drill for oil in an area of unique tourist attraction'. A.R. Timmins of Brisbane enclosed in his letter a copy of *The Australian*'s editorial from 7 January, and wrote:

> You may see what a responsible national daily newspaper thinks of your actions. Your attitude on this question seems to be to take a chance on any damage to the reef occurring as a result of drilling operations. I can only say that should you be unlucky, you will long be remembered in Australian history as a fool and worse.[16]

In the face of severe public scrutiny, the Queensland government asserted that it was 'fully conscious of its responsibility to judiciously protect and conserve the natural resources of Queensland', as opposed to the conservationists, who were only concerned with 'knocking oil drilling in coastal waters'.[17]

The government received some support for its position. Townsville resident Mr Evans telegrammed that he commended and thoroughly endorsed Bjelke-Petersen's stance on drilling Repulse Bay and drilling the Reef generally. Most correspondence from the public, however, was negative and more closely resonated with the sentiment expressed by Ms Baillieu of Victoria, who wrote: 'We deplore and regard with disgust the obstinate self-interest with which you disregard the care and preservation of the Great Barrier Reef which belongs to all Australians.'

While the Queensland government may not have been responsive to public opinion, Ampol and JAPEX were. On 21 January, JAPEX expressed its frustration with Ampol's decision to halt operations. The Japanese company indicated that public opposition had been evident for some time, but it was an issue Ampol seemed willing to disregard – until the proposed black ban. Their telegram to Ampol stated: 'We respect and share your concern for the protection of this Australian resource but we are surprised that you have delayed expressing your concern until this time even though we have previously drawn your attention to the potential problems.'[18] JAPEX was 'happy' for Ampol 'to take whatever action' it considered reasonable regarding accumulated expenditure, and would consider postponement or cancellation of the drilling program in order to minimise further costs.[19] In other words, JAPEX was content to postpone but wanted compensation.

The financial consequence of Ampol's decision was a point of angst not only for JAPEX but also for the Queensland government. In preparation for the Canberra meeting to organise a Reef inquiry, Queensland's state mining engineer, A.W. Norrie, issued a memorandum for Bjelke-Petersen. Norrie instructed the government to assert its stance of no repudiation and to express a willingness to cooperate with Ampol and JAPEX to halt operations. He then prompted the government to draw attention to other forms of possible damage facing the Reef, including tourism, defence training and oil tankers, and asked:

> Why are some people so determined to stop this drilling while allowing other human activities, that may be a greater threat to the Great Barrier Reef, to proceed? Why pick on drilling for oil and refuse to allow the people of Australia to judge whether other things may not be greater hazards?[20]

The experience of the black ban, and its financial consequences, sharpened the Queensland government's attitude towards oil drilling but left them further alienated. The government failed to accept that while the Reef held economic value, this valuation did not extend, in the public conscientiousness, to its geological resources. Whether the government was ignorant, indifferent or unwilling to recognise this was immaterial; it was determined to drill in Repulse Bay.

The Canberra conference was the first instance in which the state and federal governments discussed the Reef issue directly with one another during the Save the Reef campaign.[21] Gorton asserted at the outset that while an initial joint government committee of inquiry could be established to consider the oil issue, he envisaged a suite of interrelated committees would eventually become necessary to manage the entire Reef.[22]

Bjelke-Petersen agreed to an inquiry, but proposed an alternative that would consider the entire continent, not specifically the Queensland coast. The Queensland contingent queried why oil drilling on the Reef was an issue of concern and not, for instance, oil exploration in the Bass Strait. But, as Gorton argued, it was Queensland, not the Commonwealth, who had prompted the inquiry when they initiated the GBRRAC. He added:

> I think that if we found around Australia an area of the size of the Barrier Reef area and with the same world interest and of the same importance we would be just as interested, in conjunction with the State Government, in seeking to preserve that area [...] We have not received such a communication from any other State, but should any other State make a communication which dealt with an area of significance remotely comparable to the Barrier Reef, then of course we would take it into consideration.[23]

The Commonwealth had been lethargic in its willingness to endorse the Reef's outright protection, but, emboldened by the public following the black ban, and led by a more resolute Gorton, it rarely bought into the arguments of the Queensland government during the Canberra conference.

While both governments agreed in principle to the formation of an inquiry, Queensland was unwilling to publicly call for the postponement of oil drilling along the Reef. The financial and political ramifications of repudiation weighed heavily upon the state government. Bjelke-Petersen considered the repudiation of leases to be 'distasteful and completely unacceptable', and was determined to remain unaccountable for Ampol's decision, to avoid making the government jointly liable. Queensland would only agree to the suspension of drilling, Bjelke-Petersen asserted, if it was instigated by JAPEX, or if the Commonwealth or Ampol were willing to financially compensate JAPEX. The Commonwealth had already stipulated in March 1969 that it would not endorse new leases on the Reef, and would cooperate with any company that wished to postpone their operations pending the inquiry. The Queensland government appeared unwilling to publicly share the Commonwealth's position, lest it be interpreted as a formal request for postponement. Consequently, the Repulse Bay operation would go ahead unless Ampol and JAPEX came to terms, and the remaining oil operations along the Reef remained unresolved.

Mining minister Ron Camm proposed a solution, however, which would force oil companies to show their hands. If the Queensland government imposed new conditions upon the leases, the companies could be discouraged from drilling. 'Why not let us handle other Reef permits by imposing conditions that are unacceptable to people and let them take the initiative and fight us by saying that we have imposed conditions beyond our powers,' Camm suggested.[24]

Within this plan, however, JAPEX would still be allowed to

drill. The Queensland government confirmed it was satisfied that drilling in Repulse Bay would be safe, and offered to apply Camm's solution across other Reef leases. Gorton was 'not unhappy' with that approach, and agreed that drilling could essentially be prevented during the inquiry if conditions that 'would make it virtually impossible for people to drill' were imposed. Drilling on the Reef could be postponed by government manoeuvring, providing the space required for the inquiry to take place. But, as Camm noted, the plan would have legal ramifications. 'We cannot,' he stated, 'make it public that we are prepared to do this because that in effect would be repudiation.'[25]

The Queensland government was determined to distance itself from financial liability. The commission, according to Bjelke-Petersen, was only necessary because of public fears over oil drilling in the Reef. He indicated that the inquiry's findings would vindicate his government's attitude towards the Reef: that 'you could not destroy it if you tried'.[26] The Queensland government stipulated that, irrespective of the inquiry's findings, it would not repudiate any leases, nor ban drilling on the Reef. If the inquiry necessitated that the existing leases along the Reef be rescinded, it would play no role in financially compensating the various oil companies.

The Commonwealth did not accept Queensland's assertions of federal liability, but this did not create an impasse and the inquiry was able to proceed. Discussions on issues of compensation and liability, fuelled by the Queensland government, consumed half the meeting. The Queensland government's greatest anxiety surrounding the Reef was that it would somehow be financially responsible for compensating oil companies. The ecological hazards of drilling the Reef for oil were secondary at best.

The discussion concerning the inquiry's composition was less adversarial. Both sides agreed the nature of the inquiry would remain open, and deferred the decision of whether it should be a royal commission to a later date. Bjelke-Petersen desired to see 'the widest possible inquiry to kill this matter once and for all and to decide what we can do and what we cannot do'.[27] Impartiality of the committee was important. He stated:

> We would prefer to keep the membership apart from any men in any government departments. We do not want anybody from our departments [...] If we put in one of our men we would not feel that it was fair either. We would like to be in a position in which nobody could point a finger at us and say: 'You have loaded this committee.'[28]

Neither government desired to include conservationists or trade unionists on the committee. The Queensland government was particularly anxious for the inquiry to investigate the probable benefits of an oil industry on the Reef. Bjelke-Petersen considered this to be an oversight in the controversy, and added: 'I say: "What if we get a lot of oil?" They say: "That does not matter. You should not drill the Reef."'[29] Queensland Attorney-General Peter Delamothe agreed, and suggested that although there would be dangers inherent in drilling, they might be outweighed by the advantages.

Importantly, Gorton refused to ask the potential inquiry to make that judgement, as that would play to the strengths of Queensland's populist politics. Both governments conceded that offshore oil drilling presented possible dangers to the Reef, but disagreement emerged over how the inquiry should report on its findings. Could an inquiry rule out possible areas for oil drilling? Could it, alternatively, recommend areas where drilling could take place? Or could it make a comment on the degree to which oil companies could eliminate potential dangers? The latter possibility was considered unpalatable by Queensland, and Camm asked: 'To what extent you can [sic] act to eliminate danger? The only extent is to prohibit drilling.'[30]

The Canberra meeting revealed the various motivations and forces acting upon the Queensland government's attitude towards the Reef. Notably, the government was under enormous political pressure from several directions. It considered itself to be stuck in an almost irreconcilable dilemma between making decisions that appeased its electorate and maintaining confidence with foreign and commercial interests.[31]

Public opinion had well and truly turned against the Queensland government on the Reef issue. When the Canberra meeting came to a close and decisions on what to tell the media needed to be made, the Queensland contingent were eager to avoid any form of controversy or humiliation. 'I do not want to say anything that will embarrass anybody,' Bjelke-Petersen said. 'I have been embarrassed so much I do not think I could be embarrassed any more.'[32] Additionally, the trade unions had rendered plans to drill in Repulse Bay impossible for the time being, and the Commonwealth government was refusing to allow the Queensland government's position on repudiation to dictate the future of the Reef.

In defence, the Queensland government was determined to position the Reef issue, at least the repudiation of oil leases, as a Commonwealth responsibility. Alternatively, on Repulse Bay it asserted its responsibility and sovereignty. It was a confused position that asserted state rights on the one hand but surrendered sovereignty on the other.

The Queensland government imagined the inquiry would allay public concern on oil drilling. They had suggested that the inquiry take the form of a royal commission, since it was the only way to assure, as Bjelke-Petersen put it, 'a fairly full inquiry'.[33] It also had the benefit, Camm pointed out, of forcing 'some people to come along and divulge where they obtained their information'.[34] A royal commission could perhaps broaden the public's perception of the Reef's economic possibilities; it could assuage fears of and secure support for oil drilling.

*

The conservationists were initially thrilled with the announced black ban. Freda McLennan of the STRC wrote to Büsst: 'Hurray for Senator Georges and the Transport Worker's [sic] Union, and the only black ban I've ever cheered for in my entire life.'[35] Weeks after Georges's announcement, Büsst wrote to thank him for the intervention and signalled the importance of the black ban in the Reef campaign. 'I now feel for the first time since the original Ellison Reef case,' Büsst wrote, 'that we have a genuine chance of protecting the Barrier Reef from gross and ill-informed exploitation by Ampol-Japex, Exoil and others.'[36]

The significance of the union intervention could be read in Büsst's letters to others. He shared his elation with the *Australian* reporter Adrian Deemer, and his amusement 'at the suppressed cut-throat battle between Ampol and Japex as to who pays how much to whom!'[37] Büsst also celebrated the black ban with Wright, declaring:

> The submission I wrote some time ago for the A.C.T.U. eventually stirred things up, as did my hasty dash to Townsville to see Whitlam, to ask him to put a ban on the rig. It has taken 2½ years to bend this weapon – this is it, and the screws can be tightened still further, if the government enquiry is not over and above board, and if we are not permitted to import overseas scientists.[38]

Wright wrote that the black ban was a vindication of all Büsst's campaigning; the black ban was the 'breakthrough'.[39]

The good news continued for the conservationists. A by-election for the state seat of Albert was held on Valentine's Day, and opposition leader John Houston was determined to make the Reef a major issue.[40] So too were the conservationists. The Labor and Liberal candidates both publicly opposed drilling the Reef for oil, while the Country Party candidate sought to keep the debate to local issues. In the end the Liberal candidate won.

To Büsst, Wright wrote:

[Bjelke-]Petersen is really mad with us over the Albert by-election. What he does not yet realise is that it's better to lose a battle than a whole war; which he would have done at the next election if the Albert one had not given him a chance to save his bacon.[41]

The Albert loss created some tensions with the Queensland government, forcing Bjelke-Petersen to fight off a leadership challenge from within his Country Party. In *The Coral Battleground*, Wright recalled the importance of the Albert by-election as being the moment when the 'trades unions and the conservationists were no longer an "irresponsible minority"'.[42]

Despite their elation, the conservationists remained wary. They were concerned that the proposed inquiry would align with a conference of the Australian Petroleum Exploration Association (APEA) in March, enabling that organisation to lure witnesses to its cause. In contrast, the conservationists were unable to finance the travel and accommodation costs of supporting witnesses. The WPSQ decided to write to Gorton requesting assistance to bring 'expert witnesses forward'.[43] Büsst had already sent a letter to Gorton expressing his dissatisfaction with Bjelke-Petersen's assertion that 'people giving evidence at the enquiry would have to meet their own expenses'.[44] Büsst insisted the inquiry would be 'a complete farce and not worthwhile attending, since it will be stacked with Queensland government and oil company nominees'. Provocatively, Büsst suggested that the oil companies employed many marine biologists, 'but with the proviso that the companies retain the right to publish their findings. If the findings are unfavourable, they are not published.' Finally, Büsst listed a number of scientists who, he believed, would add important evidence to the inquiry, and requested that they be invited and their attendance paid for. If the funds were not provided, or assurances were not received, Büsst would 'have no option but to conduct a public Australia-wide appeal for funds through the Press, particularly *The Australian*, who have shown themselves to be most sympathetic to conservation matters'. Four days later, Büsst advised journalist Adrian Deemer that the Queensland government intended to draw on 'funds to import overseas geologists and others already in favour of mining the Reef, but conservationists have the funds to import exactly none'.[45]

Finances were one concern for the conservationists; the other was consistency across the various organisations and the need to rouse greater support from the scientific community. Since 1967, personal and political feuds had sullied the relationships among and between various conservationists and scientists. At a 2 February meeting, the WPSQ sharpened its stance on the Reef issue and decided to publicly declare its complete opposition to any form of mining or oil drilling. It would no longer seek appeasement through a moratorium. The organisation distanced itself from the notion of 'conservation' and 'controlled exploitation'. Finally, they had formally excluded geological exploitation from possible Reef use. They tabled a statement that asserted:

> Specifically, we believe that there should be absolute protection, sine die, against mining for limestone or other minerals, and against exploration for and extraction of oil, or natural gas [...] Progressive and controlled development of tourist and fishing industries based on the results of adequate and continuing scientific research to ensure that the type, location and extent of developments do not damage the Reef resources in the long or short term! Our attitude towards the proposed development of a marine oil industry on or near the Great Barrier Reef is therefore unequivocal, and our policy of preservation (as opposed to 'conservation' meaning 'controlled exploitation') would be maintained until it were shown that no alternative sources of oil existed elsewhere.[46]

The union black ban, Ampol's retreat and the announcement of the inquiry demonstrated that public opinion was significantly in favour of the 'preservationists'. The WPSQ's intensification of its stance sought to utilise the increased attention and sympathy for its position. Additionally, the WPSQ's decision to designate itself as 'preservationist', rather than 'conservationist', created a crucial distinction between it, the ACF and the GBRC. As Wright lamented in *The Coral Battleground*, she and the WPSQ felt frustrated by pragmatic positions on Reef conservation.[47]

The WPSQ had firmed its individual stance, but the inquiry warranted a distinct and unified case from all the conservationist bodies, including the GBRC. Patricia Mather, by this time secretary of the GBRC, prepared an agreement of the conservation organisations and presented it to a collection of WPSQ and STRC members. Mather's proposed agreement criticised the inquiry for its limited scope and its lack of ongoing statutory authority. She considered that the required interpretation of technical evidence would prove problematic and, above all, believed the entire endeavour unnecessary. Critically, the inquiry would not address whether 'an oil industry in the Great Barrier Reef waters' was 'essential for Australian development'.[48] Mather's agreement then criticised the lack of responsibility assumed by either government to conserve the Reef, and asserted that the only action that had occurred was the result of the energy and tenacity of 'citizen vigilantes' and scientists.

Much like the WPSQ's statement, Mather's provided an unequivocal list of demands on behalf of the GBRC:

> They want the conservation of the Great Barrier Reef to become law; they want an appropriate authority whose experience, expertise and resources will ensure that the area is administered under the law; they want the Great Barrier Reef removed from the arena where, for too long, it has been used politically.[49]

The new GBRC secretary was politically engaged and willing to steer the committee closer to the conservationists, but Wright's scepticism of the GBRC was entrenched. She commented that Mather's agreement seemed 'sensible enough to us', but, referring to the GBRC's previous reluctance to take a leading role, Wright lamented that 'the vigilantes [WPSQ and QLS] are to be those responsible for calling evidence'.[50] Despite an obvious need to unite before the impending royal commission, the divides between the conservationist groups remained unbridgeable, particularly that between Mather and Wright. In a letter to Büsst, Wright described Mather as 'a little like the crocodile [...] welcoming little fishes in with gently smiling jaws'.[51] The conservation groups may have all signed an agreement to present a unified message, but in practice wide divisions remained.

The decision by the GBRC to shift its position on oil drilling and support the conservationists was not taken unanimously by its executive. The GBRC had already begun to advocate for management of the Reef by a statutory authority that could appoint technical advisory bodies where necessary, but that plan had gathered little momentum. As the oil issue continued to develop in late 1969, various members of the GBRC executive voiced concerns that the committee was moving too far towards an anti-drilling stance. At the 1969 annual general meeting, Dorothy Hill expressed anxiety that the committee was about to commit to prohibiting drilling of the Reef for oil.[52] With no movement from governments towards the GBRC's policy for a single statutory authority to administer the Reef's conservation and exploitation, the GBRC's executive took a decisive step: it would advocate for a ban on oil drilling pending the establishment of the authority.[53]

The dramatic shift agitated some members of the GBRC. George Orme, a geologist and the GBRC's treasurer, had already written to Mather:

> The recent decision of the 'Executive Committee' to oppose oil drilling on the Continental Shelf off the Queensland Coast is a sudden change in the sensible attitude which has so far been maintained and supported by most members of the Committee [...] I will not support a resolution which advocates a complete ban on drilling the Queensland Continental Shelf, especially if this extends to exploratory holes. On a policy matter as important as this, I sincerely hope that an accurate and complete dossier will be obtained representing the opinions of all members of the Committee, however short the time might be, and regardless of the pressures exerted by other scientific and lay societies to support their own resolutions. I feel this is particularly important since the Executive Committee is dominated by biologists.[54]

Mather remained resolute. The GBRC, she replied, maintained its stance that the Reef's resources 'should be available to the people of Australia, with the proviso that these resources should be properly husbanded'.[55] The executive's decision, however, which she conceded was not unanimous, was '[b]ased on the fact that a delay in the accumulation of geological knowledge may be necessary to ensure that the extant biological system is not harmed by a too-rapid development in the area before the necessary technical expertise and biological information is available'.[56]

The black ban had laid bare the schism between marine geologists and biologists on the issue of the Reef's protection. There was also a clear shift in power occurring within the Reef science academy. Marine biologists asserted themselves in a world where biological knowledge about the Reef was increasing in scientific and economic relevance. Consequently, those scientists gained greater voice and control over institutions like the GBRC. Given this shift in both scientific and conservation ethics, the GBRC was clearly less willing, or likely less able, to rely on the Queensland government for meaningful Reef policies.

Whatever divisions between Reef scientists the black ban revealed, the positive reaction to it indicated the extent of the public's perception of the Reef's economic value. The public and the media overwhelmingly supported the intervention of the unions, and the black ban became a symbol of a growing frustration with government inability, at both the Commonwealth and state levels, to take resolute action on the oil issue.

Importantly, the prevalence of the anti-drilling position among the Australian public was so visceral that it provided the necessary will for the Commonwealth to push for the establishment of an inquiry. It prompted the conservationists, particularly the WPSQ, to sharpen their stance on oil drilling, and it also provided impetus for the GBRC to formulate the legislation and lobby for the establishment of a Reef authority.

Towards a Reef Commission

During the months between the black ban and the commencement of the royal commission, interested parties sharpened their positions on the Reef's conservation and exploitation. Opposition to drilling was palpable, and exposed the fragility of the Bjelke-Petersen government's pro-oil position. The black ban only intensified the media's attention and their pressure on the Queensland government to repudiate its oil leases and reverse its position. While the black ban had effectively created the moratorium, the Queensland government was determined to ensure the inquiry would endorse a future for the Reef that included oil drilling.

Since the initial reactions to the black ban, the Repulse Bay issue lingered unresolved. JAPEX expedited the situation by writing to Bjelke-Petersen. Confirming the fears of the Queensland government, JAPEX had interpreted the announcement of an inquiry as a formal recommendation by the governments to abandon operations in Repulse Bay. JAPEX explained that it was 'totally sympathetic to the public concern' for the need to protect the Reef, and did not wish to 'debate the justification or otherwise' for this concern in relation to the drilling program in Repulse Bay. The company noted, however, that because the 'recommendation' was made so late, it was impossible for it to defer drilling without substantial financial loss – a loss in that Ampol was not legally liable to share. JAPEX declared:

> This Company has come to Queensland in good faith and confident of your Government's goodwill to the investment of capital in your State. Now we find ourselves highly embarrassed by the position that your Government's recommendation has placed us in. This Company believes it must give the fullest weight to the expressed wishes of your Government and indeed for us to do otherwise is, to us, unthinkable. However, it seems to us to be neither fair nor realistic to expect our Company to abandon such a large financial investment simply to await the outcome of this inquiry which, we read in the Press, is regarded by many people as belated [...] In all the circumstances, therefore, this Company considers that it is entitled to ask your Government to compensate it for the loss that would be incurred by the deferment of the drilling programme in Repulse Bay.[1]

The losses that JAPEX sought from the Queensland government came to $1 million (approximately $12.2 million today).

Publicly and privately, the Queensland government maintained that it would not repudiate any rights it had conferred, but would agree to freeze drilling at Repulse Bay at the request of Ampol and JAPEX. Bjelke-Petersen claimed that halting the drilling in Repulse Bay was 'unlawful and unnecessary', but that concerns for the Reef had become 'so wild' that 'the only way to allay public concern' was through an inquiry. He wanted to give Australians a chance to 'judge for themselves the wisdom' of the government's politics.[2]

Legal advisers instructed the Queensland government that it had not yet infringed upon the law and was not liable. They were warned, however, against introducing new controls, as had been discussed with the Commonwealth, unless they were 'bona fide directions for the purpose of the protection of natural resources'.[3] Armed with this legal advice, Bjelke-Petersen wrote to Gorton and reminded him that Queensland would not accept financial liability for deferment or suspension of drilling as a consequence of the inquiry. He requested an 'immediate Conference' to determine whether reimbursement was warranted and whether the Commonwealth was prepared to meet such claims.[4]

That same day, JAPEX wrote to both leaders, informing them that it had decided to terminate the agreement with the company contracted to mobilise preparatory work and provisions for the oil rig *Navigator*. The decision, JAPEX claimed, minimised the cost of deferment but also acted in accordance with the wishes expressed by both governments. The letter then went on to make two substantial claims. First, JAPEX emphasised that its actions should not be interpreted as confirmation that drilling in Repulse Bay would constitute a threat to the Reef. It did accept, however, that this judgement 'should be made by the Australian people'.[5] Second, it reiterated that it expected reimbursement from the Queensland government.

The Queensland government was encouraged to 'take a strong stand' against JAPEX's claims.[6] It responded by declaring that the joint government inquiry was being organised, but it did not constitute a recommendation to any companies concerned with oil drilling on the Reef. Furthermore, Bjelke-Petersen asserted that any steps JAPEX had taken, and any loss arising from them, were matters between JAPEX and Ampol.[7] The government was now confident of its lack of liability but, believing the Commonwealth would be targeted by JAPEX, continued to press for a conference with them. Gorton, however, seemed unfazed by JAPEX's claims, and reminded Bjelke-Petersen that the requirement to have a conference depended on the inquiry's findings.[8]

JAPEX again claimed it would seek compensation for deferment, but that it and Ampol would terminate their immediate drilling agreement and defer it, subject to the outcome of the inquiry. It stipulated, however, that if any new conditions were imposed on drilling in areas covered by Ampol's authorities or permits as a result of the inquiry, then JAPEX would again seek reimbursement from either government for the costs of termination.[9] The Repulse Bay operation was now suspended, and neither government would receive any further communications from JAPEX during the five years of the royal commission. The black ban had succeeded.

Following the Canberra conference in January 1970, both governments constructed their lists of preferred candidates for the inquiry. They had agreed in Canberra that the likely committee would be a three-person panel consisting of a judge as chair, a marine biologist and an engineer. The Commonwealth recommended Justice John Nimmo as chair, marine biologist Dr Eric Smith and American petroleum engineer Mr A.D. Acuff.[10]

In a Cabinet submission, Bjelke-Petersen raised objections to the inclusions of Nimmo and Acuff. Nimmo, Bjelke-Petersen argued, was 'a Commonwealth judge', and Bjelke-Petersen thought it essential that a judge be found who would be 'sympathetically disposed' to Queensland's position. He asserted that his own 'discreet enquiries' had led him to believe that a New South Wales judge, Sir Gordon Wallace, was agreeable to having his name put forth and would be a 'suitable nominee'.[11] Acuff's inclusion was considered unacceptable because of his participation in the inquiry into the Santa Barbara oil spill, and in the 'rewriting' of the United States' offshore drilling regulations following that incident. 'I feel that in Mr Acuff there is a person who would come to the Committee with at least some pre-determined views which could be detrimental to our position,' Bjelke-Petersen told Cabinet.[12] As an alternative, Bjelke-Petersen recommended that a Canadian petroleum engineer, V.J. (John) Moroney, be nominated as the third commissioner. The premier had learnt that Melbourne-based

Queen's Counsel A.E. Woodward was prepared to have his name put forward as 'Counsel assisting the Inquiry' – a position Bjelke-Petersen thought 'every endeavour should be made' to have filled by 'a person who will allow this State's attitude to be fully presented'.[13] Finally, Bjelke-Petersen declared to his Cabinet that it was 'essential that the Mines Department should ensure that the Queensland case is adequately prepared for presentation to the Committee and that the Department be authorised to retain leading Counsel for this purpose'.[14]

The conservationists were right to assume that the Queensland government would seek to undermine, as much as legally possible, the composition of the committee. Bjelke-Petersen's argument to Gorton for Acuff's removal did not exactly align with the one he provided to Cabinet. He did not deny Acuff's credibility, but believed the position held by the petroleum engineer should be given to an 'individual with world-wide reputation as an expert on oil-drilling procedures and one who has a complete appreciation of the safety conditions imposed for well-control'.[15]

Gorton urged Bjelke-Petersen to reconsider his position, and maintained 'it would be better if the Committee were comprised of persons who have had no association with industry'.[16] In the same letter, Gorton agreed to Queensland's suggestion, made at the Canberra conference, that the 'Committee of Inquiry' become a parallel Commonwealth and Queensland royal commission.

The Queensland government circulated memorandums regarding both Moroney and Acuff following Gorton's response. The Moroney memorandum asserted that for 'the Queensland case' it was 'essential that there be a complete appreciation' of the control and safety measures being applied by the mines department. Accordingly, Moroney's long association with the oil industry and experience in oil drilling did not negate his inclusion but enhanced his suitability.[17] Acuff's independence and impartiality had been, to their mind, thrown into relief by his involvement in the investigation and follow-up to the Santa Barbara blowout. On that basis it was determined, once more, that his membership was unacceptable.[18] Bjelke-Petersen hid his concerns from the Commonwealth and argued that Acuff's lack of impartiality would be perceptible and undermine faith in the commission.[19]

Gorton made one final attempt to secure a petroleum engineer of his choosing on the committee. He nominated R.K. Dickie, who was then working as the petroleum inspector of the British minister of technology. Again Bjelke-Petersen objected, declaring that Dickie's qualifications and status did not come within the 'prescribed category'; his nomination was also unacceptable to the Queensland government. Bjelke-Petersen added that Dickie was known to officers within the Queensland mines department, who were not 'impressed with his knowledge or ability'.[20] Expressing a sense of urgency, Bjelke-Petersen nominated three new candidates, and said of the committee: 'It is now nearly two months since we agreed to its establishment and any further delay will not assist the Committee in its work when it does commence its hearings or, for that matter, our Governments' standing in the eyes of the people.'[21]

The entire episode made clear that the most pertinent issue to be considered by the royal commission, at least from the Queensland government's perspective, was the possibility of an oil leak. A recommendation in favour of Queensland's position would substantially undermine opposition to drilling the Reef.

By March, Bjelke-Petersen's eagerness to move forward with the royal commission was largely motivated by the *Oceanic Grandeur* episode in the Torres Strait. On 3 March, the oil tanker struck an uncharted rock pinnacle east of Wednesday Island. Oil gushed out from a 55-metre gash in the vessel's hull. The chemical dispersants Gamlen and Corexit were deployed to break down the spilt oil, while residual oil was transferred to another vessel, the *Leslie J.*

Thompson.[22] Neither Gamlen nor Corexit was effective: tides, winds and warm tropical water were the most active agents in the oil's dispersal and breakdown. Luckily, the spill had no impacts on the local marine or bird life.

Good fortune rather than good management meant the clean-up was successful.[23] Strong east–west tidal currents confined the spilt oil, while 'unusually calm' weather allowed for the pumping of oil between the two vessels.[24] Despite the sound management of the spill, the accident was a stark warning for the Queensland government, and this sentiment was expressed in the report by research fisheries biologist Noel Haysom, who wrote:

> I consider that we were very lucky on this occasion in that the spill was comparatively small, in that we were able to deal effectively with the spill despite the novelty of the situation for most of the officers involved [...] We may well be involved in the future with an oil spill in a location where the use of detergent may be highly inappropriate, and we have very scanty knowledge of the efficacy of other techniques and the mechanics of their application. I suggest steps be taken to remedy this situation.[25]

For the Queensland government, the *Oceanic Grandeur* was a reminder of the necessity for the impending royal commission to allay concerns over drilling the Reef for oil.

On the same day the *Oceanic Grandeur* struck rock, the Commonwealth announced its intention to address an issue close to the heart of the conservationists: who owned the waters and resources surrounding the Reef.[26] The Commonwealth had been considering the issue throughout 1969, but on 21 January Cabinet decided to assert 'Commonwealth jurisdiction over off-shore waters from low water mark outwards to the edge of the continental Shelf', and over sea areas granted to it by the *Convention on the Territorial Sea and Contiguous Zone 1958*. Sparked, in part, by former President of the International Court of Justice Percy Spender's address at the ACF symposium, it was believed that the new legislation would 'establish clear lines of authority as between the Commonwealth and the States in relation to practical issues which arise, e.g. the preservation of the resources of the Great Barrier Reef'.[27] The legislative agenda was proposed without consultation with the states, which, as the Commonwealth expected, opposed the legislation. Gorton's eventual legislation, the Territorial Sea and Continental Shelf Bill, found opposition among the states, as did a number of his other policies, creating unease within his own caucus. On 10 March 1971, Gorton was replaced as leader by William McMahon. Under McMahon, the bill lapsed; the issue of sovereignty would remain unresolved until 1975.

On 5 May 1970, letters were sent to Sir Gordon Wallace, Dr E.H. Smith and John Moroney, requesting that each man form part of the royal commission. Bjelke-Petersen had his commissioners. He had secured his preferred chairman and, even more importantly, his preferred petroleum engineer. The royal commission's terms of reference were also announced:

1. Taking into account existing world technology in relation to drilling for petroleum and safety precautions relating thereto, what risk is there of an oil or gas leak in exploratory and production drilling for petroleum in the Area of the Great Barrier Reef?

2. What would be the probable effects of such an oil or gas leak and of the subsequent remedial measures on:
   a) The coral reefs themselves;
   b) The coastline;
   c) The ecological and biological aspects of life in the area?

3. Are there localities within the Area of the Great Barrier Reef and, if so, what are their geographical limits, wherein the effects of an oil or gas leak would cause so little detriment that drilling there for petroleum might be permitted?

4. If exploration or drilling for petroleum in any locality within the Area of the Great Barrier Reef is permitted, are existing safety precautions already prescribed or otherwise laid down for that locality regarded as adequate and, if not, what conditions should be imposed before such exploration or drilling could take place?

5. What are the probable benefits accruing to the State of Queensland and other parts of the Commonwealth from exploration or drilling for petroleum in the Area of the Great Barrier Reef and the extent of those benefits?

Wright recounted the conservationists' interpretation of the terms of reference as 'unsatisfactory', 'narrow' and 'loaded against a negative answer to drilling'.[28] Wright found the lack of Australian experts on the royal commission disappointing, and noted that Dr Smith's studies of the *Torrey Canyon* disaster had been sponsored by oil companies. Three years of agitating for the Reef's protection had seen seeds of doubt blossom into outright distrust.

Moreover, the conservationists, whose concerns about the commission aligning with the APEA conference had come to nothing, were still unsure how they were to finance their case. They had had some good fortune in early April, when the Brisbane-based legal firm Lippiatt & Co. agreed to represent the five groups: the ACF, the WPSQ, the QLS, the GBRC and the STRC. The firm organised to engage various barristers, rotating them to fit in with their other commitments.[29] What remained uncertain, however, was how the costs would be met.

Consequently, the conservationists remained unconvinced that the commission would be able to come to an impartial judgement. The secretary of the Wildlife Protection Society of Australia wrote to both Gorton and Governor-General Paul Hasluck, urging the government 'pay the expenses of *all* witnesses' in the interest of impartiality, but stopped short of requesting financial support for the conservationists' legal representation.[30]

Wright recollected the anxieties surrounding Lippiatt & Co.'s ability to present the case for the conservationists. Despite the tension between herself and Mather, Wright welcomed the perceived scientific authority the GBRC provided, but was suspicious of the ACF's tendency to offer alternative views to the other conservation groups.[31] Wright believed it would be apt for the ACF to have separate representation. Lippiatt & Co., however, approached the Queensland Bar for support and was rewarded with thirty-five volunteers, including five QCs. Yet the amount of support the QCs and members of the Bar were likely able to lend without financial compensation was still unknown.

The opening day of the royal commission, 22 May 1970, gave the conservationists an opportunity to express their concerns before the commission. Arnold Bennett QC, who represented the Queensland minister for mines, stipulated that his interest was to represent 'the Crown in the administration of the Mining Laws of Queensland and in particular the Petroleum (Submerged Lands) Legislation'.[32] P.D. Connolly QC, who represented the conservationists, drew a clear distinction between the conservationists and the government and the oil companies. Connolly stated: 'The case is immensely complicated and the scientific evidence must be voluminous and extensive. It calls for continuous application both in its working up and its presentation if the Commission is to be properly assisted.'[33] He continued:

> However, on a voluntary and gratuitous basis the Bar of this State
> will do its best to ensure that the conservationist view is presented
> although obviously it will not be possible for it to be presented as
> adequately as the view of opposing interests who have the funds
> for continuous representation.[34]

Connolly's remarks prompted a response from the counsel representing the APEA, P.J. Jeffrey, who stipulated that association's own conservationist credentials. Jeffrey stated:

> In view of a remark which my friend, Mr Connolly, has just made
> adverting to opposing interests, perhaps I could be permitted to
> add that in no sense is the Association seeking representation
> for the purpose of taking a stand adverse to the conservationists
> as such. The Association for which I seek leave to appear
> subscribed completely to the objectives of conservation as the
> prudent employment of available resources and sees the natural
> environment, just as petroleum, as a resource. It is of concern
> to us how exploration and production drilling can be quite
> compatible with a viable conservation programme for the reef.[35]

Unlike the Queensland government, the APEA entered the royal commission at least willing to acknowledge the varied valuations of the Reef. The conservationists, however, who would indeed need to provide evidence to counter both the Department of Mines and the APEA, were still without financial support.

The royal commission adjourned until 14 July, but, in the meantime, the conservationists continued to lobby for financial assistance. Wright campaigned in the media for full-time legal aid.[36] She relayed Connolly's concerns over collating and delivering the immense and technical nature of the evidence, and called upon the Commonwealth to provide the necessary funding. The conservationists also endeavoured to convince

Queensland governmental departments and ministers to present evidence before the commission. David Magnus from the STRC wrote to both the minister for primary industries (John Row) and the minister for tourism (John Herbert), urging them to make submissions outlining the importance of the Reef, and the implication of potential damage to it, a responsibility held by their respective portfolios. Both ministers, however, declared that they would only make a submission if requested by the royal commission to do so.[37]

Connolly's remarks on the first day of the commission, however, had prompted the chairman, Gordon Wallace, to act. Wallace had urged both government leaders to provide financial assistance to the conservationists to enable them to have 'common legal representation before the Commission'.[38]

The Queensland government considered its position and privately negotiated its response. It concluded that the commission's finances were entirely the responsibility of the Commonwealth, and that it was not Queensland policy to pay the legal expenses of bodies seeking to appear before the commission – apart, of course, from its own. Additionally, it could create an embarrassing precedent, whereby the conservationists could call 'numerous witnesses and run up a tremendous legal bill without any real benefit to the purposes of the Commission'.[39] In the end, however, the Queensland government decided, without making it public, that they would agree 'in principle' to the proposal by Wallace. It wished to avoid a situation 'where the Commonwealth could publicly state it had been agreeable to assisting the conservationists' but Queensland had 'refused to do so'. Additionally, the government resolved that it would 'not look well to reject the Chairman's recommendations in view of his status and our acceptance of his appointment'.[40]

However, Lippiatt & Co. had 'pressed' the prime minister for funding, and Gorton folded. On 1 July, before Queensland could send its response to Wallace's letter, Gorton sent his decision to

Bjelke-Petersen via telegram: 'The Commonwealth believes that it is in the interests of the inquiry that conservationist bodies be effectively represented before the Commission. The Commonwealth will therefore meet their reasonable legal costs, including counsels [sic] fees.'[41]

Bjelke-Petersen's reply was terse: 'Have your telegram advising Commonwealth will meet reasonable costs legal representation of conservationist bodies before Barrier Reef Royal Commission. I accept that this is your prerogative.'[42]

Gorton informed the conservationists with a telegram to the WPSQ the next day.[43] The stage was now set for the royal commission, and the conservationists were adequately financed to prosecute their position.

With the beginning of the royal commission, the Save the Reef campaign moved out of the public forum and into a courtroom. The proponents of the campaign continued to be active, but most of their energies would be directed towards formulating evidence and identifying witnesses. For both governments, but especially Queensland, the commission provided some relief from the controversy. Undoubtedly, the oil issue had demonstrated the political fragility of the Queensland government on issues to do with the Reef, and public pressure had manifested most starkly in the first six months of 1970.

While the Queensland government enjoyed a minor victory by having its preferred candidates on the commission, it must have felt some anxiety when its preferred chairman began to advocate for the financial support of the conservationists. The commission would be left to consider the issue of oil drilling on the Reef. The first six months of 1970, however, revealed that the Australian public, who had historically evaluated the Reef for its combined economic and natural attributes, considered the Reef too important to be geologically exploited.

Science

When I was a full-time research student, I was desperate for money. I was fortunate enough to have a scholarship that covered living expenses, but I needed money for research, and to travel to conferences and workshops. Every week I would receive notification of available competitive grants; they were generally targeted towards the sciences, but I was in the humanities. Then one morning sometime in 2015, I got an email (like everyone else at the university) inviting me to attend a session being put on by a group called the Great Barrier Reef Foundation (GBRF). The focus of the session was how the GBRF could provide funding for Reef-related projects. I had heard of the foundation through a competition it used to run called the Bommies, which encouraged scientists to develop creative explanations of their research to engage and educate the public. A friend from high school had been a finalist. Apart from that, I knew little about the GBRF's work.

At the time, I was researching and thinking about the history of Australian science. A strong theme of that story is Australian science's place within the national project: its role in solving the problems thrown up by living as we do on this land and providing us with ways to flourish and prosper. Because of the links between Australian science and national development, Australian scientists have been historically reliant upon government funds to realise their research. This alone has made Australian science inherently political. On that day, back in 2015, the GBRF presented themselves as a solution to this problem.

They were transparent: their funds came from companies engaged in fossil-fuel extraction, land development and other forms of resource use. Nonetheless, these companies, through the GBRF, wanted to fund research into preserving the Reef. They wanted to improve the Reef's resilience. The scientists in the room seemed thrilled at this new source of research money. I couldn't locate any opportunities for myself, so I went back to my desk and did not hear another word about the GBRF. That is, until May 2018, when Prime Minister Malcolm Turnbull gave them $444 million.

The Turnbull government's announcement was shocking, because of both the amount of money and the relative obscurity of the GBRF compared to better-known organisations such as the GBRMPA, the Australian Institute of Marine Science (AIMS) and CSIRO. The huge amount of cash – a lump sum to be spent over a six-year period – was also remarkable. But as the esteemed reef scientist Ove Hoegh-Guldberg said at the time, it was 'an enormous amount of money, but the problem is huge'.[1]

The money was to be spent on specific problems faced by the Reef: improving water quality, research into coral resilience and adaptation, research into and control of the crown-of-thorns starfish, community engagement programs, greater engagement with traditional owners, and broader monitoring and management of the Reef. Some scientists at the time argued that these were bandaid solutions – that climate change remained the biggest threat to the Reef. They also hinted at the GBRF's lack of experience in leading Reef management and research. Generally, however, scientists were pleased by the funding and saw it as a commitment to preserving the Reef.

Others, particularly the Labor Party and the Greens, were more critical of the GBRF's capacity to use the huge sum efficiently and adequately. They were also sceptical of the foundation's links to fossil-fuel companies. The government defended the grant, saying it had gone to the GBRF to allow it to leverage the funds to locate additional monies from philanthropists and private donors.

At the time, the grant was just another issue that brought attention to then Prime Minister Turnbull's decision-making. Jokes were made that the grant had essentially been awarded over a cup of coffee. An anonymous scientist had told *The Sydney Morning Herald* that the grant was 'obviously' political – a brazen attempt to head off the opposition at the next election.[2] Turnbull was forced to defend the grant into August 2018, when he was dismissed as Liberal leader by his party and replaced as prime minister by Scott Morrison. Since then, the GBRF has been 'partially effective' in delivering on its promises. Nonetheless, that scientist was right: the grant was obviously political.

The politicisation of the Reef is nothing new. The Queensland and Australian governments have been using the Reef's environmental charisma and economic possibilities to achieve various political ends for over a century. There is, however, something novel about how the Reef features in contemporary environmental politics. During the Save the Reef campaign, the Queensland government needed to 'appear' informed about the Reef; now it seems that the federal and Queensland governments need to 'appear' to be saving the Reef.

Consider the following events. In 1981, the Reef was included on the United Nations Educational, Scientific and Cultural Organization's (UNESCO) World Heritage List. Since then, the Reef has lost over half of its coral cover. The steady decline of the Reef has been signposted in a sequence of outlook reports published by the GBRMPA. In 2014, its condition was described as poor. In 2015, the Australian government successfully lobbied UNESCO to ensure the Reef was not listed as 'in danger' on the World Heritage List. In 2016, the Australian government was able to have references to Australia, including the Reef, removed from a UN climate change report. Then in 2019, following the bleaching events in 2016 and 2017, the GBRMPA downgraded the Reef's outlook to very poor.

In response, in 2020, the IUCN published its own outlook for the Reef's conservation, describing the situation as 'critical'. After another bleaching event in 2020, the UNESCO World Heritage Committee in June 2021 announced it would place the Reef on its 'World Heritage in Danger' list. The Australian environment minister, Sussan Ley, said that the government had been 'blindsided', and Prime Minister Morrison expressed disgust at UNESCO's processes. As writer Anthony Ham asserted, however, the government's surprise could 'only have been because they weren't paying attention'.[3] Nonetheless, following some intense lobbying, including some 'snorkel diplomacy' (literally taking ambassadors onto the Reef to go snorkelling), the Reef was not listed as 'in danger' in 2021. Then in January 2022, Prime Minister Scott Morrison announced a further $1 billion worth of funding towards Reef research and management. But in March 2022, reports emerged that the Australian government had sought to 'water down' language in the Intergovernmental Panel on Climate Change's 2022 climate change report regarding the Reef's outlook.

Importantly, neither the Australian nor the Queensland government has ever said that the Reef's health is not declining; they just claim that it is not 'in danger'. The significant funding to the GBRF, and the additional $1 billion in 2022, is sufficient evidence to suggest that there is concern about the Reef. One criticism of that funding, at least from scientists, and from UNESCO and the IUCN towards the Reef's management, is that the government has not done enough to protect the Reef from climate change. An 'in danger' listing would likely force the Australian government to become more active in addressing the nation's relationship with fossil fuels.

Of course, these episodes brought to light the politicisation of Reef science as well. During the lobbying of UNESCO in 2021, a report on the Reef produced by AIMS was rushed to publication following a request by the government. That report suggested that during 2021 there had been an improvement in the Reef's coral cover: the Reef had experienced a brief recovery largely because while the world suffered through Covid-19, the Reef had a reprieve from mass bleaching and tropical cyclones. It had had an opportunity to recover. Apart from skating over those important nuances, demanding the report (from an apolitical organisation, to solve a political problem) early exposed the ways in which the government was willing to use scientific material, and even interfere in scientific processes, to suit its agenda.

For some, the report was confirmation of a long-held view: that the Reef is fine and scientific organisations have been ignoring or downplaying the Reef's recovery, or deceiving the public by exaggerating claims about the Reef's demise. Within this story is a broad distrust of the processes behind institutional reports on the Reef and the peer-review system. On the eve of the 2021 AIMS report's release, scientist Peter Ridd wrote that 'record coral cover means there was no disaster on the reef. The only disaster is the quality assurance at the science organisations.'[4]

For years, Ridd has been criticising the 'quality assurances' behind Reef science and the level of government funding awarded to researchers who publish what he has claimed are inaccurate, poor, exaggerated or deceptive findings.[5] Marine biologists, according to Ridd, become emotional about their science and the Reef. As a result, they lose their scientific objectivity. Beyond that, Ridd has claimed that scientific organisations have become political in their outlook. Those who support this position assert that the way to depoliticise science is to introduce greater regulation of science that assists policy agendas to ensure public funds are spent efficiently or usefully.

At the heart of Ridd's criticisms is a dispute about how 'truth' is located within the environmental sciences. He has called for a formalised, independent body to evaluate and provide quality control checks on science that informs government policy, and asserted that commercial institutions are more likely to produce more rigorously checked research.[6] Despite having his own criticisms of peer-reviewed papers responded to, along with his proposal for the review body, Ridd has maintained that what is lacking from Reef science is debate.[7]

Unsurprisingly, Ridd has found allies among conservative media personalities, think-tanks and politicians. Their support for Ridd only increased when he was dismissed by his employer, James Cook University (JCU), for continuing to make allegedly incorrect and harmful claims about the work of his colleagues at JCU, and for criticising JCU for censuring him for this conduct. The problem of 'truth' became bundled up in freedom of speech and intellectual freedom issues.

What was essentially a dispute over the extent and meaning of clauses within a workplace agreement became a rallying ground for those concerned about the deterioration of academic freedom.

Ridd's dismissal was tested first in a federal court, where he won, but JCU had the decision overturned on appeal. Then the High Court upheld JCU's dismissal of Ridd, finding that Ridd had breached confidentiality elements of his enterprise bargaining agreement and JCU's code of ethics. While he lost on this claim, the High Court found that Ridd's criticism of his colleagues, even if he did it in a manner deemed discourteous or disrespectful, was protected by intellectual freedom. Despite losing, Ridd was celebrated in conservative media for his 'monumental contribution to the High Court's robust defence of intellectual freedom'.[8]

Importantly, Ridd was also defended by the National Tertiary Education Union. His battle, notwithstanding attempts to make it seem to the contrary, was not one of left-wing and right-wing politics. Suppression of, or interference in, scientific inquiry by Australian governments and ministers, as well as universities and industries, seems prolific. A 2020 Australian study, which surveyed over 200 Australian environmental scientists, found that scientists felt they were subject to increasing undue interference from their employers. This interference reportedly included increasing the level of reviews and approvals before publishing to the outright silencing of reports signalling projects' potential biodiversity impacts. Concerningly, these processes also included, among other strategies, bullying, the threat of dismissal and warnings against attending protests critical of developments.

Of course, these Australian scientists are not alone. Globally, scientists, scientific societies and their allies have begun to mobilise against the 'silencing' of science. Part of their rationale is that science, and in this case environmental science, is shaping economic and social responses to climate change; trust in science, and its liberation from politics, is therefore paramount.

In 1974, when the Reef's future was being considered by the royal commission, a key recommendation on the Reef's management was the formation of an independent statutory body, informed and run by scientists. The eventual GBRMPA was, among other things, an attempt to depoliticise the Reef – to effectively manage the competing values that the Reef attracted without political interference. The Reef's politics have only become more vehement and foggier in the years since. Governments can invoke the 'objectivity' of science to appear both informed about and engaged in 'saving' the Reef.

In one sense, Reef science has benefited from this tactic. People care about the Reef – they want it to exist, they want to understand it – and the Reef supports a considerable component of Queensland's economy. Scientists can leverage this to receive funding. And so they should. Reef science is political and always has been. Rather than defend against claims of subjectivity, Reef scientists should feel emboldened by their practice, and encouraged to engage in the debates of our time.

In 2015 I was reading about Australian science and its history because I wanted to place Reef science within this contextual narrative. William Saville-Kent, Maurice Yonge, Charles Hedley and other early reef scientists and naturalists who studied the Reef produced brightly coloured, lyrically written and political work. These writers were crying out for governments to pay more attention to the Reef. Like their contemporaries in other scientific disciplines, these scientists wanted the Australian and Queensland governments to see the value in their work, to fund it and to look after the environment that they studied. They wanted the Reef to be valued as intrinsic to the nation's heritage. Their politics were as central to their work as the science itself. They explicitly located themselves between the two spheres and made sure that the Reef was visible to and understood by the public. Contemporary scientists can and should do the same.

Reef science is political, but this does not make it invalid. If governments are intent on utilising the science of the Reef to their own ends, then Reef scientists can protect the ideals of objectivity that inform their methods and use their work to advocate for the environment that they study. In these urgent times, this is an essential task of Reef science.

10

Royal Commission

When the royal commission resumed proceedings on 14 July 1970, both the federal and state governments hoped for a quick outcome.[1] On the second sitting day, however, counsel assisting, A.E. Woodward, signalled that the commission faced 'a most difficult and complex task'. The commissioners, he claimed, would require 'at least sufficient working knowledge' of the disciplines of petroleum chemistry, meteorology, the Reef's hydrology and marine biology before writing a report.[2] Woodward predicted that the commission would be a lengthy enterprise.[3] Government hopes of a speedy resolution were quickly dashed.[4]

From the commission's beginning, it was clear that lawyers representing the minister for mines, the APEA and conservationists would adopt combative approaches. The public campaign had built animosity between anti- and pro-drilling proponents. For instance, Arnold Bennett, the QC representing the minister for mines and therefore the interests of the Queensland government, routinely accused witnesses of bias if they had previously expressed sympathies towards conservationists, or if their evidence supported an anti-drilling position. When the Professor of Zoology of the University of California, Joseph Connell, gave evidence on the chemistry of petroleum and remedial measures for oil spills, Bennett's first question to him was: 'Dr Connell, on several public occasions you have declared that in your opinion the oil industry and the Great

Barrier Reef cannot co-exist, have you not?'[5] Similarly, when an economist argued that drilling the Reef for oil would not have sound economic benefits, Bennett suggested his views tended 'toward strong conservationism'.[6] If witnesses demonstrated conservationist dispositions, Bennett opted to dismiss their authority entirely. Dick Piesse, director of the ACF, under Bennett's questioning, conceded that his organisation had not undertaken or sponsored any scientific studies on the effects of oil on corals, or had any geologists, mining or petroleum engineers, or representatives of the oil industry, on its council. Bennett posited: 'And yet your foundation and you in this state of lack of advice in regard to certain aspects come up with the demand for a moratorium in order to carry out your research?'[7] Bennett strove to taint experts whose evidence contradicted the pro-drilling position by suggesting that their conservation leanings had biased their findings.

The Queensland government's hostilities conformed to the prevailing expectation of others that it would be inherently unsympathetic to conservation and its adherents. Consequently, officers of the Department of Mines faced accusations that the department was an arm of the oil industry. The chief government geologist, J.T. Woods, had published an article in the *Queensland Government Mining Journal* questioning the motives and sincerity of conservation campaigns. Conservationists' motives, Woods explained, under examination from lawyers representing the Australian Labor Party (ALP), 'could be ones of self-gratification – getting their names into the newspapers is one'.[8] Woods had written: '[T]he preservationists [sic] movement [...] taken in isolation, it casts a blight on progress and is a cancer in the nation's economy.'

The ALP counsel responded:

I intend to put these two questions to each Mines Department witness. It was suggested to Dr. Connell that his espousing of the conservationism cause may have introduced some bias into his approach to the question of oil drilling on the barrier reef: would you agree that ownership of shares by Mines Department employees could similarly bias their judgement as to the desirability.[9]

Woods admitted he had and still did hold shares in oil companies, but could not say whether or not those companies held interests in the Reef.

Other scientists whose evidence provided support for an oil industry on the Reef were routinely pilloried by the anti-oil proponents. Peter Woodhead, Professor of Marine Biology at the University of Newfoundland, suggested that coral recolonisation following cyclones or crown-of-thorns infestations at the Heron Island and Dabuukji (Green Island) reefs was 'better' than had been hitherto reported, and that these findings had implications for how reefs might respond to an oil pollution event.

Connolly, the conservationists' counsel, suggested that Woodhead had ignored certain areas of the Reef 'not favourable to this thesis'.[10]

Woodhead, who struggled under Connolly's rapid questions, addressed the chairman: 'I do feel in a very real sense that Mr Connolly is pushing rather hard and we are perhaps proceeding too rapidly. Certainly I become confused at points and I would prefer a more relaxed approach.'

Connolly responded harshly:

But Professor, you are on your own ground, you know, and for my part I do not understand why you should become confused at being asked simple things like, 'Can you tell me where you started something and where you finished?' Will you answer the question: what is confusing about where you started and where you finished?[11]

After being urged to move on, Connolly declared: 'The gentleman's credit is in issue as far as I am concerned.'

This adversarial tone was maintained throughout the royal commission's proceedings. In their final addresses, neither Bennett nor Connolly apologised for their tactics. Bennett defended his aggressive approach to questioning witnesses: '[W]e submit [that it is] beyond controversy that witnesses often put their case on assumptions rather than facts, sometimes extravagantly and sometimes illogically.'[12]

Connolly made similar accusations about the Queensland government:

> I ask the Commission to consider that we have been here for over two years and the only department of State of the State of Queensland which has been represented has been the Mines Department. The Commission would, I think, agree by now that no one of us can say we have a monopoly on the right attitudes and that it is inconceivable that others may have views about the question of drilling the barrier reef for oil which others might not quite rationally disagree with. It is an extraordinary thing that nobody from Queensland has said a word in opposition here.[13]

The adversarial posturing was an attempt to distinguish two competing and extreme approaches to the Reef: conservation and exploitation. The positioning of witnesses as biased sought to undermine the reliability of evidence and, accordingly, the position of the conservationists or those who were pro-drilling. Alternatively, the conservationists, the APEA and the government each sought to align themselves with a rational approach to the Reef, distinct from those of others, which incorporated appreciation of both the Reef's natural and economic attributes.

*

While the legal teams representing the conservationists and the APEA had explicitly indicated their 'rational' approaches on the commission's opening day, the Queensland government missed that opportunity. Before launching into his first cross-examination, Bennett took the opportunity to point to the rationality of the state government's own agenda:

> Perhaps I could start by making a very brief statement as to the attitude of my client in this Commission. It can be put this way: the attitude of the department is one of responsible concern for the life of the Great Barrier Reef, and also one of responsible concern for the properly controlled exploration for and development of petroleum resources. The Minister and the department will respectfully submit to the Commission that with modern technology there should be no escape of oil whatever, and that with properly applied and supervised skills, and the use of modern equipment, the risk of oil leakage is very remote.[14]

From early on, the question of 'co-existence', or whether the 'controlled exploitation' of oil and minerals was compatible with rational expectations of the Reef's conservation, was a core concern for all parties.

'Co-existence' and 'controlled exploitation' of oil and minerals was indeed possible, from the perspective of the government and the APEA. Both bodies frequently questioned scientists from the GBRC, the ACF and the WPSQ on their position on 'controlled exploitation' and 'co-existence'. On occasion, that scrutiny had the effect of highlighting conformity between the scientific community and the government and APEA. For instance, Frank Talbot, who at the time was director of the Australian Museum and deputy chairman of the GBRC, and led the One Tree Island research station, endorsed a large tourist industry on the Reef, but advocated for control to mitigate its impacts. In response to Bennett's questions about his and the GBRC's position on 'controlled exploitation', Talbot explained: 'I would put the key to the whole matter of continuance of this reef without damage [sic]; subject to that, I think controlled exploitation, usage of as many different forms as possible for the benefit of mankind, is essential.'[15] Similarly, Owen Arthur Jones, a geologist and former chairman of the GBRC, faced a series of questions on the GBRC's perceived anti-oil-drilling position. In one instance, the APEA's QC suggested that the position of Jones and the GBRC was deliberately obstructionist. The accusation provoked Jones, who had been against the GBRC's switch in position on oil drilling, to respond:

> I think on behalf of the committee that I can take considerable exception to those remarks. The Great Barrier Reef Committee, I think, has made its position perfectly clear [...] it is endeavouring to take a completely objective stand on the matter and not take any sides whatever. The committee has unfortunately been lumped together with what are loosely termed the conservationist bodies. The Great Barrier Reef Committee is interested in conservation. Its primary interest is in research and in research which leads to entirely reliable data.[16]

From the government and the APEA's perspective, the 'controlled exploitation' of tourism, or indeed any other Reef resource, was indistinguishable from the 'controlled exploitation' of the Reef's geological resources. Coercing concessions sympathetic to 'controlled exploitation' or 'co-existence' from scientists or conservationists was equated with victory.

Rather than demonstrating divisions within the ranks of the five conservationist groups, however, the tactic highlighted the various perceptions of the Reef's values they held. Throughout the course of the commission, the conservationists asserted that lack of knowledge of the Reef's biology, coupled with the potential impacts of oil pollution, necessitated the postponement of oil drilling. The paucity of information on the Reef was, Patricia Mather argued, 'especially apparent' when considering 'the development of the area and the utilization of its resources'.[17] While AIMS had been established in Townsville, Mather stressed, 'no matter how great the magnitude of effort put into the "mission oriented" research directly relevant to utilization of the reef's resources [...] the field is so enormous that the information and understanding will not be available immediately'.[18]

Mather was not alone in emphasising the dearth of research on the Reef. David Stoddart, lecturer in geography from Churchill College, Cambridge, submitted that 'less is probably known about the [Reef] than about many much smaller and intrinsically less interesting reef systems'.[19] As a consequence, 'not enough is known to document properly arguments for the conservation and management of the Reef at the present time'.[20]

Neither the government nor the APEA, however, considered this lack of knowledge an impediment to drilling. Queensland's state mining engineer, A.W. Norrie, argued:

It is a general problem, it is often suggested that we should not proceed with anything until we have made adequate studies of it, and I subscribe to this [...] At the same time, practically, there is usually a limit to this. We cannot put human beings into a refrigerator until we know everything that is likely to result from their activities in it.[21]

When asked if his views were reinforced 'by any recent statement by someone of high repute', Norrie quoted an ACF article on bushfire control, which criticised advocates of 'extreme caution' and 'impracticably complex, expensive and long-drawn out' research programs. When P.G. Jeffrey, the APEA's QC, made his final submission to the commission, he suggested that the evidence was sufficient to inform a judgement on the 'probable effects' of oil pollution on coral reefs.

Chairman Wallace, however, disagreed, holding that the evidence could not substantiate an answer either way on the issue: 'There is a strong case surely for the view to be held that the evidence before us, viewed as a whole in the case – that what we have heard is insufficient to give an answer. The evidence itself, some people might think, shows that it is quite insufficient.'[22] For Wallace, endorsements of notions of 'controlled exploitation' or 'co-existence', as they applied to geological exploitation of the Reef, were reliant upon near-consensus on the deleterious effects of oil pollution on the Reef environment.

In contrast to the evidence presented on Reef flora and fauna and the effects of oil pollution on it, the amount of evidence presented concerning the workings of the oil industry was comparatively extensive. Largely, the evidence presented by the government and the APEA sought to remove concerns around the industry's operations on the Reef. Attempts to alleviate anxieties, however, proved deficient. The commission concluded that if drilling were permitted, 'a real but small to very small risk of blowouts' would remain.[23] Additionally, the legislation and regulations stipulating operations and remedial procedures, at the time of the commission, were considered 'totally inadequate'.[24]

In his final address, Woodward argued that the existing codes required a 'complete rewriting as a matter of urgency'. At the time, the existing safety precautions left no clarity as to legal liability should a spill, blowout or leak occur, and no complete contingency plan existed. The APEA, whose approaches to oil drilling had likely been sharpened by the Santa Barbara and *Oceanic Grandeur* incidents, asserted that they would not drill if a government did not have a contingency plan.[25]

While the evidence of scientists and oil company representatives had failed to remove anxieties over the potential harm to the Reef, it was imagined that the economic value of oil drilling would outweigh the potential losses. The failure to locate oil reserves on the Reef, however, placed significant limitations on economic assessments of the possible benefits of drilling the Reef for oil. A consensus emerged that the discovery of substantial oil deposits on the Reef would lower the price of petroleum for the Australian consumer, add to the national monetary wealth, improve the balance of payments, provide increased royalties and enhance the country's self-sufficiency. Some claimed that exploration, even if no oil was discovered, would garner worthwhile benefits for the economy.[26] Broader social effects such as decentralisation and improved defence capabilities were also suggested as likely benefits from the oil industry, and some suggested that oil rigs 'attracted fish and created better fishing'.[27] The benefits for the scientific knowledge of the Reef were also considered to be significant. Drilling would provide geological information, while rigs could collect data on various issues of Reef tides, winds and currents.[28] Nonetheless, the probable benefits, however extensive, were vague.

Conversely, the potential losses, while also vague and extensive, were worrying. A research officer for the Queensland Treasury analysed the economic evidence submitted to the commission for the government. His report stipulated that an economic analysis did 'nothing to solve the problem at hand – whether the Government should even allow exploration'. The report continued:

> Economically the problem should be solved by placing a value on the possible losses to the Reef, placing a value on oil production, and choosing the best alternative. Valuing the loss to the Reef and surrounds would involve losses to tourism and other items which can be measured in money terms, but there would, of course be overriding value judgements on its maintenance as one of the wonders of the world.[29]

The report emphasised that the Reef only had an average probability of holding oil, but a significant and unknown risk existed if exploration were successful. Stuart Cochrane, who submitted an economic analysis of the potential benefits of drilling the Reef for oil, likened drilling the Reef to 'a game of chance', where ecological losses would be an unavoidable reality.[30] While the potential disadvantages of an oil industry were 'incapable of evaluation', witnesses generally agreed that the potential losses were relevant and could not be ignored.

Former governor of the Reserve Bank H.C. Coombs was willing to discuss the 'non-production effects' of an oil industry on the Reef. Coombs claimed previous economic submissions dealt only with the 'readily measurable' possibilities of drilling the Reef for oil.[31] Conversely, he contended, the Reef had to be considered as a form of accumulated natural wealth that provided the basis for goods and services, a reserve against fluctuations or permanent falls in oil production, a variety of possible economic industries and a direct source of enjoyment.[32] None of these attributes was easily measurable, but existed as a phenomenon that needed consideration. To do this, Coombs argued, the commission had to expand its temporal focus: they had to reach into a familial future. He submitted:

> The Commission is making a judgement not for a particular person or corporation but for and on behalf of the community as a whole which it seems proper to regard as having 'perpetual succession' [...] In a sense the Commission, if it were practicable, should call representatives of the grandchildren of those at present involved and indeed the grandchildren too of those grandchildren.[33]

Continuing, Coombs argued that the Reef offered unknown natural values and importance, which could only be discovered through the maintenance and research of its 'eco-systems'.[34] 'Man needs the wilderness,' Coombs declared, for knowledge, as areas of novelty and diversity, as places of refuge and reflection, and to be enjoyed. The Reef, he proclaimed, offered 'all these benefits to mankind in abundance'.[35] For Coombs, 'co-existence' or 'controlled exploitation' on the Reef was possible, to the exclusion of an oil industry.

Coombs's arguments resonated with Wright. She promoted the importance of tourism and aesthetics, and believed their inclusion in economic surveys of the Reef would ensure 'a long term decision in favour, as far as possible, of keeping such areas as the Great Barrier Reef as untouched as possible'.[36]

As had been the case in the public period of the Save the Reef campaign, the conservationists emphasised the importance of Reef tourism, proclaiming it a superior alternative to oil drilling. Importantly, they argued that the two industries could not co-exist on the Reef.

The conservationists were not alone in asserting the importance of the Reef's 'natural value' for Australian tourism and its potential as a significant economic contributor for Queensland. The ATC submitted that Reef tourism was based on a variety of activities, all of which could be impacted by oil pollution. It estimated that, in 1968, spending by people visiting the Reef was $23.5 million. It predicted that by 1975 the Reef, as part of a broader Australian tourist industry, would help attract $300 million in foreign exchange earnings. It stressed, however, that a major disaster, akin to the Santa Barbara oil spill, would have immediate and comparatively worse consequences for Reef tourism. Unlike Santa Barbara, which enjoyed close proximity to the tourist destination of Los Angeles, the Reef was dependent on the sea as a tourist drawcard. Damage to the Reef's seascape would compromise its tourist value. Also, the ATC asserted, Santa Barbara's position between Los Angeles and San Francisco on a 'popular and heavily used tourist and commercial corridor' provided a form of security that the Reef, 'thousands of miles' from 'a tourist destination', lacked.[37]

The importance of Reef tourism, as opposed to oil drilling, was further advanced by Olive Ashworth, an artist and publicist. Ashworth submitted that the Reef 'is Queensland's greatest tourist attraction', and said that greater development of the islands for tourism, along with pollution controls, would allow for continued enjoyment of it.[38] Ashworth suggested the Reef's 'harmonious distribution of colours' and 'immense diversity of living creatures' provided 'unlimited inspiration for creative artists and designers'.[39] She further claimed: 'An intensive study of the colour and form of reef life could create a new concept of Australian design, applicable to fashion and furnishing textiles, ceramics and interior design.'

Conversely, the Queensland government and the APEA devalued Reef tourism's importance. 'Tourism in itself,' Bennett asserted, 'is not productive of goods, it is more a user of good', and that tourism, 'while it contributes to the good life', was subject to external influences like economic depressions and wars. The implication was that an oil industry was not similarly disadvantaged.[40] As far as an oil industry's impact on tourism, Bennett asserted that if oil rigs compromised the aesthetics of the Reef, then accommodations could be made in terms of placement and design. He further claimed that in some overseas instances, such as the Gulf of Mexico, oil rigs 'increased greatly the amount of sports fishing done there'; he envisaged similar benefits on the Reef.[41] The APEA posited to the ATC's manager, G.W. Washington, that 'in such areas as Long Beach, California and perhaps the Mississippi mouth, one could find flourishing recreational activities alongside fairly intensive petroleum activities'.

'That relationship exists,' Washington replied, 'but I do not know whether I would agree that it is a happy relationship in all cases.'[42]

Despite attempts to convince the commission otherwise, the argument that economic value was garnered from the Reef's natural and aesthetic qualities proved salient. More importantly, the commission considered the potential disadvantages of an oil industry to be of particular concern. In its report, the commission affirmed the evidence of Coombs, Wright, Ashworth and the ATC, and concluded:

> It is essential to keep in mind that this unique and remarkable Province of the Great Barrier Reef possesses human values which are quite outstanding. However important to man's monetary and social well-being the discovery and exploitation of oil in commercial quantities within the GBRP may be, the debit side when reckoning probable net benefits must undoubtedly contain an entry to the effect that the beauty of the physical features of the Province and of man's ability to enjoy them in full will be thereby placed at some hazard.[43]

The commission added:

> The possible hazard to the tourist industry in the GBRP as the result of oil exploration and production is another disadvantage [...] which must be considered when estimating 'net' benefits [...] The importance of tourism will probably increase during the next decade, as the attractiveness of the GBRP is of outstanding and rare quality and appeals to overseas as well as Australian visitors [...] The nature of the environment of the GBRP is such that the tourist industry therein will be susceptible to reaction to any reported or publicised oil pollution and oil spills.[44]

The very inclusion of a section devoted to the probable disadvantages of an oil industry directly contradicted Bjelke-Petersen's understanding of the royal commission's purview.[45] The debate about the disadvantages of an oil industry determined that, despite the unknown biological effects of oil pollution, oil drilling on the Reef posed significant threats to important features of the Reef's natural and economic value.[46]

The Queensland government was unmoved by admiration for the Reef's beauty or its natural values. Instead, it asserted that the Reef was a vast, resilient environment that humans could realistically access only at very specific locations while enjoying limited entrée to its 'natural values'. During the cross-examination of Ashworth, for instance, Bennett suggested the difficulties of getting tourists to the outer Reef highlighted the unlikelihood that an oil industry would infringe on tourists' experience.[47] The Reef was big enough, Bennett claimed, 'to provide room for every reasonable activity properly conducted'.[48] The Reef was also resilient, stressed Bennett: it was capable of withstanding a never-ceasing cycle of disturbances.[49] For the government and APEA, the resilience of the Reef was evident in its year-to-year existence, but most pronounced in the ability of corals to recolonise reefs following periods of intense damage, particularly cyclones and attacks from the crown-of-thorns starfish.

While the Reef's size was evident and its resilience was plausible, the government's criticisms of arguments proclaiming the Reef's natural or environmental uniqueness were less credible. The government interpreted assertions of the Reef's biological uniqueness as a consequence of scientific ignorance. For instance, Bennett asked J.F. Grassle, a marine ecologist from the Woods Hole Oceanographic Institute: 'You say, "At present we do not know the details of distribution and abundance of a single reef species." I think you stressed that was literally correct, did you not?' Grassle confirmed, and Bennett then asked: 'Then how can you say any species in an area of the Great Barrier Reef is unique?'

Grassle responded:

The only evidence relative to whether a species is unique is
whether or not it has been found anywhere else. You can always
suppose that at some time in the future it may in fact be found
somewhere else. It is conceivable but the only evidence relevant to
it is that it is found nowhere else. On that basis I say it is unique.[50]

Bennett then asked, pointedly: 'Then it is the case, is it not, that you
are establishing uniqueness on the basis of your own ignorance?'

Rejecting the Reef's 'uniqueness' contravened the rationale
for the royal commission, and further demonstrated how isolated
the Queensland government was on the Reef issue. Moreover,
it compelled the commission to address the question: is the Reef
unique? Counsel Assisting, A.E. Woodward, explained that the
label of 'unique' suggested 'a heritage which requires greater care
to be taken of it than might be taken of others'. Woodward, with
reference to the Reef, later added:

There are two things to take into account. One is the diversity
and the other is the length. The very length of the reef and the
fact that it exists over a very significant north-south distance does
make it of extreme interest to marine biologists, and the fact that
it does have such a wide diversity of life on it over most of the
length does, I think, justify the use of the term 'unique'. That is
the way I read the evidence.[51]

The state government's querying of the Reef's 'uniqueness'
differentiated it from all other participants at the commission, as
Connolly noted:

The first thing I would like to suggest is that the overwhelming trend
of the evidence is to demonstrate that the barrier reef is in truth a

unique natural phenomenon of which Australia should regard itself as the trustee of the world. Curiously enough this proposition which many people have thought to be self-evident has been attacked from only one quarter. I cannot remember in the couple of years-odd that the Commission has been sitting that any interest except the Department of Mines of the State of Queensland, which apparently has a revelation all its own, doubted this.[52]

The commission would affirm the Reef's 'uniqueness' in its final report.[53]

The preceding debates indicated that the participants, with the sole exception of the Queensland government, appreciated the importance of both the economic and natural values of the Reef. A constant theme during the debates was that the lack of scientific understanding of the Reef system inhibited any proper assessments of the Reef's natural and economic values. Consequently, it was impossible to assess whether or not a Reef oil industry would compromise the Reef's perceived values. The GBRC's proposed management authority began to loom as a positive compromise for both the conservationists and the APEA.

Director of the ACF, Dick Piesse, expressed this sentiment in his submission on behalf of the ACF. When asked to explain how 'wisdom and foresight' could be adopted in a practical sense to deal with competing demands on the Reef if oil were found there, Piesse explained:

Well, it is a very broad question which in parts I could touch on but I think we would view the problem as one of the whole totality of the reef, and the reef viewed not only from an Australian conservation aspect, Australian oil industry aspect, but from the aspect of the reef being one of the principal heritages of man.

Piesse was then asked to explain if that statement meant the ACF was advocating for a total ban on oil drilling in the Reef to preserve it for 'man's' heritage. Piesse conceded: 'The Foundation has not advocated the total banning of oil drilling.' He then added:

> It advocates first of all that a body be set up by the governments concerned to look at the various competing problems of the reef, to get a scientific understanding of the basis upon which the resources of the reef should be managed, and in the meantime the Foundation is pressing for a moratorium period, in which period we would not wish to see any oil drilling whatsoever.[54]

Bennett essentially accused Piesse, and the ACF, of holding a 'one-eyed and antipathetic attitude towards the mining industry', since they would not call for a moratorium on Reef tourism. Piesse asserted, however, that the ACF made 'considered judgements'.

Mather was also questioned about her perspective on 'controlled exploitation'. When asked to clarify the GBRC's position towards mining and oil drilling, Mather asserted: 'The Committee is opposed to mining, as an operation designed to remove resources which are not renewable, until such time as it can be shown that mining does not affect the renewable resources of the reefs.' Once invited by the chairman to metaphorically divorce herself from the committee and to explain her personal views on the declaration, Mather declared: 'I personally and it is a view shared by very eminent biologists – I must stress it is my personal view – think that drilling for oil on the continental shelf of any continent is unwise, misguided. That is probably enough.'

The chairman sought clarification: 'In regard to the Great Barrier Reef area?'

To which Mather replied: 'In regard to the Great Barrier Reef area, I personally would increase the vehemence of those adjectives.'[55]

Members of the QLS and the WPSQ had been critical of the lack of agency and support provided by the GBRC in the Ellison Reef case. At the royal commission, Mather provided a clear articulation of the GBRC's and her own position on the Reef question. She did not rule out the possibility of oil drilling on the Reef, but made the strongest statement by a scientist of significance that, with the level of knowledge available, the GBRC did not, and the commission should not, endorse it.

Equally notable was Mather's recommendation for legislation that reconciled 'conflicting interests' to ensure 'that development proceeds in a manner compatible with the continuing viability of the biological system'.[56] Mather sought to fill a legislative and management vacuum. Reef management had become stretched across a suite of legislation, managed by various state and Commonwealth departments, making the reconciliation of issues like oil drilling and its existence alongside a tourist industry nearly impossible.[57] There were no personnel or facilities within the various departments with specific responsibility for administration of the Reef, there were no provisions for planned development of the area, nor were there any provisions for a scientific survey that might provide the basis for that development. Mather summarised her criticism of the legislative status quo by stating: 'In view of the national interest and responsibility one would expect some Commonwealth participation and a joint Commonwealth/State body is obviously desirable.'[58] She said the proposed GBRRAC initiative, while it 'would have provided an urgently needed interim arrangement', lacked authoritative control and the ability to administer its own recommendations. Consequently, Mather concluded that 'the only effective way of providing for the protection and/or development of an area as important and as complex as the Great Barrier Reef will be for the Parliament to legislate setting up a Statutory Authority or Commission'.[59]

Mather's proposal was thorough. The proposed authority

would administer its recommendations independent of the recommendations of other government departments; be composed of Commonwealth and state legislation as an agency of the Crown; draw up and administer its own regulations; recommend the allocation of funds to scientific, developmental or administrative purposes; employ its own staff; be run and administered by experts; and be responsive to pressing scientific problems. Crucially, it would be able to act 'outside existing political pressures and unilateral or conflicting interests'. The authority would receive its status via a bill, a draft of which Mather presented to the commission.[60] So thorough was Mather's legislative recommendations and her defence of them that Wallace at one point remarked, 'You are pretty good on all this legislation, you know.'[61]

Mather's proposition was in essence a legislative reconciliation of the competing, but co-existing, uses and values of the Reef. She returned to this rationale throughout her submission. The draft sought to 'reconcile the multiple uses compatible with the conservation of the living coral reef ecosystem' and 'the maintenance of the geological structures formed by the fossil reefs'.[62]

The need for such reconciliation was marked earlier in the proceedings even by the APEA, whose barrister, during cross-examination of B.W. Halstead of the World Life Research Institute, reasoned: 'So perhaps it is not really accurate to speak of a conflict between man on the one hand and environment on the other, rather I suggest to you it is a question of reconciling man's various interests in that environment?'[63]

Halstead replied: 'Yes, our feeling, our very strong feeling, is that this reconciliation must take place and should take place as promptly as possible.'

Mather's legislation would create a Great Barrier Reef Authority, which would be empowered to 'maintain the condition of the area and its living and non-living resources', as well as organise, plan and carry out scientific research of the area. It streamlined the process through which the Reef would be managed, clearly stipulated the responsibilities of each government, and gave 'legitimate interests' an opportunity to utilise the Reef based on a review system.

Significantly, the royal commission endorsed Mather's proposal. It, and indeed the Save the Reef campaign, had made clear that the Reef's management was hindered by the lack of clear authority by either the state or Commonwealth governments, as well as a dearth of scientific knowledge. Mather's legislation was a remedy for this.

The APEA also proposed a statutory committee, one that would be comprised of public servants 'and specialist citizens having knowledge of oil'.[64] Its committee, however, would solely be concerned with the 'controlled management' of any future oil industry on the Reef. Mather's authority held a much broader purview.

The commission, after considering both propositions, reported: 'It seems sound that conflicting albeit legitimate interests and issues should go for review and decision to one statutory body responsible to the appropriate Parliament or Parliaments. The views of Dr Mather as stated [...] attract serious governmental consideration.'[65] Mather's bill, and the commission's endorsement of it, were the most authoritative acknowledgement of a composite perception of the Reef's natural and economic values, and of the need to formally and legislatively reconcile those two elements.

The royal commission and the Save the Reef campaign were principally concerned with the possibility that the Reef might be drilled for oil. But the commission in particular also prompted broader questions on the Reef's various other competing uses, and in doing so created an opportunity for discussion of how competing values should be reconciled into the future. Importantly, the commission, in its transcripts of proceedings and its exhibits, made clear that although the oil issue had been dominated by the anti-oil-drilling and pro-oil-drilling positions, there was a shared understanding of the Reef's composite value in economic and natural terms. What impeded assessments, for the purposes of evaluating the Reef's management, was a lack of understanding of Reef life, its systems, and the impacts of various forms of pollution and exploitation upon them. Evidently, a single authority equipped with the requisite legislative powers was required to reconcile conflicting approaches to the Reef and to manage its exploitation and conservation in line with the Reef's ecology and public expectations of resource use and conservation.

The royal commission therefore recommended that Mather's legislation for a Great Barrier Reef Authority be considered for implementation. Ultimately, this would lead to the creation of the GBRMPA.

11

The Great Barrier Reef Marine Park Authority

When the royal commission's report was released to the public at the end of 1974, the Reef's future was no longer dependent upon its findings. The Labor federal government of Gough Whitlam, elected in 1972, had claimed Commonwealth sovereignty over the offshore oil reserves in 1973, and would quickly find itself in a High Court challenge against the states. The Commonwealth government had also begun drafting the *Great Barrier Reef Marine Park Act* in 1974.[1]

The High Court challenge and the GBRMPA's eventual introduction in 1975 overshadowed the royal commission's findings, then and since. The High Court challenge had, in some eyes, rendered the 1967 *Petroleum (Submerged Lands) Act* invalid, and ensured Commonwealth control over oil drilling on the Reef.[2] In *The Coral Battleground*, Judith Wright wrote only two paragraphs on the commission's findings, and contended that the report sparked both the Commonwealth and the Queensland governments to assert their control over the Reef.[3] An alternative view was put forth by Iain McCalman, who considered the commission's 'affirmative report' and the High Court's judgement as instrumental in paving the way for 'an eventual settlement'.[4]

In the end, oil drilling on the Reef was banned, but few have suggested the royal commission unequivocally informed that decision. A deeper consideration of the commission's transcripts and exhibits, however, suggests its role in the eventual changes to the Reef's management was more significant than has hitherto been recognised.

The report was provided to the Commonwealth and Queensland governments on 1 November 1974, and released to the public on 19 December 1974. It stated clearly that if the Reef were to be drilled, substantial legislative and bureaucratic controls must be introduced, and that greater knowledge of the Reef's biology and the consequences of oil pollution were required before any oil drilling commenced.

There was disagreement, however, among the commissioners. Commissioners Moroney and Smith concluded that 'weathered oil' – oil that had been spilt and exposed to the elements – would probably be 'depleted of the toxic components originally present in the freshly spilt crude oil to the point where it is virtually non-toxic to marine organisms'.[5] They also considered that drilling could take place in the Reef area as long as strict buffer zones were established and the recommended safety precautions (including contingency plans) were adopted.[6] Chairman Wallace, however, claimed that insufficient evidence on the properties of freshly spilt crude and weathered oil prohibited him from 'defining any locality' for oil drilling. He recommended that further experiments be carried out, and noted the Reef's natural value as an important point of consideration. Referring to former governor of the Reserve Bank H.C. Coombs, Wallace stated:

> As Dr Coombs indicated, the present generation is in a real sense a trustee of this unique wilderness, and it is undoubtedly the fact that at present there is a complete lack of scientific knowledge of possible damage of an indirect and long-term nature, and which according to the evidence is scientifically possible.[7]

Despite unanimous decisions on most of the evidence, the commission had failed to come to a common conclusion on whether or not the Reef could be drilled.

The differing conclusions allowed for conflicting interpretations. The conservationists considered the report disappointing. In *The Coral Battleground*, Wright recounted that the 'split in the view' was predictable. She lamented that much of the biological and economic evidence provided by the conservationists had not been given the emphasis they hoped it would. Wright surmised that the commissioners had ultimately 'too much accepted the view that their terms of reference were to state whether and how the Reef could be drilled – not whether it should be protected from drilling'.[8]

The APEA, while slightly more positive in its appraisal of the report, was not completely enamoured with its findings either. Summarising the report in the *APEA Journal*, Bob Foster (a BHP employee) considered it 'a good report [...] easy to read'.[9] The review considered the report's findings, especially Moroney and Smith's sanctioned drilling zones, as 'generally consistent' with the APEA's position, and said the protection of reefs within drilling areas was a 'sensible and cautious compromise'.[10] The review lamented, however, that 'the dismal discovery record' of oil in Australia had tempered the interests of the exploration industry, and rising world oil prices had made other countries more 'financially rewarding exploration targets'.

Foster's review also considered that the commission had taken a 'pessimistic' view towards the likelihood of an oil or gas blowout or leak, despite having conceded during the commission that a risk would 'always' remain. Much like the conservationists, the APEA considered the responses by both governments to be the significant factor in the future of the Reef.

Despite the four years they had invested, neither the oil industry nor the conservationists received the commission's report with great enthusiasm.

The report also did little to calm the strained relationship between the Commonwealth and the Queensland governments over the

Reef. The Whitlam government had chosen to assert its sovereignty as a means of protecting the Reef from oil drilling. The minister for minerals and energy, Rex Connor, in his introduction of the Seas and Submerged Lands Bill, resolved 'to remove any doubt about the exclusive right of the Commonwealth to sovereign control over the resources of the seabed off the coast of Australia and its territories, from the low water mark to the outer limits of the continental shelf'. His comments on the need for 'national' environmental protection measures indicated that the bill was perhaps intended to resolve issues emanating from the royal commission:

> There is a greater awareness these days of the need for conservation of our resources and preservation of our environment, and there is much more urgency to find and adopt suitable methods to prevent or control pollution. All these aspects require careful consideration – consideration on a uniform national level. Moreover, some of them may require quick and decisive action, as in the case of a major pollution threat, with little time for lengthy consultation or for passing of special legislation, as has been necessary in the past, for example in the case of the stranding on a reef in our northern waters of the tanker 'Oceanic Grandeur'.[11]

The opposition, despite its earlier attempt to resolve the sovereignty issue in the Commonwealth's favour in 1970, criticised the government for not seeking the cooperation of the states. Nonetheless, the bill passed into law on 4 December 1973. As expected, all the state governments launched a High Court challenge against the legislation.

In 1974, before the royal commission released its final report and, despite the High Court challenge, the Whitlam government began implementing its agenda for the Reef's protection as part of its broader environmental policy. The centrepiece of this legislative agenda was the creation of a Barrier Reef Marine Park based on

Mather's draft legislation. Any attempt to incorporate the Reef into a single marine park, however, would require the assistance of the Queensland government, principally because it, whatever the outcome of the High Court challenge, still controlled the Reef's islands and their surrounds within 3 miles (4.8 kilometres) of the high-water mark. Furthermore, as Reef historians James and Margarita Bowen asserted, any law would have to ensure 'that Commonwealth legislation overrode that of Queensland if inconsistencies were to arise'.[12]

On 23 September, Whitlam wrote to Bjelke-Petersen declaring his intention 'to introduce legislation [...] as soon as possible to establish a Great Barrier Reef Marine Park Authority'.[13] Whitlam was in equal parts resolute and conciliatory in his approach. He declared that the Commonwealth would create the marine park 'over those parts of the Reef and surrounding waters' that were Commonwealth responsibility, but sought cooperation with Queensland and acknowledged their history of conservation in the Reef area. The authority would be responsible to the Commonwealth minister for the environment and conservation, and would have a full-time chair and two part-time commissioners (appointed by the governor-general) and be supported by a consultative committee (nominated by both governments).

The Queensland government's response was indicative of the uncertainty surrounding the outcomes of the royal commission's findings and the High Court challenge. The Queensland attorney-general, William Knox, advised the premier's department that since neither had been resolved, the government should not participate in the establishment of the proposed authority.[14]

In response to Whitlam, Bjelke-Petersen wrote: 'It seems to me that consideration of the Great Barrier Reef area is not a matter for impulsive action but rather a question where, in addition to the national heritage aspect being granted its due acknowledgment, all other matters should be accorded their just priority.'[15] He reminded Whitlam that Commonwealth responsibility for the Reef was contingent on the High Court, and declared 'it is not my Government's wish to be associated with an arrangement which might prove to be unconstitutional'. He did not wish his response to 'be taken as a matter of unwillingness to co-operate', but as a proposal to postpone the initiative until 'a clear definition of authority' was established.

Despite Bjelke-Petersen's response, Whitlam wrote back explaining that the legislation would be introduced 'as soon as possible', and Queensland would be given opportunities to participate and make submissions after the High Court decision.[16] Bjelke-Petersen ceded to Whitlam's agenda, welcomed the opportunity to make submissions after the High Court decision and declared that 'nothing will be done to prejudice the preservation of the Reef'.[17]

Meanwhile, perhaps unbeknown to the Commonwealth, Queensland was investigating the possibility of introducing its own marine park legislation. The Queensland government had begun preparing for the declaration of the reefs surrounding Dabuukji (Green Island), Heron Island and Wistari Reefs as marine parks in 1973, these being finally declared in February 1974.[18] Further work was underway in October 1974 for the creation of marine park status for the reefs surrounding Teerk Roo Ra (Peel Island) and Jiigurru (Lizard Island).[19]

In a submission to Cabinet, the minister for lands and forestry, Wallace Rae, stated that further proposals were being considered for areas of importance as bird nesting sites, and noted that 'in many cases an island and its associated coral reef are so interdependent that they must be considered as a whole and not as two separate entities'.[20] Sites that were being considered held importance for recreation, science, conservation (especially of turtles and birds), or were locations of historical significance, or held notable diversity of life and habitats and showed the least effects of 'human activities'.[21]

Furthermore, despite the uncertainty surrounding offshore sovereignty, the Queensland government was prepared to include the area from the high-water mark along the Queensland coast and its islands to the continental shelf to the northern Torres Strait limit within the marine parks.[22] As the government prepared to make a public announcement, however, enthusiasm for the stretched offshore sovereignty waned, and settlement on the 3-nautical-mile (5.6-kilometre) limit was 'strongly' recommended by an interdepartmental committee.[23] By October 1974, the establishment of a 'State Authority to preserve and manage the Great Barrier Reef area' and the declaration of a marine park area was a major priority of the Queensland government. It even established a 'top-level committee' to advise on their formation.[24]

However, establishing marine parks in Queensland did not prohibit oil drilling. Crucially, a declared marine park area did little more than define an area 'under the jurisdiction of the State of Queensland and within which it may set aside specific Marine National Parks'.[25] Under the *Forestry Amendment Act 1971*, oil drilling was permitted in marine parks and in marine national parks, a fact that attracted protests from the Queensland Conservation Council.[26] It was suggested that the declaration of marine parks and marine national parks was not an earnest effort of nature conservation by the Queensland government but rather a way of placating public opinion.[27] That claim is not unfounded, considering the legal and political realities within which the Bjelke-Petersen government was operating. It is worth recognising, however, that the Bjelke-Petersen government at least endeavoured to introduce forms of conservation over the Reef – however insufficient.

Nonetheless, the Commonwealth and Queensland governments' parks initiatives demonstrated the political imperative of introducing bureaucratic mechanisms that sought protection over large sections of the Reef, while allowing for continued use of it by a range of competing industries. Some level of 'co-existence' or 'controlled exploitation' was central to both initiatives. The Queensland proposals, however, demonstrated not only their adherence to the notion that an oil industry could co-exist alongside other Reef industries, but also a continued willingness to test public opinion on the matter.

The divide between the two governments was widened once more with the release of the royal commission's report. On 22 May 1975, the federal minister for environment and conservation, Moss Cass, introduced the *Great Barrier Reef Marine Park Act* to the House of Representatives, declaring that the authority would:

> Examine the entire Barrier Reef region, determine which sections of the region should be proclaimed as part of the Great Barrier Reef Marine Park, and decide appropriate uses for its various sections [...] Other zones will be set aside for tourist development, for shipping, fishing, and other appropriate uses. However, conservation and protection of the Great Barrier Reef will be the paramount aim of the Authority in all zones of the Marine Park.[28]

The next day, in a letter to Bjelke-Petersen, Whitlam declared:

> My Government has considered the Report and taken decisions on its Recommendations. We support the Chairman's position that drilling not be permitted in the area of the Reef until such time as reliable scientific information is available on the effects of oil on the Reef's ecosystems. I seek your Government's support for this stand and propose that the relevant Ministers of our Governments consult as soon as possible on arrangements to implement the decision.[29]

The co-ordinator general advised Bjelke-Petersen that since the Queensland government's review of the report was still ongoing, 'it would seem reasonable to advise the Prime Minister that the Queensland Government agrees to a stay of drilling for a period of twelve months when it will again review the position'.[30] Mining minister Ron Camm's suggested response was more inflammatory:

> It is noted that the Commonwealth Government does not accept the majority report of the Commission and has rejected the advice of the two commissioners, acknowledged world-wide as experts in marine biology and control of petroleum drilling, for the minority advice of the commissioner whose background is legal. The Queensland Government does not propose to support the Prime Minister's stand, which appears to make a mockery of the Royal Commissions for short-term political expediency, but intends to make its own decision after proper consultation.[31]

Clearly, some within the Queensland government were more willing than others to cooperate with the Commonwealth and relinquish their pro-drilling stance.

Whitlam would never receive a reply to his 23 May letter, but continued to engage with the Queensland government over the introduction of the Great Barrier Reef Marine Park Authority (GBRMPA), which had been assented to in the Senate on 16 July 1975. The Queensland government continued to stress that the GBRMPA legislation was contingent on the outcome of the High Court case on the *Seas and Submerged Lands Act*.

In the meantime, however, and to ensure that Queensland could wield 'the greatest possible' influence over the Reef, the government elected to utilise the opportunities presented through the nominations of the part-time member of the authority and the members of the consultative committee.[32] Various Queensland ministers were also concerned by the consequences the GBRMPA would have for their departments. But these apprehensions did not extend to outright opposition to the bill, and ministers usually suggested nominees for the respective positions in order to retain some input.[33] The Queensland government was beginning to show signs of cooperation with the Commonwealth over the Reef and anticipated the passing and establishment of the GBRMPA by the Whitlam government.

Things move slowly in politics – until they do not. Whitlam was dismissed on Remembrance Day 1975. Liberal leader Malcolm Fraser was elected prime minister on 13 December. Two days later, the Queensland government held a Cabinet meeting to resolve its position on the GBRMPA. It decided to cooperate by nominating members to the authority and to the consultative committee. It would not, however, abandon its claim of sovereignty over Queensland territories, and would challenge actions taken under the Act that affected aspects within its jurisdiction. A decision was also reached on the appointment of a part-time member, Sir Charles Barton, who would join the appointed chairman, Don McMichael.[34]

Two days later, the High Court passed down its ruling on the *Seas and Submerged Lands Act*, decided five to two in favour of the Commonwealth. The High Court decision was the final piece required for the Commonwealth to ensure that oil drilling would be prohibited on the Reef. Fraser had maintained the Whitlam government's interpretation of the royal commission's report, and pressed ahead with the implementation of the GBRMPA, with the Queensland government's assistance.[35] Although its implementation would be drawn out over several more years, legislation, along with public opinion and expectation, had moved the notion of oil drilling on the Reef beyond the realms of probability.

The Reef was saved – or, at least, saved from oil drilling.

Change

In 2009 and 2010, the Australian historian Susan Marsden interviewed Patricia Mather for the National Library of Australia. In that discussion, Marsden asked Mather about the issues facing the Reef at the time of the interview. Mather, after recollecting about her time with Judith Wright, said:

> I believe that we've set up a machinery that, if the Australian public want it in regard to the Great Barrier Reef, is there forever. But stupid people who don't understand what they're saying are still talking about, 'Saving the Great Barrier Reef'. How can they? They can't [...] as far as I'm aware I saved it.

As a chief architect of the GBRMPA legislation, Mather's words carry weight. She passed away in 2012. That year, scientists from AIMS and the University of Wollongong published data indicating a major loss of coral cover on the Barrier Reef since 1985. They warned that things were likely to get worse without stabilisation of the climate. That did not occur, and the Reef has continued to decline. Nonetheless, Mather's remarks pose serious questions, ones at the heart of this book: how can the Reef be saved? Can it be saved?

Since 1975, when the GBRMPA was founded, the known threats to the Reef and the methods to manage those threats have changed considerably. Back then, the major known threats – indeed, the only notable threats, once mineral and oil exploitation were abandoned – were the crown-of-thorns starfish, tourism and fishing. Management goals were focused on ensuring the abundance of iconic Reef animals such as dugongs and turtles and ensuring plentiful fish stocks. Those concerns and goals remain, but since then, and especially since 2010, they have been overshadowed by the threats of marine debris, water quality, extreme weather and climate change. Managers of the Reef are less concerned with fish stocks and the iconic Reef species, and more focused on the Reef's biodiversity and building its resilience.[1]

But how can climate change fit into, or be addressed by, day-to-day management? Bleaching events are likely to increase in frequency and severity; so too are cyclones. Indeed, even the most optimistic modelling of carbon emissions reductions suggests that water temperatures will continue to rise through to 2050. How can Reef managers save the Reef from a changing climate that is inhospitable to the corals that construct its reefs?

One attempt to address these questions is the Reef Restoration and Adaptation Program (RRAP). This significant research and development program – orchestrated across a number of research institutions and funded through the GBRF's 2018 grant – is endeavouring to 'provide a level of health insurance for the Reef' by developing interventions that will allow managers to keep the Reef resilient and 'sustain critical functions and values'.[2] These interventions are varied, and include erecting or placing floating structures over corals to provide shade, localised cooling of reefs using fogging technology, the stabilisation of damaged reefs with large netting to assist recovery, coral seeding by collecting coral spawn and transferring it to high-risk areas, and the seeding of corals from lab-held stocks for deployment on degraded reefs. The huge suite of research projects that fall under the RRAP program are, in essence, racing against time to produce affordable, feasible and scalable measures that can be implemented across the Reef and the world.

The creation of the RRAP represents a new paradigm in the history of Reef science. Coral reef science has shifted through various phases, each characterised by different focuses of inquiry. In the nineteenth century, and well into the twentieth, the major challenge was to understand the geological processes involved in the formation of coral reefs. After that question was substantively resolved, and largely because of the accessibility that scuba diving provided, coral reef biology began to rise in both importance and popularity among scientists. Since the 1970s, research questions have become increasingly varied, but are largely derived from both a need to understand coral reefs, in the broadest sense, and a desire to manage human impacts upon them in the optimal fashion. From a marine conservation perspective, the paradigm has been one of 'passive habitat protection'.[3] Increasingly, as both the funding to the GBRF and the creation of the RRAP suggests, the key question being asked is: what elements of coral reefs are saveable? Emerging from this field of inquiry is a plethora of Reef restoration or rehabilitation projects (including those that do not receive funding through the RRAP), which seek to provide localised methods of assisting coral reefs to adapt to the warming planet.

These projects also throw up the question of which reefs should be saved. All projects begin as small-scale. Some can be scaled up, but generally the sites for these interventions must meet certain thresholds of value. Coral reefs with significant cultural heritage value, tourism appeal or functional importance will be the top targets. Selecting these locations obviously creates tensions around what is to be valued. Much of this work to date has focused on developing the science; the other job is to understand public perceptions of which reefs are important and why.

Beyond this, there is also the question of what is achievable. Is this really restoration, or is it rehabilitation? Can we really bring coral reef ecosystems back to a predetermined level where no further 'assistance' is required? Or will we be constantly, if intermittently, upgrading our sites of rehabilitation? Is the latter really 'saving' the Reef? One irony of this work is that it involves the use of emissions-intensive materials such as cement, as well as plastics and steel. It may not be marine pollution, but there are important social and environmental considerations and questions that must be faced.[4]

Of course, there is debate about this shift in focus within the broader discipline of reef science. And, as in many twenty-first-century debates, some participants take to social media to voice their frustrations. One of the most reported-upon restoration projects is something called 'coral IVF': coral eggs and sperm are collected from corals during spawning events and then, after *in situ* or *ex situ* fertilisation and culturing, larvae are distributed over degraded reefs in the hope that the eventual survivors breed and repopulate depleted reefs.

The metaphor of coral IVF attracts media attention both within Australia and abroad. Terry Hughes, former director of the ARC Coral Reef Research Centre at James Cook University, tweeted in response to *The Times'* coverage of this program: 'The way the media portrays and misrepresents these tiny-scale interventions, while ignoring inaction on anthropogenic climate change, is nothing short of criminal. (and it's not IVF).'[5] Here lies the major criticism of coral reef restoration projects: they detract from mitigating climate change and other threats to the marine environment. Coral reef restoration provides a political convenience, especially for the Australian government, which has dragged its feet on addressing climate change: they can fund projects that 'save' the Reef without addressing its major threat. If the argument is taken further, it suggests that funding of this research should be abandoned.

It isn't just reef restoration that attracts this criticism. If you have been on a Reef tourism boat in the last decade, chances are you have been warned about applying sunscreen immediately prior to entering the water. Two highly cited studies, published in 2008 and 2016, found that sunscreen caused increased rates of coral bleaching.[6] The findings prompted some reef jurisdictions to place bans on certain sunscreens. Again, Terry Hughes argues that these studies involved exposing corals to higher concentrations of sunscreen than typically found on reefs. More critically, Hughes, and others, assert that blaming bleaching on sunscreen misses the biggest reason bleaching occurs: increased water temperatures.

The other popular reef-saving initiative that has achieved considerable traction with the general public and government alike has been the removal of plastic drinking straws from circulation. Indeed, Molly Steer, the founder of the Straw No More project, which highlighted the impacts plastic straws have on oceans and encouraged consumers and businesses to abandon their use, will have her likeness installed as a statue – ironically, surrounded by sculptured straws – as part of the Museum of Underwater Art. Again, however, Hughes has criticised this focus. 'I've never seen a plastic straw underwater on the #GreatBarrierReef,' he tweeted. 'Can we deal with the REAL problems please?'[7]

The other issue with these measures, particularly restoration, is one of scale. Passive marine park management, bans on sunscreen, removal of plastic straws and small-scale Reef restoration fail to address, at least according to their critics, the spatial or temporal scale of intervention required to 'save' coral reefs. Reefs require the functional elements of their ecosystems to be preserved and maintained. The Reef – and coral reefs more generally – require ecosystem-wide interventions; they need globalised cooperation to protect corals in the Anthropocene.

To this end, critics of Reef restoration advocate for nationwide rethinks on the use of fossil fuels, and the establishment of and investment in transnational institutions pivoted towards protecting coral reef ecosystems. On the former, Australia has performed poorly, while the latter issue throws up a whole suite of issues and tensions emerging from balancing biodiversity conservation, socio-economic equality and food security. Nonetheless, detractors of Reef restoration programs suggest that these are the only real ways of 'saving' reefs in any meaningful and widespread way.

Proponents of Reef restoration accept that their projects aren't designed to counter or mitigate climate change and declining water quality. These initiatives are, however, a method that can protect coral biodiversity in the short term, especially the protection of disappearing species. Restoration scientists want to ensure that there are corals available to repopulate reefs once zero emissions are achieved and the climate stabilises. Significantly, these interventions can place a great deal more of the stewardship and conservation responsibility upon the local communities who live with the reefs. Restoration scientists are capable of working with communities and traditional owners on specific needs and desires to achieve workable conservation outcomes. Without saying so, restoration advocates accept that their capacities are restricted to managing and intervening in coral reef biology; they can't shift the world's consumption of fossil fuels, nor redirect a nation's energy policies. They are doing what is achievable within their skill set: locating the functional mechanisms of coral reefs and seeking to protect them. Reef restoration therefore acts as a 'temporal bridge' between immediate protection for reefs and effective global action on climate change.

The divisions within the scientific community also obscure the fact that there are issues Reef scientists agree on. Both sides of this debate accept that there is coral reef 'decline', or at least changes occurring in coral reef diversity. They both accept that climate change is the major driver of these shifts, and that changes will continue to occur even with the unlikely achievement of zero carbon emissions. Also, they both recognise that if their science is to be realised by the masses and governments, then they will need to confront the ways in which their science is entangled with social and cultural dynamics.

In this sense, restoration advocates have an advantage. Theirs is a relatively simple message (albeit with complicated science) that can be readily understood by citizens and governments. For the public, these interventions draw them in and allow them to feel like they are contributing to a broader cause. While they may have minimal impact, it creates a connection between people and their environment.

Additionally, although the practices are complicated, and yet to be developed, restoration interventions, along with sunscreen and plastic-straw bans, provide simple messages for governments to convert into policies. Even if coral IVF is a misnomer, it is a familiar and comforting comparison for the public to latch on to, and a tantalising concept for governments to fund. In Australia, where governments have at best laboured over and at worst stonewalled meaningful action on climate change, saving the Reef through restoration provides a suitable temporal solution to match the election cycle, while kicking the climate concerns down the road. While both the Queensland and Commonwealth governments could and should do more to contribute to the global effort, they can't stop climate change. But they can do all sorts of other remedial things within their reach, including Reef restoration.

Beyond all that, stories about 'success' within Reef restoration projects gives the public a message of hope in an otherwise gloomy news cycle. Whether or not that hope is warranted can be debated, but at a social level, a sense of optimism may provide the continued interest and action needed to effect change.

The Reef is a magnificent environment, and one of the best-managed marine parks on the planet. Within the context of global reefs, however, it is not alone. Coral reefs are changing across the world. When scientists express concerns for reefs, they may do so with specific reference to the Barrier Reef, but their view is much wider. Nonetheless, the Reef matters. One could argue, as many have, that if the Reef is in decline, then other coral reef ecosystems have little chance. Notwithstanding the sincerity and deep care for the environment that those who tread this line hold, this is a form of messaging the importance of the science as well as the urgency of things. The Reef is a charismatic environment known throughout the world. Scientists and coral reef managers need people who live close to and far from reefs to care, and to advocate for change. The issue is, however, that while this is a simple enough message, the policy and governance are not. And creating a transnational system that accomplishes the effective management of people and reefs feels like an insurmountable challenge, given the state of global climate politics (not to mention the state of global power politics).

Patricia Mather knew that 'values' were at the heart of saving the Reef. The GBRMPA legislation was an acknowledgement of that. Much of that legislation, and the rationale behind it, was informed by a need to tackle the ethics of environmental use. Decisions had to be made about how the Reef could be used, and by whom, and the GBRMPA could be the system through which those decisions could be made.

In 1975, however, those competing values were easier to manage. Climate change has meant that the Reef's management poses a much more complex dilemma. The GBRMPA alone, despite Mather's claims, was never sufficient to 'save' the Reef. It can, as it has for over a decade, emphasise that climate change is having the biggest impact on the Reef's conservation outlook, but it cannot accomplish profound changes in this space.

Yet the GBRMPA does provide a model. It acknowledges that there is no single 'truth' of how the Reef can be used, understood or imagined. The common thread among those who value the Reef has always been the desire to keep it. Saving the Reef, if it is to be achieved, will need traditional management methods, restoration interventions and significant global action on climate change. We just need the will to accomplish it.

Epilogue

The historian David Lowenthal wrote that 'the past is a foreign country'. It is a bold move to equate cross-cultural similarities and differences with the millennia of human existence, but it is a comforting and convincing idea. We visit the past and take from its vibrant ideas, beliefs and values to inform and enrich our own. There is also the tendency to compare our own conditions with those who have come before us. At times it is heartening to locate continuities with our ancestral kin, and reassuring to see how much we have changed. Ultimately, we see ourselves there; we locate our present circumstances; we define ourselves by it. The past is always there to inform, but ultimately it is a crafted story that can't help but do some damage. The past is used to amplify some voices and silence others, to include and exclude. Like travel, our experiences of the past are often curated and catered excursions rather than *real* encounters, no matter how sincere our efforts.

For me, thinking about the Reef requires considering its past. When I was young, my family would often take the short ferry ride over to Yunbenun (Magnetic Island) for the school holidays. As we approached its shores, I would look towards the island's rocky edges, scattered with hoop-pine leading upwards into rolling, forested hills, and ponder what it must have been like before me. That place would kick-start my imagination into creating ideas and stories about what life was like. I think this was a learnt behaviour:

my father would often talk to my brothers and me about the past; he would rationalise our presence at certain places and times as a combination of circumstance and happenstance beyond our control. Our existence in place was the function of systems and narratives both human-made and earthly driven. He would tell us the histories of places, and in my young mind I would begin editing those stories to suit my desires. Although I have tried to leave the Reef's past within these pages untainted, I can't escape that this book is the same. There will be aspects of the Reef's past and present crises that I have overlooked, provided too little attention to or ignored, while highlighting and even exaggerating others. Nonetheless, I have sought in this book to show the ways in which the Reef's past has woven itself into the present.

We are not at our current crisis because of one single moment in the Reef's past. Our current crisis is a messy knot that has threads entangling back through time that can't be unravelled but can be seen.

Time is confounding. The past can be retraced, but we only ever recover fragments and hear echoes. The present fades before us, and the future is either rushing towards us or approaching too slowly, or it exists too distantly to warrant proper consideration. The Reef's contemporary crisis has a temporal element. Compounding the spatial scale of change occurring across the Reef is the pace at which it is occurring. It is urgent, but its change doesn't have a steady tempo.

Saving the Reef has become a constant element of the way we talk about the Reef, but the moments that remind us of the threats it faces appear suddenly, sometimes in clumps, but at other times after long intervals. There is a disconnect between our immediate need to respond and the apparent slowness of the catastrophe.[1] Between these spaces, doubt, denial and disillusionment can emerge. The AIMS report released in 2021, which indicated coral regrowth and was used to suggest that the Reef was in recovery, spoke to this temporal element. Maintaining the Reef within the minds of people becomes part of the struggle. People care about the Reef, but in a world where concern seems to prevail and is preyed upon by news cycles and politicians, the constant threat to the Reef – a place that most people don't live in but hold within their imagination – becomes marginalised.

Yet as I write these words in 2022, the United States National Oceanic and Atmospheric Administration (NOAA) has just released its forecast for a mass bleaching event across large swathes of the Reef.[2] This would be the fourth such event since 2016, and any future bleaching, cyclones or crown-of-thorns outbreaks must be considered alongside past events. In these moments, the Reef's story inevitably becomes one of loss. The Reef's destruction through human action and human-induced climate change will understandably permeate the way we think about its past, present and future. While we place those events within our own lived histories of the Reef, we will be drawn to place them within a longer continuum, searching for a time when things began to go wrong or for a time when alternatives will emerge, and solutions will be secured. All the while counting the costs of our misdeeds.

For the Reef, this is routinely done through dollars. Deloitte Access Economics published a report in 2017 outlining that the Reef's value could be calculated at about $6.4 billion annually to the Australian economy and, as a single asset, $56 billion. These huge numbers serve as important economic rationales for increased Reef preservation and further investment in research. It can, however, create an obvious problem if, for instance, the value of extractive industries such as coal and gas are valued more highly than the Reef.

One element of Deloitte's analysis included asking respondents from both Australia and abroad how much they would personally be willing to pay to help preserve the Reef. Australian respondents, on average, suggested they would be able to part with $1.30 a week, while the international respondents would pay $1.98. The report included comments from the participants that suggested how much the Reef means to them, and the angst they feel at the thought of losing it. These calculations, as hopeful as they appear, were also accompanied by comments that showed people's individual financial strains: 'The amount I specify is not how much I would like to pay, but the amount I am able to pay (on a pension) [...] It would be tragic to watch the GBR die,' said one participant from South Africa.[3] In a way, assigning a value to the Reef showcases the competition that exists for saving it.

An alternate way of measuring the loss is through biological data. Scientists who have been working on the Reef for decades lament the visible changes they have witnessed. Their mourning is substantiated by research that indicates the Reef has indeed seen declining coral cover, biodiversity loss and increased nutrient and sediment loads over time. In doing the work of stabilising baselines, scientists (unlike historians) can make helpful generalisations about this historical data to forecast future scenarios, and they are grim.

Loss can also be counted through stories. These are less easily quantified, but just as powerful. The traditional owners who remember collecting now-disappeared molluscs, those scientists who recall seeing more coral or more fish, or the fishermen who had more catch available to them will bewail the loss of the product, but also the process. They and others have lost a source of tangible and emotional connection to place.

In many cases, the stories we hear about the Reef have already initiated a form of grieving.[4] Conversely, contemporary conservationists use the Reef's past as a source of optimism. For many of them, the Save the Reef campaign is a source of hope. It provides a clear success story of a time when ecological concerns won over economic pursuits. The historic campaign becomes the poster material to motivate contemporary conservationists to safeguard past successes and to energise slacktivists. This is part of their battle.

I don't want this book to increase the sense of fear about the Reef's future. By presenting the story of how the Reef has become an icon and a source of national pride over time, illustrating the episodes in which communities fought to conserve it, and considering the commonalities between the way we perceive the Reef, my goal has been to provide an alternative narrative to complement our contemporary concerns. The Reef's current crisis has a history, as does our fear of its destruction, but so too does our desire to protect it. Our admiration and love for the Reef, and our connection with it, are all part of our story with it.

I want this book to be a source of hope: a positive reminder to see the Reef, to imagine the Reef, and to save the Reef.

Acknowledgements

This book has come after nearly ten years of thinking about, researching and writing about the Reef's history. I am thrilled that it has been published and am immensely grateful to those who have supported me in seeing it through.

First, thank you to University of Queensland Press for taking on this project. In particular, I want to thank Madonna Duffy, Felicity Dunning and Julian Welch for both championing my manuscript and helping me to shape it into a more polished piece of prose.

There is a huge community of historians and friends who were generous enough to read my material and provide helpful insights and comments on elements of this book. Thank you to Claire Brennan, Charlie Veron, Tim Bonyhady, Margaret Cook, Andrea Gaynor, Tom Griffiths, Iain McCalman, Russell McGregor, Lyndon Megarrity, Ruth Morgan, Theresa Petray, Henry Reese and Liz Tynan.

None of my research would have been possible without the work and assistance of librarians and archivists. I am indebted to those who work at CityLibraries Townsville, the Cairns Historical Society, James Cook University's Eddie Koiki Mabo Library, the Mitchell Library at the State Library of New South Wales, the State Library of Queensland, Griffith University's Nathan Library, the Fryer Library at The University of Queensland, the Queensland State Archives, the National Archives of Australia and the National Library of Australia.

I was awarded a National Library of Australia Summer Scholarship in 2015. That scholarship allowed me to stay in Canberra for six weeks to research the Save the Reef campaign in considerable depth. I would like to thank the National Library for providing the opportunity, and the anonymous donor, the McCann family, and John and Heather Seymour for funding it.

Since completing my PhD, apart from a delightful year of travel, I have been working as a teacher at Ignatius Park College in Townsville. I extend my gratitude to the students, for their constant interest in this 'hobby', and to my colleagues, for their friendship and support in my work beyond the classroom.

There are also a number of people who have played roles in getting this book through. I'll more than likely miss someone, so I won't allow myself that indignity and will instead name no-one. There are roommates, group chat members, relatives and family friends, PhD comrades, sailing and boating buddies, teammates, bandmates, neighbours, colleagues, school chums and friends on whom I have leant for support during the writing of this book: thank you. I would, however, like to extend a hearty thanks to the members of Bookies – my book club – for broadening my appreciation and understanding of the world of books and writing, and the possibilities for vegan baked goods and book-inspired cocktails.

A warm thank you to the entire Wessell family – Christo, Mimi, Coreen and Chris – with a particular thanks to Mercia.

I would like to thank my own family too. This book likely provides the first opportunity for my brothers, David and Gareth, to read my work, but you have both always encouraged and celebrated it. This book is dedicated to my parents, Ron and Wendy. They are my first teachers, biggest champions and most important editors. I am forever grateful for their love and support.

Thank you to Tess Smith (dog), for listening to me read my manuscript aloud, laying across my feet and welcoming me home each day with great enthusiasm.

Finally, thank you, Hillary Smith, for your love, care, humour and support. Writing needs energy and inspiration, and you have been a limitless source of both.

Notes

Introduction

1   J. Wright, *The Coral Battleground* (New Edition), Spinifex Press, Geelong, 2015, p. xxiii. Permission to quote from *The Coral Battleground* (New Edition) granted by the publisher, Spinifex Press.

2   J. Veron, *A Reef in Time: The Great Barrier Reef from Beginning to End*, The Belknap Press of Harvard University, Cambridge, 2008, p. 5.

3   D. Hutton and L. Connors, *A History of the Australian Environment Movement*, Cambridge University Press, Cambridge, 1999, p. 17.

Chapter 1: European Arrival and Settlement

1   R. Lloyd, 'An Extraordinary Barrier: European exploration, shipwrecks and early heritage values on the Great Barrier Reef 1770–1860', *History Australia*, vol. 17, issue 1, 2020, pp. 40–58.

2   J. Hawkesworth, *An Account of the Voyages Undertaken by the Order of His Present Majesty, for Making Discoveries in the Southern Hemisphere, and Successively Performed by Commodore Byron, Captain Wallis, Captain Carteret, and Captain Cook, in the Dolphin, the Swallow, and the Endeavour: Drawn up from the Journals Which Were Kept by the Several Commanders and from the Papers of Joseph Banks, Esq.*, W. Strahan and T. Cadell, London, 1773, p. 601.

3   Hawkesworth, *An Account ...*, pp. 606–7.

4   See M. Flinders and Q. & W. Nicol (Firm), *Chart of Terra Australis*, G.W. Nicol, London, 1814. Retrieved 20 June 2016 from nla.gov.au/nla.obj-232590021.

5   P.P. King, [No title], *The Sydney Herald*, 20 January 1834, p. 1.

6   J.B. Jukes, *Narrative of the Surveying Voyage of H.M.S. Fly: Commanded by Captain F. P. Blackwood, R. N., in Torres Strait, New Guinea, and Other Islands of the Eastern Archipelago, During the Years 1842–1846: Together with an Excursion into the Interior of the Eastern Part of Java*, vol. 2, T. and W. Boone, London, 1847, p. 257.

7   Jukes, *Narrative of the Surveying Voyage of H.M.S. Fly*, pp. 255–57.

8   F.P. Blackwood in P.P. King, *Directions for the Inner and Outer Routes from Sydney to Torres Strait / By ... Phillip Parker King and F.P. Blackwood to Accompany the Surveys Made by Order of the Lords Commissioners of the Admiralty*, F.P. Blackwood (ed.).

Directions for the outer route from Sydney to Torres Strait. Printed for the Hydrographic Office, Admiralty, London, 1849, p. 4.

9   M. Gibbs and E. McPhee, 'The Raine Island Entrance: Wreck traps and the search for a safe way through the Great Barrier Reef', *The Great Circle*, vol. 36, no. 2, 2004, pp. 24–54, 36.

10   'The Colonial Agent for New South Wales', *The Maitland Mercury and Hunter River General Advertiser*, 27 September 1845, p. 1.

11   'The Colonial Agent for New South Wales', p. 1.

12   J. MacGillivray, *Narrative of the Voyage of H.M.S. Rattlesnake: Commanded by the Late Captain Owen Stanley During the Years 1846–1850, Including Discoveries and Surveys in New Guinea, the Louisiade Archipelago, Etc., to Which Is Added the Account of Mr. E.B. Kennedy's Expedition for the Exploration of the Cape York Peninsula*, vol. 1, Libraries Board of South Australia, Adelaide, 1967, p. 2.

13   MacGillivray, *Narrative of the Voyage of H.M.S. Rattlesnake*, p. 7.

14   MacGillivray, *Narrative of the Voyage of H.M.S. Rattlesnake*, p. 7.

15   Abstracts of his report appeared in various Australian newspapers. Eventually, the Council of the Royal Geographical Society published a memoir giving details of the *Herald*'s voyages. Apparently, the Admiralty did not consider Denham's work to be a remarkable enough achievement to warrant further immediate glory, although he was later promoted to rear admiral. See A. David, *The Voyage of HMS Herald: To Australia and the South-West Pacific 1852–1861 under the Command of Captain Henry Mangles Denham*, The Miegunyah Press, Melbourne, 1995, pp. 432–33.

16   Cited in J. Bowen and M. Bowen, *Great Barrier Reef: History, Science, Heritage*, Cambridge University Press, Cambridge, 2002, p. 106.

17   I. McCalman, *The Reef: A Passionate History*, Viking, Melbourne, 2013.

18   King, *Directions for the Inner and Outer Routes …*, p. 352.

19   In King's voyages there are a number of episodes in which he encounters the 'fin-back' whales. See, for instance, King, *Directions for the Inner and Outer Routes …*, p. 367; Jukes, *Narrative of the Surveying Voyage of H.M.S. Fly*, pp. 1, 13.

20   MacGillivray, *Voyage of the H.M.S. Rattlesnake*, pp. 97–98.

21   Hawkesworth, *An Account …*, p. 140.

22   M. Flinders, *A Voyage to Terra Australis: Undertaken for the Purpose of Completing the Discovery of That Vast Country, and Prosecuted in the Years 1801, 1802 and 1803 in His Majesty's Ship the Investigator, and Subsequently in the Armed Vessel Porpoise and Cumberland Schooner: With an Account of the Shipwreck of the Porpoise, Arrival of the Cumberland at Mauritius, and Imprisonment of the Commander During Six Years and a Half in That Island*, vol. 2, Libraries Board of South Australia, Adelaide, 1966, p. 85.

23   Flinders, *A Voyage to Terra Australis*, pp. 87–88.

24   Flinders, *A Voyage to Terra Australis*, p. 94.

25   J. Bowen and M. Bowen, *Great Barrier Reef*, pp. 44–55, 65–73.

26   J.L. Stokes, *Discoveries in Australia: With an Account of the Coasts and Rivers Explored and Surveyed During the Voyage of HMS Beagle in the Years 1837–38–39–40–41–42–43. By Command of the Lords Commissioners of the Admiralty, Also a Narrative of Captain Owen Stanley's Visits to the Islands in the Arafura Sea*, T. and W. Boone, London, 1846, pp. 1, 338.

27   'H.M. Ship *Fly*', *Australian*, 26 March 1844, p. 2.

28   Jukes, *Narrative of the Surveying Voyage of H.M.S. Fly*, pp. 1, 311–48.

29   Jukes, *Narrative of the Surveying Voyage of H.M.S. Fly*, pp. 342–43.

30   Jukes, *Narrative of the Surveying Voyage of H.M.S. Fly*, p. 332.

31   'Domestic Intelligence', *The Sydney Morning Herald*, 16 December 1847, p. 2; 'Miscellaneous Extracts – Geology of Torres Straits', *The Sydney Morning Herald*, 22 March 1848, p. 3; 'Review', *The Sydney Morning Herald*, 21 December 1850, p. 2.

32   Jukes, *Narrative of the Surveying Voyage of H.M.S. Fly*, pp. 1, 10.

33   Jukes, *Narrative of the Surveying Voyage of H.M.S. Fly*, p. 122.

34   Jukes, *Narrative of the Surveying Voyage of H.M.S. Fly*, pp. 17–18.

35   MacGillivray, *Narrative of the Voyage of H.M.S. Rattlesnake*, pp. 1, 94.

36   MacGillivray, *Narrative of the Voyage of H.M.S. Rattlesnake*, p. 109.

37   P. King, *Narrative of a Survey of the Intertropical and Western Coasts of Australia: Performed between the Years 1818 and 1822*, vol. 1, Libraries Board of South Australia, Adelaide, 1969, pp. 2, 18.

38   Stokes, *Discoveries in Australia*, pp. 1, 346–47.

39   Jukes, *Narrative of the Surveying Voyage of H.M.S. Fly*, pp. 1, 94, 97.

40   'The Barrier Reef', *The Perth Gazette and West Australian Times*, 11 May 1866, p. 3.

41   C. Lack, 'The Taming of the Great Barrier Reef', *Journal of the Royal Australian Society of Queensland*, vol. 6, no. 1, 1959, pp. 130–35.

42   'Reuter's Cablegrams', *Northern Miner*, 19 October 1883, p. 2.

43   'Townsville', *Queenslander*, 3 May 1879, p. 551.

44   'Cairns', *Queenslander*, 29 December 1877, p. 8.

45   C.H. Eden, *My Wife and I in Queensland: An Eight Years' Experience in the Above Colony with Some Account of Polynesian Labour*, Longmans, Greens & Co., London, 1872, p. 293. 'Nutmeg pigeon' is one of a number of common names ('white nutmeg pigeon', 'Australian pied imperial pigeon' and 'Torres Strait pigeon') that refer to the Torresian imperial pigeon, or *Ducula spilorrhoa*.

46   'The Coral Islands on the Coast', *Capricornian*, 13 December 1884, p. 7.

47   E. Reclus, *Australasia*, Rex Nan Kivell Collection, A.H. Keane (ed.), Virtue and Co., London, 2008, p. 366.

48   Eden, *My Wife and I in Queensland*, pp. 86, 241.

49   'A Cruise along the Great Barrier Reef', *The Sydney Morning Herald*, 12 January 1875, p. 7.

50   'The Ministerial Tour in the North', *The Brisbane Courier*, 24 June 1885, p. 5.

51   'Towards the Sun-Line', *The Sydney Morning Herald*, 6 September 1889, p. 3.

52   'Townsville Health Resort', *Northern Miner*, 19 October 1900; and 'Notice to Holiday Makers', *Northern Miner*, 5 October 1900.

53   See Bowen and Bowen, *Great Barrier Reef*, pp. 173–213, and McCalman, *The Reef*, pp. 225–50.

54   Bowen and Bowen, *Great Barrier Reef*, p. 194.

55   Sea Urchin, 'The Great Barrier Reef', *Toowoomba Chronicle and Darling Downs General Advertiser*, 5 June 1886, p. 5.

56   See, for instance, 'Coral Formations', *The Sydney Morning Herald*, 13 January 1873, p. 3, and 'The Barrier Reef', *The Brisbane Courier*, 26 March 1875, p. 3.

57   J.E. Tennison-Woods, 'The Wonders of Nature in Australia', *The Sydney Mail and New South Wales Advertiser*, 7 June 1879, p. 889.

58   G. Bowen, 'New Settlement at Cape York, and Survey within Great Barrier Reef', *Proceedings of the Royal Geographical Society of London*, vol. 8, no. 4, 1863, pp. 114–21.

59 Eden, *My Wife and I in Queensland*, pp. 292–93.

60 The first noted capture of a dugong in Moreton Bay by European fishermen can be found in 'News from the Interior', *The Sydney Morning Herald*, 19 August 1846, p. 3.

61 G. Bennett, *Gatherings of a Naturalist in Australasia 1860*, Currawong Facsimile Classic, Currawong Press, Milsons Point, NSW, 1982, p. 165.

62 For a discussion of the development of the Queensland dugong fishery in the mid-nineteenth century and the subsequent advertisements and promotion of the medicinal qualities of dugong oil, see V. Folkmanova, 'The Oil of the Dugong: Towards a history of an Indigenous medicine', *History Australia*, vol. 12, no. 3, 2015, pp. 97–112.

63 Bennett, *Gatherings of a Naturalist ...*, p. 166.

64 Eden, *My Wife and I in Queensland*, p. 296.

65 E. Thorne, *The Queen of the Colonies; or, Queensland as I Knew It*, Sampson Low, Marston, Searle & Rivington, London, 1876, p. 248.

66 'Curing Dugong Hides', *Queenslander*, 30 August 1873, p. 5.

Chapter 2: Exploitation and Enjoyment

1 R. Lloyd, 'Optimism Unlimited: Prospects for the pearl-shell, bêche-de-mer and trochus industries on Australia's Great Barrier Reef, 1860–1940', in Nancy Cushing and Jodi Frawley (eds), *Animals Count: How Population Size Matters in Animal-Human Relations*, Milton Park, Routledge, 2018.

2 'Pearl Shell, Bêche-de-Mer and Dugong', International Exhibition, Rise and Progress of Queensland Industries (ed.), Brisbane, 1880, p. 1.

3 W. Saville-Kent, 'Pearl and Pearl-Shell Fisheries of Northern Queensland', in *Fisheries of Queensland, 1889–1905*, Government Printer, Brisbane, pp. 2, 10.

4 Letter to the Editor, Pearlshell, 'The Pearlshell Industry', *The Courier*, 25 May 1894, p. 7.

5 'Pearlshell Controversy', *The Courier*, 26 November 1894, p. 4.

6 Treasury Department batch file – Royal Commission – Pearl-Shell and Beche-de-Mer, 'Report on the Marine Department for the Year 1900–1901', 13, Queensland State Archive (QSA), SRS 16785 Batch Files, ID 315197.

7 W. Saville-Kent, *The Great Barrier Reef of Australia: Its Products and Potentialities*, W.H. Allen, London, 1893, p. ix.

8 Saville-Kent, *The Great Barrier Reef of Australia*, p. 317.

9 T.P. Austin, 'A Visit to the Great Barrier Reef', *Emu*, vol. 7, 1907, p. 178.

10 W. MacGillivray, 'Along the Great Barrier Reef', *Emu*, vol. 7, 1910, p. 217.

11 L. Robin, *The Flight of the Emu: A Hundred Years of Australian Ornithology 1901–2001*, Melbourne University Press, Melbourne, 2001.

12 E. Banfield, *Confessions of a Beachcomber*, Angus & Robertson, Sydney, 1968, p. 92.

13 T. Griffiths, *Hunters and Collectors: The Antiquarian Imagination in Australia*, Cambridge University Press, Cambridge, 1996, pp. 121–49.

14 The Beachcomber, 'Rural Homilies', *The Northern Miner*, 11 November 1908, p. 2.

15 Banfield, *Confessions of a Beachcomber*, p. 116.

16 E.M. Cornwall, 'The Nutmeg Pigeon', *Emu*, vol. 2, 1903, pp. 175–76.

17 'Report for 1901–2', *Emu*, vol. 2, 1903, p. 185.

18 'Protection of the Nutmeg-Pigeon', *Emu*, vol. 3, 1903, pp. 77–78.

19 *Queensland Government Gazette*, vol. 85, 28 October 1905, p. 937.

20 *Queensland Government Gazette*, vol. 84, 13 May 1905, p. 1546.

21 E. Banfield, 'A Queensland Bird Sanctuary', *Emu*, vol. 5, 1906, p. 204.

22 Robin, *The Flight of the Emu*, p. 80.

23 C. Barrett, '"The Beachcomber" and His Tropic Isle', *Australian Museum Magazine*, vol. 1, no. 10, 1923, p. 304.

24 A. Chisholm, 'Introduction', in *Last Leaves from Dunk Island*, Angus & Robertson, Sydney, 1925, p. xviii.

25 E. Banfield, 'Dunk Island: Its General Characteristics', *Queensland Geographical Journal*, vol. 23, 1908, p. 64.

26 Queensland Government Intelligence and Tourist Bureau (QGITB), *Whitsunday Passage: Within and Without*, QGITB, Brisbane, 1915.

27 'The Riviera of the Commonwealth', *The Australian Worker*, 29 June 1916, p. 14.

28 QGITB, *The Great Barrier Reef of Australia: A Popular Account of Its General Nature*, QGITB, Brisbane, 1923, pp. 20–21.

29 R. Bedford, 'Wonders of the Nor'-East', *Queensland Geographical Journal*, vol. 21, 1905–6, pp. 14–17.

30 H.C. Richards, 'Problems of the Great Barrier Reef', *Queensland Geographical Journal*, vol. 36/37, 1922, pp. 53–54.

31 See, for instance, L. Ayscough, 'The Barrier Reef', *The Townsville Daily Bulletin*, 23 January 1915, p. 3; 'The Barrier Reef', *The Brisbane Courier*, 18 October 1917, p. 3.

32 The Beachcomber, 'Rural Homilies', *Townsville Daily Bulletin*, 7 January 1915, p. 6.

33 Richards, 'Problems of the Great Barrier Reef', p. 52.

34 Richards, 'Problems of the Great Barrier Reef', p. 54.

35 M. Nathan, 'Presidential Address', *Queensland Geographical Journal*, vol. 38, no. 24, 1923, p. 95.

36 H.C. Richards, *The Great Barrier Reef of Australia*, Government Printer, Melbourne, 1923, p. 1.

37 Richards, *The Great Barrier Reef of Australia*, pp. 4–5.

38 M. Nathan, 'Presidential Address', *Queensland Geographical Journal*, vol. 39, no. 25, 1924, p. 82.

39 'Naturalists' Expedition to the Capricorn Islands', *The Sydney Morning Herald*, 20 November 1925, p. 10.

40 'Scientific Expedition', *The Brisbane Courier*, 18 July 1927, p. 20.

41 *The Embury Story*, Mitchell Library, PXA 642, Embury Scientific and Holiday Expeditions on the Great Barrier Reef: Pictorial Material.

42 This arrangement is borne out in letters between Embury, the Office of the Commissioner for Railways and the Chief Secretary's Office between 1930 and 1937. QSA, SRS 1043, Premier's Batch Files, ID 538150, Great Barrier Reef – General, 75, Part 1.

43 H. Marks, *A Christmas Holiday on the Great Barrier Reef, 1932–1933*, Harris and Sons, Sydney, 1933, pp. 8–9.

44 Advertisement material, Mitchell Library, PXA 642, Embury Scientific and Holiday Expeditions on the Great Barrier Reef: Pictorial Material.

45 T. Barr, *No Swank Here? The Development of the Whitsundays as a Tourist Destination to the Early 1970s*, Department of History and Politics / Department of Tourism, James Cook University (JCU), Townsville, 1990, p. 9.

46 'Whitsunday Islands', *The Telegraph*, 1 December 1932, p. 13.

47   C.M. Yonge, *Origin, Organization and Scope of the Expedition*, Museum British and Expedition Great Barrier Reef (ed.), Scientific Reports (Great Barrier Reef Expedition [1928–1929]), vol. 1, no. 1, British Museum (Natural History), London, 1930.

48   'Barrier Reef: British Expedition Objects Outlined', *The Brisbane Courier*, 10 July 1928, p. 13.

49   Bowen and Bowen, *Great Barrier Reef*, p. 278.

50   C.M. Yonge, *A Year on the Great Barrier Reef: The Story of Corals & of the Greatest of Their Creations*, Putnam, London, 1930, p. 210.

51   S.E. Napier, *On the Barrier Reef: Notes from a No-ologist's Pocket-book*, Angus & Robertson, Sydney, 1928, p. 24.

52   T.C. Roughley, *Wonders of the Great Barrier Reef*, Angus & Robertson, Sydney, 1936, p. 29.

53   E.M. Embury, *The Great Barrier Reef*, The Shakespeare Head Press, Sydney, 1933, p. 9.

54   Yonge, *A Year on the Great Barrier Reef*, p. 75.

55   E.H. Rainford, 'The Destruction of the Whitsunday Group Fringing Reefs', *The Australian Museum Magazine*, vol. 2, no. 5, 1925, pp. 175–77.

56   'Mining on the Reef', *The Cairns Post*, 11 February 1922, p. 4; 'Certificate of Application for Mining Lease', *The Cairns Post*, 5 June 1922, p. 1; 'Applications for Mineral Leases', *The Cairns Post*, 5 June 1922, p. 4; 'Mineral Leases', *The Cairns Post*, 13 July 1922, p. 4.

57   'Green Island – Application for Mineral Lease', *The Cairns Post*, 15 July 1922, p. 5.

58   Telegram, Cairns Mayor to Queensland Minister for Mines printed in 'Mineral Leases – Cairns Town Council and Recent Application', *The Cairns Post*, 18 July 1922, p. 8.

59   E. Sanders [sic], letter to the editor, 'Correspondence', *The Cairns Post*, 20 July 1922, p. 2.

60   'Bird Life on the Reef', *The Cairns Post*, 18 October 1922, p. 5.

61   'Cairns City Council', *The Cairns Post*, 20 February 1924, p. 12.

62   'Green Island Mineral Lease', *The Cairns Post*, 5 February 1925, p. 4.

63   'Cairns City Council', *The Cairns Post*, 25 March 1925, p. 10.

64   See 'Cairns Deputations to Minister for Lands', *The Cairns Post*, 6 June 1925, p. 5, and 'City Council', *The Cairns Post*, 11 December 1925, p. 10.

65   Embury, *The Great Barrier Reef*, p. 83.

66   Roughley, *Wonders of the Great Barrier Reef*, p. 209.

67   Napier, *On the Barrier Reef*, p. 50.

68   Bowen and Bowen, *Great Barrier Reef*, p. 291. See also 'Oyster Cay', *The Cairns Post*, 23 July 1926, p. 5, and 'The Barrier Reef', *The Cairns Post*, 5 January 1932, p. 4.

69   A. Musgrave and G.P. Whitley, 'From Sea to Soup: An Account of the Turtles of North-West Islet', *Australian Museum Magazine*, vol. 2, 1926, pp. 335–36.

70   Roughley, *Wonders of the Great Barrier Reef*, p. 225.

71   Yonge, *A Year on the Great Barrier Reef*, p. 205.

72   *Queensland Government Gazette*, vol. 138, 17 December 1932, p. 1867.

73   F. Moorhouse, 'Notes on the Green Turtle (*Chelonia mydas*)', *Reports Great Barrier Reef Committee*, vol. 4, Part 1, 1933, p. 20.

74   Napier, *On the Barrier Reef*, pp. 126–27.

75   C. Pocock, 'Tourists riding turtles', *Australian Zoologists*, vol. 33, no. 4, 2006, pp. 425–35.

76   B. Daley, *Great Barrier Reef: An Environmental History*, Earthscan from Routledge, Abingdon, 2014, pp. 60–67.

77   V. Palmer, 'Trochus and Beche-de-Mer Fishing', *Walkabout*, August, 1935, pp. 44–46.

78   Yonge, *A Year on the Great Barrier Reef*, p. 167.

79   Yonge, *A Year on the Great Barrier Reef*, p. 176.

80   For discussions of the company boat scheme, see J. Beckett, 'The Torres Strait Islanders and the Pearling Industry: A Case of Internal Colonialism', *Aboriginal History*, vol. 1, 1977; R. Ganter, *The Pearl-Shellers of Torres Strait: Resource Use, Development and Decline, 1860s–1960s*, Melbourne University Press, Melbourne, 1994, pp. 61–98; S. Mullins, 'Company Boats, Sailing Dinghies and Passenger Fish: Fathoming Torres Strait Islander Participation in the Maritime Economy', *Labour History*, no. 103, 2012, pp. 39–58.

81   Embury, *The Great Barrier Reef*, p. 35.

82   For instance, see Yonge, *A Year on the Great Barrier Reef*, p. 173.

83   Palmer, 'Trochus and Beche-de-Mer Fishing', p. 46.

84   Roughley, *Wonders of the Great Barrier Reef*, p. 194.

85   Napier, *On the Barrier Reef*, pp. 126–27; Roughley, *Wonders of the Barrier Reef*, p. 7.

86   C. Pocock, 'Romancing the Reef: History, Heritage and the Hyper-Real', PhD thesis, James Cook University, 2003, p. 25.

87   G. Francis to Premier W. Forgan Smith, 7 January 1939, QSA, SRS 1043, ID 538150.

88   North Queensland Naturalists Club, 'Tourist Guides', *The North Queensland Naturalist*, vol. 1, 1932, p. 2.

89   See articles from *Cummins & Campbell's*: 'Barrier Reef Development', issue 4, 1930, p. 81; 'Reef Fishing in North Queensland – Continued', issue 4, 1930, p. 13; 'Cruising Around Hinchinbrook', issue 4, 1930, p. 33; 'The Great Barrier Reef', January 1932, pp. 76–77; 'Queensland's Coral Gems', July 1934, p. 7; 'Whitsunday Islands', July 1935, pp. 35–40; 'Dunk Island: New Developments', August 1935, p. 35; 'The Great Barrier Reef: One of the World's Greatest Wonders', May 1936, pp. 39–40; 'Islands of the Barrier: North Queensland Attractions', May 1937, pp. 9–13; 'Magnetic Island: Health and Pleasure Resort', August 1939, pp. 44–46.

90   Bowen and Bowen, *Great Barrier Reef*, pp. 294–95.

91   Secretary of Queensland Railways Commissioners Office to Chief Secretary's Office, 19 October 1939, p. 3, QSA, SRS 1043, ID 538150.

92   'The Great Barrier Reef', *Cummins & Campbell's*, August 1939, p. 53.

Knowledge

1   Banfield, *Confessions of a Beachcomber*, p. 7.

2   Eden, *My Wife and I in Queensland*, pp. 86, 241.

3   'Islands of the Barrier: North Queensland Attractions', *Cummins & Campbell's*, May 1937, p. 11.

4   C. Pocock, 'Aborigines, Islanders and Hula Girls in Great Barrier Reef Tourism', *The Journal of Pacific History*, vol. 49, no. 2, 2014, pp. 170–92.

5   See M. Fine, O. Hoegh-Guldberg, E. Meroz-Fine and S. Dove, 'Ecological changes over 90 years at Low Isles on the Great Barrier Reef', *Nature Communications*, vol. 10, paper 4409, 2019.

6   A. Antonello and R. Morgan, 'Making and Unmaking Bodies: Embodying knowledge and place in environmental history', *International Review of Environmental History*, vol. 4, issue 1, 2018.

Chapter 3: Emerging Concern

1   Minute for Chief Secretary's Department, 'Barrier Reef Advertising', 10 May 1944, QSA, SRS 1043, ID 538150.
2   Chief Secretary's Department minute, 'Barrier Reef Advertising', 10 May 1944, QSA, SRS 1043, ID 538150. Emphasis in original.
3   A. Calwell to E.M. Hanlon, 13 January 1947, QSA, SRS 1043, ID 538150.
4   T.C. Roughley, 'Appendix No 1: The Great Barrier Reef as a Tourist Attraction', in Queensland Tourist Development Board (QTDB), *Report of the Queensland Tourist Development Board on the Tourist Resources of Queensland and the Requirements for their Development*, Government Printer, Brisbane, 1947, p. 95.
5   W.J. Dakin, *The Great Barrier Reef: And Some Mention of Other Australian Coral Reefs*, Angus & Robertson, Sydney, 1950, p. 95.
6   'Shell-gathering earns them a living', *The Australian Women's Weekly*, 6 September 1947, p. 21.
7   J.K. Jarrott (Hon Secretary NPAQ) to E.M. Hanlon, 3 October 1947, p. 1, QSA, SRS 1043, ID 538150, 2.
8   Department of Forestry memorandum, 'Spoliation of Great Barrier Reef', 26 November 1947, QSA, SRS 1043, ID 538150.
9   QTDB, *Report*, pp. 18–23, 35.
10   QTDB, *Report*, p. 62.
11   QTDB, *Report*, p. 71.
12   QTDB, *Report*, p. 74.
13   QTDB, *Report*, p. 74.
14   R.B. McAllister (Under Secretary Chief Secretary Department) to Queensland Government Offices London, 14 September 1949, 1, QSA, SRS 1043, ID 538150.
15   Barr, *No Swank Here?*, pp. 23–32. Also see Department of Forestry memorandum, 'Spoilation of Great Barrier Reef', 26 November 1947; McAllister to Queensland Government Offices London, 1.
16   Barr, *No Swank Here?*, p. 38.
17   Barr, *No Swank Here?*, pp. 35–41.
18   *Isles of the Sun, Queensland*, ed. Bureau Queensland Government Tourist (Brisbane: Queensland Government Tourist Bureau, c. 1950).
19   The issues of coral collecting during this period are covered in Daley, *Great Barrier Reef*, pp. 137–40.
20   E. Evans, Legislative Assembly, *Hansard*, 18 October 1955, p. 781.
21   J. Pizzey, Legislative Assembly, *Hansard*, 18 October 1955, p. 787.
22   D. Jolly to V. Gair, 9 January 1956, QSA, SRS 1043, ID 538150.
23   T. Foley to V. Gair, 15 February 1956, QSA, SRS 1043, ID 538150.
24   W.H. Bryan (Deputy Chairman of GBRC) to Premier Hanlon, 21 September 1950, QSA, SRS 6232 General Correspondence, ID 959329 'Establishment of marine biological station – Heron Island, Great Barrier Reef'.
25   Department of Harbours and Marine memorandum, 'Tour ref: 50/18601 H. Bds. G'stone Gen.', 15 December 1950, QSA, SRS 6232, ID 959329.

26   Secretary Land Administration Board to W.H. Bryan, 8 November 1950, QSA, SRS 6232, ID 959329; Under Secretary (Chief Secretary's Department) to W.H. Bryan, 15 June 1951, QSA, SRS 6232, ID 959329.

27   'Science Centre on Barrier Reef', *The Courier Mail*, 14 June 1951, p. 3.

28   Bowen and Bowen, *Great Barrier Reef*, p. 309.

29   Prime Minister Chifley to Premier Hanlon, 23 September 1947, QSA, SRS 1043, ID 538150.

30   D. Hill, Report for Maurice Mawby, 'The Geology of the Great Barrier Reef in Relation to Oil Potential', UQ Fryer Library, UQFL25, Dorothy Hill Collection, pp. i, 36.

31   Hill, 'The Geology of the Great Barrier Reef', pp. i, 127–37.

32   Premier G.F.R. Nicklin, 'Personally Speaking', *The Cairns Post*, 5 February 1959, p. 6.

33   Department of Mines memorandum, 'Petroleum, offshore, exploration and production', 19 August 1969, QSA, SRS 1043 Premier's Batch Files, ID 538159 'Committee of Inquiry into the Possible Effects of Oil Drilling – Great Barrier Reef.'

34   Statement of A.W. Norrie, National Library of Australia (NLA), MS 3990, Exhibits of the Great Barrier Reef petroleum drilling Royal Commissions 1964–1972, 2/3(ii), Exhibit 80.

35   Nicklin, 'Personally Speaking'.

36   F. McNeill, 'Wealth in Coral Gravels', *Australian Museum Magazine*, vol. 10, no. 6, June 1951, pp. 190–92.

37   McNeill, 'Wealth in Coral Gravels', p. 191.

38   McNeill, 'Wealth in Coral Gravels', p. 192.

39   'Turtle Carcases for England', *The Central Queensland Herald*, 12 January 1950, p. 21.

40   'Turtle Hunting "Cruel Trade"', *The Daily Mercury*, 17 May 1950, p. 2.

41   'Turtle Hunting "Cruel Trade"', p. 2.

42   F. McNeill, 'Saving the Green Turtle of the Great Barrier Reef', *Australian Museum Magazine*, vol. 11, no. 9, March 1955, pp. 278–82.

43   McNeill, 'Saving the Green Turtle', p. 281.

44   *Queensland Government Gazette*, vol. 175, 9 September 1950, p. 1333.

45   McNeill, 'Saving the Green Turtle', p. 282.

46   C.J. Limpus, J.D. Miller, C.J. Parmenter and D.J. Limpus, 'Green Turtle, *Chelonia mydas*, Population of Raine Island and the Northern Great Barrier Reef: 1843–2001', *Memoirs of the Queensland Museum*, vol. 49, part 1, 2003, pp. 349–440, 365.

47   C.J. Limpus et al., 'Green Turtle', p. 366.

48   *Queensland Government Gazette*, vol. 199, 6 September 1958, p. 22.

49   'Slaughtering of Turtles', *The Cairns Post*, 18 May 1959, p. 5.

50   Editorial, *The North Queensland Naturalist*, no. 123, 1959, p. 8.

Chapter 4: Towards Saving the Reef

1   Büsst to Wright, 24 July 1966, JCU, John Büsst Papers (hereafter Büsst Papers), 2/13.

2   For an example of how Büsst and Webb's relationship manifested in terms of scientific and literary output, see J. Büsst, 'Nesting of Grey Swiftlet on Bedarra Island', *North Queensland Naturalist*, no. 116, September 1956, pp. 1–3.

3   P. Clare, *Struggle for the Great Barrier Reef,* Collins, London, 1971, p. 89.

4   Clare, *Struggle for the Great Barrier Reef,* p. 90.

5   'Littoral' refers to area on the shore of a sea or a lake, or a region lying along a shore. The ambiguity of the name 'Queensland Littoral Society' was criticised by John Büsst to one of its executive on 22 July 1968. See Büsst to Owen Kelly, JCU, Büsst Papers, 2/11. The organisation has since changed its name to the more identifiable Australian Marine Conservation Society.

6   Hutton and Connors, *A History of the Australian Environmental Movement,* p. 89.

7   Wright, *The Coral Battleground,* p. 5.

8   The theme of a 'David v Goliath' narrative has become an important part of the memorialisation of this period and the Save the Reef campaign. For a criticism of this theme, and a discussion of the connections and strategies of the conservationists, see R. Lloyd, M. Newlands and T. Petray, 'Coral Battleground? Re-examining the "Save the Reef" campaign in 1960s Australia', *Environmental Sociology,* vol. 3, no. 1, 2017, pp. 54–63.

9   Wright, *The Coral Battleground,* p. 2.

10   Clare, *Struggle for the Great Barrier Reef,* p. 56.

11   N. Monkman in Clare, *Struggle for the Great Barrier Reef,* p. 63.

12   Wright, *The Coral Battleground,* p. 3.

13   V. Serventy, 'Tourists and Wild Life at Green Island', *North Queensland Naturalist,* vol. 33, no. 139, 1965, pp. 5–6.

14   B.J. Dalton and H. Reynolds, *Incidence of Crown-of-Thorns on the Great Barrier Reef: An Oral History Project,* History Department of James Cook University, Townsville, 1984, p. 18.

15   Dalton and Reynolds, *Incidence of Crown-of-Thorns,* pp. 19–20.

16   Dalton and Reynolds, *Incidence of Crown-of-Thorns,* p. 23.

17   V. Vlasoff to R.A. Armstrong (Member for Mulgrave), 28 August 1969, QSA, SRS 9187 General Correspondence Batches, ID 294333 General Correspondence: Code 22 (G) – Crown of Thorns Starfish, Great Barrier Reef.

18   Vlasoff to Armstrong (Member for Mulgrave), 28 August 1969.

19   Dalton and Reynolds, *Incidence of Crown-of-Thorns,* pp. 24–25. For a statistical report, see R. Endean, *Report on Investigation Made into Aspects of the Current Acanthaster Planci (Crown of Thorns) Infestations of Certain Reefs of the Great Barrier Reef,* Queensland Department of Primary Industries, Fisheries Branch, Brisbane, 1969, pp. 9–11.

20   Starfish Committee on the Problem of the Crown-of-Thorns, *Report of the Committee Appointed by the Commonwealth and Queensland governments on the Problem of the Crown-of-Thorns Starfish (Acanthaster Planci),* R.J. Walsh (ed.), CSIRO, Melbourne, 1971, p. 9.

21   B.L. Hayles (Managing Director of Hayles Magnetic Island Pty Ltd) to Gordon Chalk, 7 February 1966, QSA, SRS 9187, ID 294333.

22   Cabinet Minute, Decision 8601, Measure to Combat Star Fish Infestation – Great Barrier Reef, 1 February 1966, QSA, p. 1.

23   Cabinet Minute, Decision 8601, p. 3.

24   Cabinet Minute, Decision 8601, pp. 2–3.

25   See, for instance, Bowen and Bowen, *Great Barrier Reef,* p. 325, and Dalton and Reynolds, *Incidence of Crown-of-Thorns,* p. 27.

26   'Starfish dines on the Barrier Reef', *Australasian Post,* 17 February 1966, p. 24, and

'Weird starfish eating miles of Barrier Reef', *The Sun Herald*, 20 February 1966, p. 13.

27 J. Barnes, 'The Crown of Thorns Starfish as a Destroyer of Coral', *Australian Natural History*, vol. 15, no. 8, 1966, pp. 257–61.

28 'Starfish dines on the Barrier Reef', p. 24.

29 'Publisher's Column', *Walkabout*, vol. 33, no. 7, July 1967, p. 11.

30 'Protecting the Reef attraction', *The Courier Mail*, 28 September 1965, p. 3.

31 Editorial, *The Courier Mail*, 29 September 1965, p. 2.

32 T. Hiley, Legislative Assembly, *Hansard*, 30 September 1965, p. 728.

33 T. Hiley, Legislative Assembly, *Hansard*, 30 September 1965, p. 729.

34 R. Jones, Legislative Assembly, *Hansard*, 24 August 1965, p. 85.

35 P. Tucker, Legislative Assembly, *Hansard*, 10 November 1966, p. 1530.

36 Cabinet Minute, Decision 9864, Offshore Petroleum Legislation, 31 January 1967, p. 1, QSA.

37 See Cabinet Minute, Decision 9864 and Statement of A.W. Norrie, NLA, MS 3990, Exhibits of the Great Barrier Reef petroleum drilling Royal Commissions 1964–1972, 2/3 (ii), Exhibit 80.

38 R. Camm, Legislative Assembly, *Hansard*, 16 November 1965, p. 1581.

39 Cabinet Minute, Decision 9864, p. 2.

40 R. Casey, Senate, *Hansard*, 21 February 1967, p. 9.

41 I. Wood, Senate, *Hansard*, 9 March 1967, p. 433.

42 R. Patterson, House of Representatives, *Hansard*, 20 April 1967, p. 1562.

43 B. Wentworth, House of Representatives, *Hansard*, 3 May 1967, p. 1669.

44 H. Turner, House of Representatives, *Hansard*, 3 May 1967, p. 1678.

45 J. Rosewater, 'The Giant Clams', *Australian Natural History*, vol. 15, no. 8, 1966, p. 256.

46 O.A. Jones, 'Geological Questions Posed by the Reef', *Australian Natural History*, vol. 15, no. 8, 1966, p. 248.

47 D.F. McMichael, 'The Future of the Reef', *Australian Natural History*, vol. 15, no. 8, 1966, pp. 269–72.

48 McMichael, 'The Future of the Reef', p. 270.

49 McMichael, 'The Future of the Reef', p. 271.

50 McMichael, 'The Future of the Reef', p. 272.

51 McMichael, 'The Future of the Reef', p. 272.

Catchment

1 A. Phillips, T. Major and J. Gunders, 'Great Barrier Reef protection laws see farmers rally against agricultural run-off limits in Townsville', *ABC News*, 3 September 2019. Accessed from www.abc.net.au/news/rural/2019-09-03/farmers-protest-against-reef-regulations-in-townsville/11473136.

2 See M. Star, J. Rolfe, P. Long, G. Whish and P. Donaghy, 'Improved Grazing Management Practices in the Catchments of the Great Barrier Reef, Australia: Does climate variability influence their adoption by landholders', *The Rangeland Journal*, vol. 37, 2015, pp. 507–15; E. Hamman and F. Deane, 'The Control of Nutrient Run-Off from Agricultural Areas: Insights into governance from Australia's sugarcane industry and the Great Barrier Reef', *Transnational Environmental Law*, vol. 7, no. 3, 2018, pp. 451–68; C. Creighton, J. Waterhouse, J.C. Day and J. Brodie,

'Criteria for Effective Regional Scale Catchment to Reef Management: A case study of Australia's Great Barrier Reef', *Marine Pollution Bulletin*, vol. 173, 2021, p. 112882; F. Deane, C. Wilson, D. Rowlings, J. Webb, E. Mitchell, E. Hamman, E. Sheppard and P. Grace, 'Sugarcane farming and the Great Barrier Reef: The role of a principled approach to change', *Land Use Policy*, vol. 78, 2018, pp. 691–98.

3   Creighton et al., 'Criteria for Effective Regional Scale Catchment to Reef Management'.

4   Hamman and Deane, 'The Control of Nutrient Run-Off from Agricultural Areas', p. 452.

Chapter 5: The Save the Reef Campaign: Ellison Reef

1   'Certificate of Application for Special Mining Lease No. 9 – Innisfail District', *The Cairns Post*, 23 August 1967, p. 14.

2   Clare, *Struggle for the Great Barrier Reef*, p. 105.

3   Clare, *Struggle for the Great Barrier Reef*, pp. 105–7.

4   B. Wain, 'Artist and wife near victory to save coral reef', *The Australian*, 18 December 1967, p. 2.

5   'Lease of reef to obtain lime', *The Cairns Post*, 28 August 1967.

6   Büsst to N. Monkman, 31 August 1967, JCU, Büsst Papers, 1/4.

7   Büsst to Wright, 2 September 1967, JCU, Büsst Papers, 2/13.

8   'Mining "threat" to reef is opposed', *The Courier Mail*, 21 September 1967, p. 21.

9   'Dredging on the Barrier Reef?', *The Courier Mail*, 22 September 1967, p. 22.

10   Wright to Büsst, 25 September 1967, JCU, Büsst Papers, 2/13.

11   G.E. West to O.C. Shaul (General Manager of the ATC), 28 August 1967, QSA, SRS 9187 General Correspondence Batches, ID 294293 General Correspondence: Code 22 (G) – Extraction of lime from Ellison Reef.

12   Romano to Director General QGTB, 2 September 1967, QSA, SRS 9187, ID 294293.

13   Büsst to Director General QGTB, 11 September 1967, QSA, SRS 9187, ID 294293.

14   Department of Labour and Tourism memorandum, 7 September 1967, QSA, SRS 9187, ID 294293.

15   Büsst to R. Camm, 11 September 1967, QSA, SRS 9187, ID 294293.

16   Büsst to Camm, 11 September 1967.

17   R. Endean (Chairman GBRC) to Arthur Fenton (WPSQ Secretary), 15 September 1967, JCU, Büsst Papers, 1/4.

18   Endean to Fenton, 15 September 1967. Emphasis in original.

19   Endean to Fenton, 15 September 1967.

20   Wright, *The Coral Battleground*, pp. 9–10; Queensland Littoral Society (QLS), 'Ellison Reef Report', *Aquatic Conservation Series*, no. 2, 1968, pp. 1–2.

21   Wright, *The Coral Battleground*, pp. 9–10.

22   Wright, *The Coral Battleground*, p. 13.

23   B. Wain in *The Australian*: 'Test case on bid to mine Barrier Reef', 21 November 1967, p. 4; 'Lime mine "would damage the Reef"', 22 November 1967, p. 1; 'Plea for qualified probe on Barrier Reef', 23 November 1967, p. 4; 'Barrier Reef mining "like bulldozing Taj Mahal"', 25 November 1967, p. 3; 'Mining on Barrier Reef is ruled out', 9 December 1967, p. 3; 'Artist and wife near victory to save coral reef', 18 December 1967, p. 2.

24   QLS, 'Ellison Reef Report', p. 10.

25 Wildlife Preservation Society of Queensland, *Wildlife*, no. 12 (January 1968), pp. 3–4.

26 *Wildlife* (January 1968), p. 4; *Wildlife*, no. 11 (December 1967), p. 3.

27 *Wildlife* (January 1968), p. 4.

Chapter 6: We Must Appear to Be Well Informed

1 J. Houston, Legislative Assembly, *Hansard*, 18 October 1967, p. 949.

2 D. Sherrington, Legislative Assembly, *Hansard*, 18 October 1967, p. 953.

3 A. Dewar, Legislative Assembly, *Hansard*, 18 October 1967, p. 956.

4 R. Camm, Legislative Assembly, *Hansard*, 18 October 1967, p. 960.

5 William Fulton, House of Representatives, *Hansard*, 2 November 1967, p. 2735.

6 'Heads in the Sand Again', *The Courier Mail*, 1 December 1967, p. 2.

7 Legislative Assembly, *Hansard*, 8 November 1967, p. 1491; 'Fear Chinese may wipe out clams', *The Courier Mail*, 9 November 1967, p. 12.

8 House of Representatives, *Hansard*, 2 November 1967, p. 2736; 'Extend limits', *The Courier Mail*, 6 November 1967, p. 3.

9 Endean, *Report on Investigation Made into Aspects of the Current Acanthaster Planci (Crown of Thorns) Infestations*, p. 16.

10 Secretary of Keppel Bay Shell Club to John Herbert (Minister for Labour and Tourism), 27 June 1968, QSA, SRS 9187, ID 249333.

11 Kelly to Büsst, 3 April 1968, JCU, Büsst Papers, 2/11.

12 K. McArthur to Büsst, JCU, Büsst Papers, 2/14.

13 Kelly to Büsst, 28 July 1968, JCU, Büsst Papers, 2/11.

14 Cairns Chamber of Commerce to Don Chipp, 25 October 1967, QSA, SRS 9187, ID 294333.

15 QGTB Memorandum, 16 April 1969, QSA, SRS 9187, ID 294333.

16 Peel (Director Department of Harbours and Marine) to Muhl (Under Secretary Department of Labour and Tourism), 14 May 1969, QSA, SRS 9187, ID 294333.

17 Vlasoff to R.A. Armstrong (Member for Mulgrave), 28 August 1969, QSA, SRS 9187, ID 294333.

18 Cairns Chamber of Commerce to Minister for Labour and Tourism, 15 September 1969, QSA, SRS 9187, ID 294333.

19 Cabinet Minute, Decision 12684, Crown of Thorns Starfish, 4 March 1969, QSA.

20 See QSA Cabinet Minutes: Decision 13349, Crown of Thorns Starfish, 4 August 1969; Decision 13455, Crown of Thorns Starfish, 1 September 1969; Decision 13500, Crown of Thorns Starfish, 8 September 1969. Also see letter, G. Chalk to J. Gorton, 24 March 1969, QSA, SRS 9187, ID 294333.

21 See QSA Cabinet Minute, Decision 13349, and Endean, *Report on Investigation Made into Aspects of the Current Acanthaster Planci (Crown of Thorns) Infestations*, p. 24.

22 Cabinet Minute, Decision 13455, p. 3.

23 D. Jack, 'GBR Graveyard', *Australian: Weekend Edition*, 4 October 1969, p. 15.

24 Starfish Committee on the Problem of the Crown-of-Thorns, *Report of the Committee Appointed by the Commonwealth and Queensland Governments*, pp. 6–7.

25 T. Willy and K. Brown, *Crown of Thorns: The Death of the Great Barrier Reef?*, Angus & Robertson, Sydney, 1972; P. James, *Requiem for the Reef: The Story of Official Distortion About the Crown-of-Thorns Starfish*, Foundation Press, Brisbane, 1976.

26 Anecdote from correspondence with Coralie Endean, 28 August 2018.

27 P. Mather in *Patricia Mather Interviewed by Susan Marsden [sound recording]*, 2009, access open for research, personal copies and public use, 41:06–41:21.

28 J. Sapp, *What Is Natural? Coral Reef Crisis*, Oxford University Press, Oxford, 1999, p. 151.

29 I. Bennett in *Isobel Bennett Interviewed by Amy McGrath [sound recording]*, 1980, access open for research, personal copies and public use, 31:43–38:13.

30 Correspondence, 27 October 2019.

31 M. Pratchett, C. Caballes, J. Wilmes, S. Matthews, C. Mellin, H. Sweatman, L. Nadler, J. Brodie, C. Thompson, J. Hoey, A. Bos, M. Byrne, V. Messmer, S. Fortunato, C. Chen, A. Buck, R. Babcock and S. Uthicke, 'Thirty Years of Research on Crown-of-Thorns Starfish (1986–2016): Scientific advances and emerging opportunities', *Diversity*, vol. 9, no. 4, pp. 41, 35.

32 Wright, *The Coral Battleground*, p. 29.

33 D.W. Connell, 'The Great Barrier Reef Conservation Issue – a Case History', *Biological Conservation*, vol. 3, no. 4, 1971, pp. 249–54.

34 'Move for laws to protect Reef', *The Courier Mail*, 23 November 1967, p. 13.

35 R.J. Walsh (AAS) to F. Nicklin, 13 December 1967, QSA, SRS 1043, Premier's Batch Files, ID 538154 Great Barrier Reef-Resources Advisory Committee (GBRRAC).

36 P. Mather (Hon. Secretary GBRC) to J. Pizzey, 31 January 1968.

37 Mather to Pizzey, 31 January 1968, attachment 'Proposal relating to the conservation and controlled exploitation of the Great Barrier Reefs'.

38 Mather to Pizzey, 31 January 1968, attachment, pp. 2, 4.

39 J. Pizzey to G. Chalk, 1 February 1968, QSA, SRS 1043, ID 538154.

40 Pizzey to Chalk, 1 February 1968.

41 Cabinet Minute, Decision 11409, subcommittee report, Proposal by Australian Academy of Science for a Scientific Investigation of the Great Barrier Reef, 1 April 1968, QSA.

42 Pizzey to Chalk, 1 February 1968.

43 Cabinet Minute, Decision 11244, Great Barrier Reef – Scientific Investigations by Australian Academy of Science, 26 February 1968, QSA.

44 Cabinet Minute, Decision 11591, Proposal by Australian Academy of Science for a Scientific Investigation of the Great Barrier Reef, 28 May 1968, QSA.

45 Cabinet Minute, Decision 11409, subcommittee report, p. 4.

46 Decision 11409, subcommittee report, p. 1.

47 Decision 11409, subcommittee report, p. 2.

48 Decision 11409, subcommittee report, p. 3.

49 G. Chalk to J. Gorton, 7 June 1968, QSA, SRS 1043, ID 538154.

50 Cabinet Minute, Decision 11864, Marine National Parks, 30 July 1968, p. 1, QSA.

51 Cabinet Minute, Decision 11864, Marine National Parks, 30 July 1968, p. 2, QSA.

52 Decision 11409, subcommittee report, p. 2.

53 Decision 11409, subcommittee report, p. 2.

54 Decision 11409, subcommittee report, p. 3.

55 Cabinet Minute, Decision 11402, Visit of Eminent Overseas Marine Biologist – The Great Barrier Reefs Special Investigations – Special Consolidated Revenue Allocation, 1 April 1968, QSA.

56 Unknown to Büsst, 24 February 1968, JCU, Büsst Papers, 1/6.

57 J. Kikkawa to Büsst, 8 March 1968, JCU, Büsst Papers, 1/6.

58 Minute of Wildlife Preservation Society of Queensland Innisfail Branch, 7 February 1968, National Archives of Australia (NAA), A1838, ID 558106.

59 E. Hegerl to Büsst, 25 March 1968, JCU, Büsst Papers, 2/11.

60 Hegerl to Büsst, 25 March 1968.

61 President of QLS to Department of Labour and Tourism, received 30 April 1968, QSA, SRS 9187, ID 294293.

62 Department of Mines memorandum, 13 May 1968, QSA, SRS 9187, ID 294293.

63 Letter to the editor, 'Mining threat to Barrier Reef?', *Truth*, 31 March 1968; Letter to the editor, 'Dead reef very alive', *The Courier Mail*, 21 March 1968.

64 R. Camm to J. Herbert, 2 May 1968, QSA, SRS 9187, ID 294293.

65 Camm to Herbert, 2 May 1968.

66 H.S. Ladd, *Preliminary Report on Conservation and Controlled Exploitation of the Great Barrier Reef*, Government Printer, Brisbane, 1968, pp. 1–6.

67 Ladd, *Preliminary Report*, p. 42.

68 Ladd, *Preliminary Report*, p. 44.

69 'Strict control urged in any mining of reef', *The Courier Mail*, 4 September 1968, p. 9.

70 H.S. Ladd to J. Woods (Chief Government Geologist, Geological Survey of Queensland), 9 January 1969, Smithsonian Institute Archives, RU7396, Harry Stephen Ladd Papers.

71 Undated report, 'Notes on Mining and Petroleum Exploration and Possible Future Exploitation on the Great Barrier Reef', QSA, SRS 1043, ID 538154.

72 For Grassle's full letter to *The Courier Mail*, which published pieces of it, see J.F. Grassle to Editor of *The Courier Mail*, 7 September 1968, JCU, Büsst Papers, 1/8. For the *Courier Mail* article, see 'Ladd report on reef is challenged', *The Courier Mail*, 11 September 1968, p. 3.

73 C. Burdon-Jones address to Apex Club at Cairns, c. 14 September 1968, pp. 9–11, QSA, SRS 1043, ID 538150 Great Barrier Reef – General.

74 Büsst to D. McMichael, 15 September 1968, JCU, Büsst Papers, 1/7.

75 Wright, *The Coral Battleground*, p. 29.

Chapter 7: The Save the Reef Campaign: Oil Drilling

1 Chairman of People the North Committee to Camm in Memorandum Premier's Department, 5 September 1968, QSA, SRS 1043, ID 538150.

2 F. Ratcliffe to Büsst, 20 September 1968, JCU, Büsst Papers, 1/7.

3 Wright to Büsst, 9 September 1968, JCU, Büsst Papers, 2/13.

4 Ratcliffe to Büsst, 20 September 1968.

5 Büsst, quoted in Clare, *Struggle for the Barrier Reef*, p. 98.

6 Büsst to J. Gorton, 27 August 1968, JCU, Büsst Papers, 2/16.

7 See Büsst to Owen Kelly (QLS), 22 July 1968, and Büsst to Kelly, 2 August 1968, JCU, Büsst Papers, 2/11.

8 Connell, 'The Great Barrier Reef Conservation Issue', pp. 249–54.

9 See Kelly to Büsst, 28 July 1968, JCU, Büsst Papers, 2/11, and Barry Wain, 'The Bingil Bay Bastard', *The Nation*, 1 May 1971, p. 14. 'Bingil Bay Bastard' was a name Büsst gave himself prior to the Save the Reef campaign, when he fought to preserve a tract of rainforest near his home from military use. Evidently, Büsst continued to use the name and would occasionally use it as his signature at the end of a letter.

10 QLS, *Newsletter*, no. 27, July–August 1968, p. 8.

11 Wright, *The Coral Battleground*, p. 31.

12 QLS, *Newsletter*, no. 27, pp. 2–8.

13 P. Mather, *Patricia Mather Interviewed by Susan Marsden*, Session 5, 17:59–18:27. Ellipses in original transcript.

14 McCalman, *The Reef*, pp. 278, 292.

15 J. Kikkawa to Büsst, 8 March 1968, JCU, Büsst Papers, 1/8.

16 Büsst to Barwick, 8 February 1968, JCU, Büsst Papers, 2/12.

17 Australian Conservation Foundation (ACF), *Newsletter,* October 1968, p. 2.

18 ACF, *Newsletter,* p. 3.

19 Wright to Büsst, 22 November 1968, JCU, Büsst Papers, 2/13.

20 Wright to Büsst, 4 December 1968, JCU, Büsst Papers, 2/13.

21 M. Fox, Senate, *Hansard*, 26 February 1969, p. 83.

22 Wright, *The Coral Battleground*, p. 51.

23 Büsst to *The Townsville Bulletin*, 10 February 1969, p. 3, JCU, Büsst Papers, 1/9. Emphasis in original.

24 P. Mather to K. Bradshaw (Senate Select Committee), 19 February 1969, QSA, SRS 1043, ID 538156 Oil and Mineral Exploration on the Great Barrier Reef.

25 R. Patterson, House of Representatives, *Hansard*, 26 February 1969, pp. 156–57.

26 See Cabinet Minutes, Decision 860, Urgency Motion – Control of Oil Drilling and Mining in the Great Barrier Reef, 4 March 1969, and Decision 915, Law of the Sea: Gulf of Carpentaria and Great Barrier Reef, 25 March 1969, NAA.

27 'Government pledges to guard Reef', *The Courier Mail*, 29 April 1969, p. 3.

28 Wright, *The Coral Battleground*, p. 60.

29 Piesse to Büsst, 28 March 1969, JCU, Büsst Papers, 1/7.

30 Wright, *The Coral Battleground*, p. 60.

31 Kelly to Büsst, 15 May 1969, JCU, Büsst Papers, 2/11.

32 WPSQ Innisfail branch to Barwick (ACF), 19 June 1969, JCU, Büsst Papers, 1/7.

33 Wright, *The Coral Battleground*, p. 65.

34 Ratcliffe to D. Connell (Pres. QLS), 5 June 1969, JCU, Büsst Papers, 1/9.

35 Copy of letter Barwick to Gorton, n.d., JCU, Büsst Papers, 1/9.

36 Wright, *The Coral Battleground*, p. 40.

37 McCalman, *The Reef*, pp. 292–93.

38 ACF, *The Future of the Great Barrier Reef: Papers of an Australian Conservation Foundation Symposium*, Parkville, Victoria, Special Publication, 1969, p. 68.

39 Hutton and Connors, *Australian Environment Movement*, p. 106.

40 J. Bowen, 'The Great Barrier Reef: Towards Conservation and Management', in S. Dovers (ed.), *Australian Environmental History*, Oxford University Press, Melbourne, 1994, p. 248.

41 ACF, *The Future of the Great Barrier Reef*, pp. 38–39.

42 Cabinet Submission 599, Decision 1222, 26 August 1969, p. 1, NAA.

43 Cabinet Submission 599, Decision 1222, 26 August 1969; Protection of the Great Barrier Reef – Report of the Inter-Departmental Committee, p. 6, NAA.

44 These facts were revealed in Extracts from Mines Department File re Mackay No. 1 (Repulse Bay). NLA, MS 3990 Exhibits of the Great Barrier Reef petroleum drilling Royal Commissions 1964–1972, 5/9 (ii), Exhibit 255.

45 Ministerial Statement, Ron Camm, 'Ampol-Japex Mackay No.1 Well', 19 August 1969, QSA, SRS 1043, ID 538161 Committee of Inquiry into Possible Effects of

Drilling – Great Barrier Reef 75B-1, Part 3. A slightly altered version of this speech was made on the same date to the Legislative Assembly. See *Hansard*, 19 August 1969, pp. 64–65.

46 Extracts from Mines Department File re Mackay No. 1 (Repulse Bay), NLA, MS 3990 Exhibits of the Royal Commission.

47 See, for instance, O. Kelly, letter to the editor, 'All this and oil wells, too?', *The Australian*, 16 May 1969; O. Kelly, letter to the editor, 'A Barrier Reef or oil industry', *The Age*, 6 September 1969, p. 8; 'Oil and troubled waters', *The Australian*, 16 September 1969, p. 11; O. Kelly, letter to the editor, 'Call for oil moratorium', *The Australian*, 18 September 1969; G. Williams, 'The calm Miss Wright fights to save reef', *The Australian*, 26 November 1969.

48 See, for instance, 'Balance in conservation', *The Australian*, 1 May 1969; 'Juggling the Barrier Reef issue', *The Australian*, 24 December 1969, p. 6.

49 J. Gorton, House of Representatives, *Hansard*, 26 August 1969, p. 640.

50 See telegrams: 18 September 1969, QSA, SRS 1043, ID 538155 Oil and Mineral Exploration on the Great Barrier Reef.

51 B.A. Walton to Bjelke-Petersen, 27 August 1969, QSA, SRS 1043, ID 538155.

52 L.J. Jones to Bjelke-Petersen, 28 August 1969, QSA, SRS 1043, ID 538155.

53 J. Campbell to Bjelke-Petersen, 1 October 1969, QSA, SRS 1043, ID 538155.

54 O.K. White to Bjelke-Petersen, 25 September 1969, QSA, SRS 1043, ID 538155.

55 See letters: Bowen Shire Council to Premiers Department, 1 September 1969; Humanist Society of Queensland to Bjelke-Petersen, 11 September 1969; Zoological Society of Frankfurt to Bjelke-Petersen, 1 October 1969; Townsville and District Tourist Development Association to Bjelke-Petersen, 8 October 1969, QSA, SRS 1043, ID 538155.

56 See, for instance, O. Kelly, letter to the editor, *The Australian*, 16 May 1969.

57 Büsst to Whitlam, 5 September 1969, JCU, Büsst Papers, 2/16.

58 Garland (Commonwealth Secretary AEU) to Bjelke-Petersen, 16 September 1969, QSA, SRS 1043, ID 538155.

59 D.W. Goode to Bjelke-Petersen, 17 October 1969, QSA, SRS 1043, ID 538155.

60 Büsst to Gorton, 31 December 1969, JCU, Büsst Papers, 2/16.

61 Büsst to Gorton, 31 December 1969, JCU, Büsst Papers, 2/16.

62 Büsst to L. Naylor (Arthur Robinson & Co.), JCU, Büsst Papers, 2/14.

Seeing

1 R. Jacobsen, 'Obituary: Great Barrier Reef (25 Million BC-...)', *Outside*, 11 October 2016, accessed from www.outsideonline.com/outdoor-adventure/environment/obituary-great-barrier-reef-25-million-bc-2016/.

2 A. Remeikis, 'Great Barrier Reef tourism spokesman attacks scientist over slump in visitors', *The Guardian*, 13 January 2018, accessed from www.theguardian.com/environment/2018/jan/13/great-barrier-reef-tourism-spokesman-attacks-scientist-over-slump-in-visitors.

3 'Pauline Hanson visits healthy reef to dispute effects of climate change', *ABC News*, 25 November 2016, accessed from www.abc.net.au/news/2016-11-25/pauline-hanson-visits-the-great-barrier-reef-climate-change/8059142.

4 Media release, 'Reef tourism operators make historic climate change declaration', Fight for our Reef, 3 May 2018, accessed from www.marineconservation.org.au/

reef-tourism-operators-make-historic-climate-change-declaration.

5   P. Hannam, '"Huge step": Tourist industry wakes up to reef's climate risks', *The Sydney Morning Herald*, 7 July 2018, accessed from www.smh.com.au/environment/climate-change/huge-step-tourist-industry-wakes-up-to-reef-s-climate-risks-20180706-p4zq0x.html.

6   G. Wong-Parodi and I. Feygina, 'Engaging People on Climate Change: The role of emotional responses', *Environmental Communication*, vol. 15, issue 5, 2021, pp. 571–93.

7   Tourism Australia, 'Tourism and the Great Barrier Reef', accessed 16 October 2021 from www.ecotourism.org.au/assets/Resources-Hub-Ecotourism-Research/Tourism-and-the-Great-Barrier-Reef.pdf.

8   G.S. Cumming and K.A. Dobbs, 'Understanding Regulatory Frameworks for Large Marine Protected Areas: permits of the Great Barrier Reef Marine Park', *Biological Conservation*, vol. 237, 2019, pp. 3–11.

Chapter 8: The Black Ban

1   A black ban is a mass refusal to supply or purchase goods or services. Jack Mundey in 1973 would eventually coin the term 'green ban' to distinguish traditional union 'black bans' from those with a distinct environmentalist agenda. Georges referred to the 1970 intervention as a 'black ban'; few, however, could doubt its environmentalist underpinnings.

2   'Senator to lead black ban move on reef oil rig', *The Australian*, 6 January 1970.

3   Clare, *Struggle for the Barrier Reef*, p. 197.

4   'Senator to lead black ban move on reef oil rig', *The Australian*.

5   'Forcing the public to direct action', *The Australian*, 7 January 1970, p. 6.

6   Wright to Bjelke-Petersen, 8 January 1970, QSA, SRS 1043, ID 538156 Oil and Mineral Exploration on the Great Barrier Reef.

7   Telegram, Ampol to JAPEX, 13 January 1970, NLA, MS 7984, Bib ID 42626, Papers of Sir John Gorton, Box 11.

8   This inquiry into the crown-of-thorns was the same that was discussed briefly in the previous chapter.

9   Copy of telegram, Bjelke-Petersen to Dr D.F. Martyn (Australian Academy of Science), 14 January 1970, QSA, SRS 1043, ID 538159 Committee of inquiry into the possible effects of oil drilling – Great Barrier Reef.

10 Press statement, 'Drilling on the Barrier Reef', 14 January 1970, NLA, MS 7984, Papers of Sir John Gorton, Box 11.

11 Press statement, 'Drilling on the Barrier Reef', 15 January 1970, NLA, MS 7984, Papers of Sir John Gorton, Box 11.

12 Telegram, Bjelke-Petersen to Gorton, 16 January 1970, QSA, SRS 1043, ID 538159.

13 Telegram, Gorton to Bjelke-Petersen, 19 January 1970, QSA, SRS 1043, ID 538159.

14 See Clare, *Struggle for the Great Barrier Reef*, p. 119; Wright, *The Coral Battleground*, p. 116; Bowen and Bowen, *Great Barrier Reef*, p. 335.

15 See telegram, Bjelke-Petersen to Gorton, 20 January 1970, and Gorton to Bjelke-Petersen, 21 January 1970, QSA, SRS 1043, ID 538159.

16 Timmins to Bjelke-Petersen, 14 January 1970. This correspondence, along with those listed above and the telegrams below, can be found in QSA, SRS 1043, ID 538156 Oil and Mineral Exploration on the Great Barrier Reef.

17 Press release, 'Government's attitude to criticism of Repulse Bay drilling', 15 January 1970, QSA, SRS 1043, ID 538156.

18 Telegram, JAPEX to Ampol, 21 January 1970, QSA, SRS 1043, ID 538162 Royal Commission, Risk of Damage, Drilling Great Barrier Reef for Petroleum.

19 Telegram, JAPEX to Ampol, 21 January 1970, QSA, SRS 1043, ID 538162 Royal Commission, Risk of Damage, Drilling Great Barrier Reef for Petroleum.

20 Draft memorandum, A.W. Norrie, 21 January 1970, p. 1, QSA, SRS 1043, ID 538162.

21 Those present at the conference were Prime Minister John Gorton, Minister for National Development R.W.C. Swartz, Minister for Education and Science N.H. Bowen, (federal) Attorney-General T.E.F. Hughes, Premier Joh Bjelke-Petersen, Minister for Mines and Main Roads Ron Camm, Minister for Justice and (Queensland) Attorney-General P.R. Delamothe.

22 Proceedings Conference of Commonwealth and State Ministers, 29 January 1970, pp. 3–4, NLA, MS 7984, Papers of Sir John Gorton, Box 11. The information in the following paragraphs is only drawn from this source. Only significant quotes are paginated.

23 Proceedings Conference of Commonwealth and State Ministers, pp. 6–9.

24 Proceedings Conference of Commonwealth and State Ministers, p. 16.

25 Proceedings Conference of Commonwealth and State Ministers, p. 18.

26 Proceedings Conference of Commonwealth and State Ministers, p. 56.

27 Proceedings Conference of Commonwealth and State Ministers, p. 69.

28 Proceedings Conference of Commonwealth and State Ministers, p. 72.

29 Proceedings Conference of Commonwealth and State Ministers, p. 76

30 Proceedings Conference of Commonwealth and State Ministers, p. 76.

31 Bjelke-Petersen, submission to Conference of Commonwealth and State Ministers, 29 January 1970, p. 6, NLA, MS 7984, Papers of Sir John Gorton, Box 11.

32 Proceedings Conference of Commonwealth and State Ministers, p. 94.

33 Proceedings Conference of Commonwealth and State Ministers, p. 70.

34 Proceedings Conference of Commonwealth and State Ministers, p. 71.

35 McLennan to Büsst, 7 January 1970, p. 1, JCU, Büsst Papers, 2/12.

36 Büsst to Georges, 27 January 1970, JCU, Büsst Papers, 2/12.

37 Büsst to Deemer, 28 January 1970, JCU, Büsst Papers, 2/12.

38 Büsst to Wright, 4 February 1970, p. 2, JCU, Büsst Papers, 2/13.

39 Wright, The Coral Battleground, p. 105.

40 'Reef drilling a major issue in Albert poll', The Courier Mail, 17 January 1970.

41 Wright to Büsst, 20 February 1970, JCU, Büsst Papers, 2/13.

42 Wright, The Coral Battleground, p. 131.

43 See Minutes of Meeting of WPSQ, 3 February 1970, p. 4, NLA, MS5781 Papers of Judith Wright, 1944–2000, 3/19. The letter was sent on 21 February 1970. See Wright to Gorton, JCU, Büsst Papers, 2/13.

44 Büsst to Gorton, 2 February 1970, JCU, Büsst Papers, 2/16.

45 Büsst to Deemer, 6 February 1970, JCU, Büsst Papers, 2/12.

46 Minutes of Meeting of WPSQ, 3 February 1970, p. 5, NLA, MS5781 Papers of Judith Wright, 1944–2000, 3/19. The statement had been circulated among the WPSQ senior members from 22 January.

47 Wright, The Coral Battleground, p. 52.

48 Draft by Dr P. Mather for Agreement of Conservation Organisations, attachment in Wright to Büsst, 6 February 1970, p. 1, JCU, Büsst Papers, 2/13.

49 Draft by Dr P. Mather for Agreement of Conservation Organisations.

50 Wright to Büsst, 6 February 1970, p. 1, JCU, Büsst Papers, 2/13.

51 Wright to Büsst, 20 February 1970, JCU, Büsst Papers, 2/13.

52 Great Barrier Reef Committee Meeting No. 114, 27 November 1969, p. 21, UQFL, UQFL25 Dorothy Hill Collection, Box 24, Great Barrier Reef, Minutes, etc. Publications.

53 P. Mather to Members of the GBRC, 2 April 1970, UQFL, UQFL25 Dorothy Hill Collection, Box 24, Reef Matters.

54 Orme to Mather, 20 February 1970, UQFL, UQFL25 Dorothy Hill Collection, Box 24, Reef Matters.

55 P. Mather to Members of the GBRC, 2 April 1970, p. 1.

56 P. Mather to Members of the GBRC, 2 April 1970, p. 2.

Chapter 9: Towards a Reef Commission

1   S. Oka (JAPEX GM) to Bjelke-Petersen, 6 February 1970, p. 2, QSA, SRS 1043, ID 538160 Committee of Inquiry into the Possible Effects of Oil Drilling – Great Barrier Reef.

2   Statement made by Bjelke-Petersen, 'Drilling of Mackay No. 1 Well', 10 February 1970, pp. 1–2, QSA, SRS 1043, ID 538160.

3   Opinion from Arnold Bennett QC Regarding Ampol Exploration (Queensland) Pty Limited and Japex Australia Pty Ltd, 12 February 1970, p. 2, QSA, SRS 1043, ID 538160.

4   Bjelke-Petersen to Gorton, 13 February 1970, QSA, SRS 1043, ID 538160.

5   Oka to Bjelke-Petersen, 13 February 1970, p. 2, QSA, SRS 1043, ID 538160.

6   Memorandum Arnold Bennett, 16 February 1970, p. 2, QSA, SRS 1043, ID 538160.

7   Bjelke-Petersen to Oka, 17 February 1970, p. 1, QSA, SRS 1043, ID 538160.

8   Gorton to Bjelke-Petersen, 25 February 1970, QSA, SRS 1043, ID 538160.

9   Pavey, Wilson, Cohen and Carter Solicitors (on behalf of JAPEX) to Bjelke-Petersen, 3 March 1970, p. 2, QSA, SRS 1043, ID 538160.

10 Gorton to Bjelke-Petersen, 4 February 1970, QSA, SRS 1043, ID 538160.

11 Copy of Cabinet Minute, Committee of Inquiry – Barrier Reef, 10 February 1970, pp. 1–2, QSA, SRS 1043, ID 538162.

12 Cabinet Minute, Decision 14082, Committee of Inquiry – Barrier Reef, 10 February 1970, p. 2, QSA.

13 Cabinet Minute, Decision 14082, p. 3.

14 Cabinet Minute, Decision 14082, p. 3.

15 Bjelke-Petersen to Gorton, 12 February 1970, p. 2, QSA, SRS 1043, ID 538160.

16 Gorton to Bjelke-Petersen, 19 February 1970, p. 1, QSA, SRS 1043, ID 538160.

17 Undated memorandum regarding Mr V.J. Moroney, QSA, SRS 1043, ID 538160.

18 Undated memorandum regarding Mr A.D. Acuff, QSA, SRS 1043, ID 538160.

19 Bjelke-Petersen to Gorton, 25 February 1970, p. 2, QSA, SRS 1043, ID 538160.

20 Bjelke-Petersen to Gorton, 19 March 1970, p. 1, QSA, SRS 1043, ID 538161, Committee of Inquiry into Possible Effects of Drilling – Great Barrier Reef.

21 Bjelke-Petersen to Gorton, 19 March 1970, p. 3.

22   Queensland Parliament, 'Report on the Grounding of the oil tanker *Oceanic Grandeur* in the Torres Strait on 3rd March, 1970 and the Subsequent Removal of Oil from Waters', Government Printer, Brisbane, 1970, pp. 1–5.

23   'The grounding of the oil tanker *Oceanic Grandeur* in the Torres Strait', and B.S. Newell and D.J. Tranter, 'Report on Oil Pollution from the Tanker *Oceanic Grandeur*', CSIRO Division of Fisheries and Oceanography, 1970.

24   Newell and Tranter, 'Report on Oil Pollution from the Tanker *Oceanic Grandeur*', pp. 5–6.

25   'The grounding of the oil tanker *Oceanic Grandeur* in the Torres Strait', p. 14.

26   House of Representatives, *Hansard*, 3 March 1970, p. 11.

27   Cabinet Minute, Submission 72, Protection of the Great Barrier Reef, 21 January 1970, pp. 1–6, NAA, SRS A5873, 76.

28   Wright, *The Coral Battleground*, p. 153.

29   Wright to Büsst, 3 April 1970, JCU, Büsst Papers, 2/13.

30   Meisenhelter to Gorton and Hasluck, 1 May 1970, QSA, SRS 1043, ID 538162. Emphasis in the original.

31   Wright, *The Coral Battleground*, p. 154.

32   'Royal Commissions on Great Barrier Reef', p. 6.

33   'Royal Commissions on Great Barrier Reef', p. 7.

34   'Royal Commissions on Great Barrier Reef', p. 7.

35   'Royal Commissions on Great Barrier Reef', p. 8.

36   Wright, 'Full-time legal aid for Reef case is urged', *The Courier Mail*, 30 May 1969, p. 2.

37   Herbert to Magnus, 8 June 1970, QSA, SRS 1043, ID 538162. Row's response is explained in the postscript of Herbert's reply.

38   Premier's Department Memorandum, 22 June 1970, p. 1, QSA, SRS 1043, ID 538162.

39   Premier's Department Memorandum, 22 June 1970, p. 1.

40   Premier's Department Memorandum, 22 June 1970, p. 2.

41   Gorton to Bjelke-Petersen, 1 July 1970, QSA, SRS 1043, ID 538162.

42   Bjelke-Petersen to Gorton, 1 July 1970, QSA, SRS 1043, ID 538162.

43   Gorton to WPSQ (Judith Wright), 2 July 1970, JCU, Büsst Papers, 2/16.

Science

1   P. Hannam, '"Like winning lotto": Reef Foundation minnow braces for $444 m windfall', *The Sydney Morning Herald*, 13 May 2018, accessed from www.smh.com. au/environment/conservation/like-winning-lotto-reef-foundation-minnow-braces-for-444m-windfall-20180511-p4zeud.html.

2   Hannam, '"Like winning lotto"'.

3   A. Ham, 'The spin and secrecy threatening the Australian environment', *The Monthly*, November 2021, accessed from www.themonthly.com.au/issue/2021/november/1635685200/anthony-ham/spin-and-secrecy-threatening-australian-environment.

4   P. Ridd, 'Science and media doomsayers ignore good news on reef', *The Australian*, 23 July 2021, accessed from www.theaustralian.com.au/commentary/science-and-media-doomsayers-ignore-good-news-on-reef/news-story/28125321d6f1f2d2f6fec1a90c728e12.

5   P. Ridd, 'It's the science that's rotten, not the Reef', *The Australian*, 6 December 2020, accessed from www.theaustralian.com.au/commentary/its-reef-science-thats -rotten-not-the-great-barrier/news-story/1d95f63bc1a2651f5f7c4f9837750513.

6   P. Larcombe and P. Ridd, 'The need for a formalised system of Quality Control for environmental policy-science', *Marine Pollution Bulletin*, vol. 126, 2018, pp. 449–61.

7   B. Schaffelke, K. Fabricius, F. Kroon, J. Brodie, G. De'ath, R. Shaw, D. Tarte, M. Warne and P. Thorburn, 'Support for improved quality control but misplaced criticism of GBR science. Reply to viewpoint "The need for a formalised system of Quality Control for environmental policy-science" by P. Larcombe and P. Ridd', *Marine Pollution Bulletin*, vol. 129, 2018, pp. 357–63.

8   J. Albrechtsen, 'Decision a blow for Ridd but a win for the country', *The Weekend Australian*, 15 October 2021, accessed from www.theaustralian.com.au/inquirer/ decision-a-blow-for-ridd-buta-win-for-the-country/news-story/75d568d354dadb2 6941fc5bd4241c15d.

Chapter 10: Royal Commission

1   Gorton to Bjelke-Petersen, 29 May 1970, QSA, SRS 1043, ID 538162.

2   'Royal Commissions on Great Barrier Reef', pp. 27–28. Strictly speaking, both the state and federal government were called royal commissions, and in some cases, like the title used in the official documents, the plural format remained in use. Here, however, I will only use the singular form. Two collections of the 'Transcript of proceedings' have been consulted: one at the National Library of Australia and the other at the James Cook University Eddie Koiki Mabo Library. The binding conducted by the libraries mean that the collections number 46 and 66 volumes respectively. Thus, rather than referring to the volume numbers, I will cite the page numbers, which are common to both.

3   'Royal Commissions on Great Barrier Reef', p. 28.

4   An undated internal memo likely from September 1970, two months into the commission's proceedings, asserted that a 'conservative estimate' indicated that sittings would last for fifteen weeks, ending in February 1971. With a period allowed for the writing of the report, the memo suggested governments should not expect a report before late 1971. See undated memorandum, 'Great Barrier Reef Petroleum Drilling Royal Commissions', QSA, SRS 1043, ID 538162.

5   'Royal Commissions on Great Barrier Reef', p. 499.

6   'Royal Commissions on Great Barrier Reef', pp. 9529–30.

7   'Royal Commissions on Great Barrier Reef', p. 13456.

8   'Royal Commissions on Great Barrier Reef', p. 901.

9   'Royal Commissions on Great Barrier Reef', pp. 901–2; see J.T. Woods, 'Some facts of life', *Queensland Government Mining Journal*, vol. 71, no. 824, June 1970, pp. 256–57.

10   'Royal Commissions on Great Barrier Reef', pp. 5415–16.

11   'Royal Commissions on Great Barrier Reef', p. 5426.

12   'Royal Commissions on Great Barrier Reef', p. 14783.

13   'Royal Commissions on Great Barrier Reef', pp. 18167–68.

14   'Royal Commissions on Great Barrier Reef', p. 168.

15   'Royal Commissions on Great Barrier Reef', p. 1053.

16 'Royal Commissions on Great Barrier Reef', p. 1885.

17 Statement of Dr P. Mather, p. 18, NLA, MS 3990, Exhibits of the Great Barrier Reef petroleum drilling Royal Commissions 1964–1972, 9/16 (i), Exhibit 447. Hereafter, the exhibits will be referred to as Exhibits of the Royal Commission.

18 Statement of Dr P. Mather, p. 23.

19 Statement of Mr D.R. Stoddart, p. 10, NLA, MS 3990, Exhibits of the Royal Commission, 6/11 (i), Exhibit 284.

20 Statement of Mr D.R. Stoddart, p. 12.

21 'Royal Commissions on Great Barrier Reef', pp. 2221–22.

22 'Royal Commissions on Great Barrier Reef', pp. 17100–1.

23 Australian Royal Commission into Exploratory and Production Drilling for Petroleum in the Area of the Great Barrier Reef, 'Report: Royal Commissions into Exploratory and Production Drilling for Petroleum in the Area of the Great Barrier Reef', Government Printer, Canberra, 1975, p. 324.

24 'Report: Royal Commissions into Exploratory and Production Drilling for Petroleum in the Area of the Great Barrier Reef', p. 606.

25 'Report: Royal Commissions into Exploratory and Production Drilling for Petroleum in the Area of the Great Barrier Reef', p. 629.

26 See Statement of A.W. Norrie, p. 10, NLA, MS 3990, Exhibits of the Royal Commission, 2/3 (ii), Exhibit 80; R.H. Fields (Under Treasurer) to A.W. Norrie, 18 March 1971, QSA, SRS 6232 General Correspondence, ID 958199 Department Mines – Problem of the quantification of economic effects on Great Barrier Reef; 'Transcript of proceedings', pp. 2213–16.

27 'Royal Commissions on Great Barrier Reef', pp. 15029–30.

28 Statement of A.W. Norrie, p. 11, NLA, MS 3990, Exhibits of the Royal Commission, 2/3 (ii), Exhibit 80.

29 Treasury memorandum, Summary of the Problem of Quantification of Economic Effects on Reef Drilling as Discussed, 8 January 1971, QSA, SRS 6232, ID 958199.

30 Statement of Mr S.M. Cochrane, p. 3, NLA, MS 3990, Exhibits of the Royal Commission, 7/13 (iii), Exhibit 341.

31 Statement – Dr H.C. Coombs, p. 8, NLA, MS 3990, Exhibits of the Royal Commission, 8/15 (ii), Exhibit 406.

32 Statement – Dr H.C. Coombs, p. 9.

33 Statement – Dr H.C. Coombs, p. 10.

34 'Royal Commissions on Great Barrier Reef', pp. 11337–38.

35 Statement – Dr H.C. Coombs, p. 12.

36 'Royal Commissions on Great Barrier Reef', p. 7831.

37 Evidence to be presented on behalf of the Australian Tourist Commission, p. 15. NLA, MS 3990, Exhibits of the Royal Commission, 2/4 (ii), Exhibit 107.

38 Statement of Miss O. Ashworth, p. 1, NLA, MS 3990, Exhibits of the Royal Commission, 5/9 (ii), Exhibit 251.

39 New statement by Miss O. Ashworth (in lieu of Exhibit 251), p. 13, NLA, MS 3990, Exhibits of the Royal Commission, 7/13 (ii), Exhibit 325.

40 'Royal Commissions on Great Barrier Reef', pp. 7728–29.

41 'Royal Commissions on Great Barrier Reef', p. 16458.

42 'Royal Commissions on Great Barrier Reef', pp. 7699–700.

43 'Report: Royal Commissions into Exploratory and Production Drilling for Petroleum in the Area of the Great Barrier Reef', p. 952.

44 'Report: Royal Commissions into Exploratory and Production Drilling for Petroleum in the Area of the Great Barrier Reef', p. 984.

45 'Proceedings Conference of Commonwealth and State Ministers', 29 January 1970, p. 74, NLA, MS 7984, Papers of Sir John Gorton, p. 11.

46 'Report: Royal Commissions into Exploratory and Production Drilling for Petroleum in the Area of the Great Barrier Reef', p. 985.

47 'Royal Commissions on Great Barrier Reef', pp. 7793–95.

48 'Royal Commissions on Great Barrier Reef', p. 5851A.

49 'Royal Commissions on Great Barrier Reef', p. 5368.

50 'Royal Commissions on Great Barrier Reef', p. 6272.

51 'Royal Commissions on Great Barrier Reef', p. 16115.

52 'Royal Commissions on Great Barrier Reef', p. 17834.

53 'Report: Royal Commissions into Exploratory and Production Drilling for Petroleum in the Area of the Great Barrier Reef', pp. 952–58.

54 'Royal Commissions on Great Barrier Reef', p. 13315.

55 'Royal Commissions on Great Barrier Reef', pp. 14124–26.

56 Statement of Dr P. Mather, pp. 2–3, NLA, MS 3990, Exhibits of the Royal Commissions, 9/16 (i), Exhibit 447.

57 Statement of Dr P. Mather, pp. 4–12. The pieces of legislation identified by Mather were: the *Fauna Conservation Act* of 1952 (which stipulated all Queensland Islands as fauna sanctuaries above the high-tide mark); the *Native Plants Protection Act 1930* (listed protected species); the *Forestry Act 1959*, the Forestry Regulations of 1960 and the *Forestry Amendment Act 1964* (which provided for protection of fauna and flora of 'attractive islands (for tourist purposes)' that were within national parks, and stipulated that any area could be excised from a national park to make it available for other uses); the *Fisheries Act 1957–1962* (this Act protected coral in all Queensland waters and a subsequent Order in Council extended it to cover all marine life, excluding fish caught by hook and line, for the reefs surrounding Dabuukji [Green Island] and Heron Island, as well as Wistari Reef in July 1963); the *Harbours Acts 1955–1964* (which prohibited the removal of rock, stone, gravel, sand and other materials from Queensland waters, including beaches below the high-water line, without authority); the *Fisheries* and *Pearl Oyster Fisheries* Acts (which provided jurisdiction to the Commonwealth over Australian and foreign nationals in Australian proclaimed waters); and the *Petroleum (Submerged Lands)* legislation. Mather asserted that the following Queensland departments had some role in overseeing the administration of the Reef area: Primary Industries, Forestry, Mines, Native Affairs, Tourism, Harbours and Marine. The relevant Commonwealth departments were: Primary Industry, National Development, Bureau of Mineral Resources, Education and Science and the Bureau of Meteorology.

58 Statement of Dr P. Mather, p. 12.

59 Statement of Dr P. Mather, p. 16.

60 Statement of Dr P. Mather, pp. 16–18. As part of her own statement, Mather included a copy of 'A Draft of a Bill for an Act relating to the Great Barrier Reef and the Surrounding Submerged Lands of the Continental Shelf Adjacent to the Australian Coast and Contiguous with the Queensland Coast '.

61 'Royal Commissions on Great Barrier Reef', p. 14086. The exchange begins with the chairman asking if Mather has a 'law degree tucked away'. Mather does not,

prompting the chairman's referenced response. Mather replies, 'I have been very involved with this particular area for some years.'

62 P. Mather, 'A Draft of a Bill for an Act relating to the Great Barrier Reef', p. 1 in Statement of Dr Patricia Mather, NLA, MS 3990, Exhibits of the Royal Commissions, 9/16 (i), Exhibit 447.

63 'Royal Commissions on Great Barrier Reef', p. 7430.

64 'Report: Royal Commissions into Exploratory and Production Drilling for Petroleum in the Area of the Great Barrier Reef', p. 960.

65 'Report: Royal Commissions into Exploratory and Production Drilling for Petroleum in the Area of the Great Barrier Reef', p. 962.

Chapter 11: The Great Barrier Reef Marine Park Authority

1 The legislation was presented to the royal commission by Patricia Mather, but the Whitlam government had already moved ahead with their own version of the bill.

2 Bowen and Bowen, *Great Barrier Reef*, p. 349.

3 Wright, *The Coral Battleground*, p. 175.

4 McCalman, *The Reef*, p. 299.

5 'Report: Royal Commissions into Exploratory and Production Drilling for Petroleum in the Area of the Great Barrier Reef', p. 32.

6 'Report: Royal Commissions into Exploratory and Production Drilling for Petroleum in the Area of the Great Barrier Reef', pp. 584–88. Based on Smith and Moroney's recommendations, three basins were considered suitable for drilling: the southern end of the Capricorn Channel, an area stretching between Cairns and Townsville called the Halifax Basin, and the Papuan Basin at the northern end of the Reef.

7 'Report: Royal Commissions into Exploratory and Production Drilling for Petroleum in the Area of the Great Barrier Reef', pp. 588–89.

8 Wright, *The Coral Battleground*, p. 175.

9 B. Foster, 'Barrier Reef Revisited: An appraisal of the Royal Commission report', *APEA Journal*, vol. 15, no. 2, 1975, p. 32.

10 Foster, 'Barrier Reef Revisited', pp. 34–36.

11 R. Connor, House of Representatives, *Hansard*, 10 May 1973, pp. 2005–6.

12 Bowen and Bowen, *Great Barrier Reef*, p. 346.

13 Whitlam to Bjelke-Petersen, 23 September 1974, QSA, SRS 1043, ID 538172 Great Barrier Reef Marine Park Bill 1975 Commonwealth Legislation.

14 Knox to Maher (Under Sec. Premier's Department), 7 October 1974, QSA, SRS 1043, ID 538172.

15 Bjelke-Petersen to Whitlam, 25 November 1974, QSA, SRS 1043, ID 538172.

16 Whitlam to Bjelke-Petersen, 29 January 1975, QSA, SRS 1043, ID 538172.

17 Bjelke-Petersen to Whitlam, 24 February 1975, QSA, SRS 1043, ID 538172.

18 See copy of Department of Forestry memorandum, Marine National Parks, 8 January 1974, and Cabinet Minute, Decision 21270, Marine National Parks, 7 October 1974, QSA, SRS 1043, ID 538170 Marine National Parks.

19 Cabinet Minute, Decision 21270, p. 2.

20 Cabinet Minute, Decision 21270, p. 2.

21 Cabinet Minute, Decision 21309, Marine National Parks, 14 October 1974, pp. 2–3, QSA, SRS 1043, ID 538170.

22 Marine National Parks Planning Committee in Cabinet Minute, Decision 21385, Marine Park Area, 28 October 1974, QSA, SRS 1043, ID 538170.

23 Cabinet Minute, Decision 21437, Report of Inter-Departmental Committee on Marine Park Areas, 11 November 1974, p. 2, QSA, SRS 1043, ID 538170.

24 Cabinet Minute, Decision 21385, Marine Park Area, 28 October 1974, p. 1, QSA, SRS 1043, ID 538170.

25 Cabinet Minute, Decision 21437, p. 1.

26 D. Tarte (Co-ordinator Queensland Conservation Council) to Bjelke-Petersen, 25 November 1974, QSA, SRS 1043, ID 538170.

27 See Bowen and Bowen, *Great Barrier Reef*, p. 352; Wright, *The Coral Battleground*, p. 175.

28 M. Cass, House of Representatives, *Hansard*, 22 May 1975, p. 2690. The bill was assented on 16 July 1975.

29 Whitlam to Bjelke-Petersen, 23 May 1975, QSA, SRS 1043, ID 538165 Royal Commission, Risk of Damage Drilling Great Barrier Reef for Petroleum.

30 Co-ordinator general to Premier's Department, 28 May 1975, QSA, SRS 1043, ID 538165.

31 Camm to Bjelke-Petersen, 1 July 1975, QSA, SRS 1043, ID 538165.

32 Co-ordinator general to Premier's Department, 23 October 1975, p. 2, QSA, SRS 1043, ID 538172.

33 See Newbery (Minister for Tourism and Marine Services) to Bjelke-Petersen, 27 October 1975; Wharton (Minister for Aboriginal and Islanders Advancement and Fisheries) to Premier's Department, 17 November 1975; Tomkins (Minister for Lands, Forestry, National Parks and Wildlife Service) to Bjelke-Petersen, 20 November 1975, QSA, SRS 1043, ID 538172.

34 *The Great Barrier Reef Marine Park Act 1975*, 15 December 1975, QSA, Cabinet Minute, Decision 23664.

35 Fraser to Bjelke-Petersen, 19 March 1976, QSA, SRS 1043, ID 538172.

Change

1 D.R. Bellwood, M.S. Pratchett, T.H. Morrison, G.G. Gurney, T.P. Hughes, J.G. Álvarez-Romero, J.C. Day, R. Grantham, A. Grech, A.S. Hoey, G.P. Jones, J.M. Pandolfi, S.B. Tebbett, E. Techera, R. Weeks and G.S. Cumming, 'Coral Reef Conservation in the Anthropocene: Confronting spatial mismatches and prioritizing functions', *Biological Conservation*, vol. 236, 2019, pp. 604–15.

2 RRAP, 'The program', accessed on 28 November 2021 from gbrrestoration.org/the-program.

3 L. Bostrom-Einarsson, R.C. Babcock, E. Bayraktarov, D. Ceccarelli, N. Cook and S.C.A. Ferse, 'Coral Restoration: A systematic review of current methods, successes, failures and future directions', *PloS ONE*, vol. 15, no. 1, 2020.

4 Bostrom-Einarsson et al., 'Coral Restoration'.

5 T. Hughes, tweet, 10.47am, 8 December 2021, accessed from twitter.com/ProfTerryHughes/status/1468381638912458756.

6 R. Danovaro, L. Bongiorni, C. Corinaldesi, D. Giovannelli, E. Damiani, P. Astolfi, L. Greci and A. Pusceddu, 'Sunscreens Cause Coral Bleaching by Promoting Viral Infections', *Environmental Health Perspectives*, vol. 116, no. 4,

2008, pp. 441–47, and C.A. Downs, E. Kramarsky-Winter, R. Segal, J. Fauth, S. Knuston, O. Brontsein, F.R. Ciner, R. Jeger, Y. Lichtenfeld, C.M. Woodley, P. Pennington, K. Cadenas, A. Kushmaro and Y. Loya, 'Toxicopathological Effects of the Sunscreen UV Filter, Oxybenzone (Benzophenone-3), on Coral Planulae and Cultured Primary Cells and Its Environmental Contamination in Hawaii and the U.S. Virgin Islands', *Archives of Environmental Contamination and Toxicology*, vol. 70, 2016, pp. 265–88.

7   T. Hughes, tweet, 9.00am, 27 June 2018, accessed from twitter.com/profterryhughes/status/1011745940603064321.

Epilogue

1   I am appropriating the term 'slow catastrophe' used by Rebecca Jones in her history of Australian drought. See R. Jones, *Slow Catastrophes: Living with Drought in Australia*, Monash University Publishing, Melbourne, 2017.

2   NOAA's forecast was correct and the Reef did suffer a further major bleaching event in 2022.

3   Deloitte Access Economics, 'At what price? The economic, social and icon value of the Great Barrier Reef', 2017, p. 36.

4   M.I. Curnock, N.A. Marshall, L. Thiault, S.F. Heron, J. Hoey, G. Williams, B. Taylor, P.L. Pert and J. Goldberg, 'Shifts in tourists' sentiments and climate risk perceptions following mass coral bleaching of the Great Barrier Reef', *Nature Climate Change*, vol. 9, 2019, pp. 534–41.

Index

Aboriginal and Torres Strait Islander peoples *see* First Nation peoples
Aboriginal reserves
  Bwgcolman Aboriginal reserve 43, 46
  forced relocation to 43
  Yarrabah mission 46, 47
acidification xvii
activism *see* Reef conservation; 'Save the Reef' campaign
Adani coal mine xi
air travel
  Brisbane to Mackay route 53–4
  Catalina Flying Boat Services 53
  Proserpine aerodrome 54
  tourism on the Reef 53–4
Albert by-election 1970 141–2
Ampol 118, 120
  black ban xiii, 131–7, 141–7
Ansett, Reginald 54
Association of Marine Park Tourism Operators (AMPTO) 125
  climate change declaration 127
  crown-of-thorns control 126
Attenborough, David 48
  Great Barrier Reef 42
Australian Academy of Science (AAS) 100–1, 102
Australian Conservation Foundation (ACF) 66
  Ellison lime mining application 87, 89, 90
  management authority, call for 185
  moratorium on oil drilling movement 110, 113–14
  symposium on geological exploitation 114, 115, 116–17
Australian Institute of Marine Science (AIMS) 47, 162, 175, 200
  2021 report 164, 165, 209
Australian Labor Party (ALP) 170
Australian Marine Conservation Society 127
Australian Mining and Smelting Co
  Authorities to prospect 59

Australian Museum 60, 62, 77, 116, 173
Australian Museum Magazine 35–6, 63
Australian National Travel Association (ANTA) 39
Australian Natural History
  1966 Reef edition 76–7
Australian Petroleum Exploration Association (APEA) 142
  see also royal commission into oil drilling in the Reef
  APEA Journal 192
  report of royal commission, response 192
Australian Primary Producers Union 120
Australian Tourist Commission (ATC) 75
  royal commission evidence 179–80, 181

Banfield, Bertha 22, 44–5
Banfield, Edmund ('The Beachcomber') 32, 44–6
  bird protection 22–3, 24
  call for economic development 25, 27
  First Nations people 44–6
  My Tropical Isle 45
  national park 25
Barrett, Charles 24
Barwick, Sir Garfield 67, 113
Bass Strait oil reserves 74
Beagle 6, 7
bêche-de-mer fishery 1, 6, 17–18, 27, 28
  depletion of stock 18, 20, 38
  Indigenous labour force 18
  Japanese and Chinese labour 21
  Pearl Shell and Bêche-de-Mer Fishery Act 1881 18, 19
  post–World War I 38
Bennett, Arnold, QC 157
  comments on tourism 180, 182
  witnesses, questioning 169–70, 172, 173–4, 182–3, 185
Bennett, George 15, 19
Bennett, Isobel 99

Bingil Bay 65, 66, 87–8, 105, 111
birdlife
    bird protection 22, 34–5
    early twentieth century ornithologists 21–2
    feral cats, protection from 35
    muttonbirds 35
    Native Bird Protection Act 1905 24
    nutmeg pigeon *see* nutmeg pigeon
    sanctuaries, creation 24
    shooting 12, 22, 35
Bjelke-Petersen, Joh 98, 107–8, 119, 120
    see also Queensland government; royal
      commission into oil drilling in the Reef
    black ban, response to 132
    GBRMPA and 194–5
    GBRRAC conference 136–40
    pro-oil position, criticisms about
      134–5, 148, 149
Bowen 12
Bowen, James 31, 56, 116–17, 194
Bowen, Margarita 31, 56, 194
Bowen Shire Council 120
Breaksea Spit 4
Broad Sound 59
Brook Islands 24
Bunker Group 6, 12, 59
Burdekin 84
Büsst, Alison 87
Büsst, John 65, 66, 67, 82, 87, 96
    Ampol-JAPEX drilling proposal 121, 122
    black ban 141
    Ellison lime mining application 87, 88–9,
      90, 91–2, 105
    Ladd report 108
    moratorium on oil drilling movement
      109–15
    royal commission into oil drilling 142–3

Cairns 6, 10
    Chamber of Commerce 96
    turtle industry 64
Cairns City Council
    1922–1924 Dabuukji (Green Island) mining
      lease 33
Cairns Naturalists Society 89
Camm, Ron 74–5, 88, 91, 93, 94, 198
    conditions on permits, imposing 137
    deputy premier 107
    Ellison decision 104, 105, 106
    moratorium on oil drilling movement
      109, 115
    Repulse Bay drilling 118–19
Cape Grenville 12
Cape Melville 59
Cape York xvii, 3, 4
Capricorn Group 12, 29, 59
    deep oil prospect wells 60
Capricornian 12

Cardwell 11, 12, 15
Carson, Rachel 99
    Silent Spring 65
Chalk, Gordon 70, 95, 102
Charles Eaton 2
Charters Towers 11, 14
charting the Reef
    Beaufort, Francis 5
    Blackwood, Francis 4–5
    Cook and Flinders 1, 3, 4, 10, 80
    King, Phillip Parker 4
    marking of safe channels 5
    Stanley, Owen 5
Chinese fishing vessels 94, 95
Chipp, Don 96
Chisholm, Alec 24
clams, giant 76–7
Clare, Patricia 66, 82, 131
    Struggle for the Great Barrier Reef 68, 86–7
climate change xvii, 80, 201, 206, 207
    see also coral bleaching
    anthropogenic xix, 203
    culture wars about 83
    deniers xvi
    inaction on, governmental 203
    moral contingencies 85
    One Nation 125
    Reef as symbol of national heritage xvii
    Reef management and 201, 207
    Reef Restoration and Adaption Program
      (RRAP) 201–2
coal mining
    expansion xi
    search for coal 58
    value of 210
coastal development
    water quality, decline in 80, 81, 85, 201
Commonwealth government
    approval of oil exploration permits xiii
    decision not to approve future permits 115
    moratorium on oil drilling movement 110–15
    sovereignty over offshore oil 190, 193, 198,
      199
    sovereignty over Reef, proposal for 110, 113,
      114, 118
Connell, Dr Joseph 169, 170
Connolly, P.D., QC 157–8, 159, 171–2,
    183–4
'controlled exploitation of the Reef'
    APEA position 174
    GBRC positions 101–2, 174, 185
    Ladd report 108
    Queensland government position 114, 173,
      174
    Reef conservation and 173–4
    WPSQ rejection of 143
*Convention on the Territorial Sea and Contiguous
    Zone 1958* 154

Cook, Captain James 1, 2–3
  channels in and out of the Reef, locating 3, 10
  charting 80
  description of Reef 7
Cooktown 27
Coombs, H.C. 178–9, 181, 191
Coonanglebah (Dunk Island) 22, 24, 25
  ferry service 54
  First Nations people 44–6
  nutmeg pigeons 23, 24
coral
  coral loss since 1985 200
  coral polyps 8, 32, 129
  foot traffic over 73
  growth rates and water quality 80
  licence required to collect 73
  over-collection of 50, 51, 52, 68, 72–3
  prohibition on collection 52, 54–5, 56, 78–9
  recolonisation 171, 182
  sale of collected coral 53
coral bleaching xix, 82, 201
  2016 mass event 124, 127, 163
  2017 mass event 124, 163
  2020 mass event 163
  2022, forecast of mass event 210
  Cape York xvii
  increased water temperatures 124, 203
  mass bleaching events 124, 210
  media reports 124–5
  sunscreen and 203, 204, 205
coral gravels, collection of 60–1
coral IVF 203, 205–6
coral mining xiii, 14, 15, 33–4, 35
coral reef science xv
  see also Reef science
coral reefs
  coral, collection and sale 1, 50, 51, 52, 68,
    72–3
  decline 82
  dredge spoil 82
  restoration projects 201–6
  vulnerability to increased ocean temperatures
    xvii, xix
Coral Sea 4
  1860 survey of 5–6
Country Party 55, 106 141, 142
crown-of-thorns starfish (Acanthaster planci)
  1940s emergence of 69
  1960s plague 69–72, 79
  2016 and 2018 Commonwealth funding 126
  AMPTO assistance in control 126
  cause, theories as to 95, 97
  conservationists and 100
  control method 126
  coral, destruction of 69
  Endean publicity 96–100, 125–6
  giant triton shell, removal 95, 97
  impact on attitudes to Reef protection 72

  lack of scientific knowledge about 70, 71–2
  physical removal 70
  recolonisation of coral 171, 182
cruises
  Whitsunday Passage 13, 25–6
CSIRO 66, 87, 113, 162
cyclones 164, 171, 182, 201

Dabuukji (Green Island) 25, 69
  1870s, holiday/picnic visits 11
  1922 coral mining lease 33–4
  1924 resort application 34
  1930s guided tours 39
  coral and shell removal, damage caused by 68
  crown-of-thorns starfish plague 69–71, 79,
    96–7, 171
  marine park, declaration as 195
  nutmeg pigeons 23
  underwater observatory 54, 69, 97
Dakin, William 51
Darwin, Charles 8, 14, 58
Daydream Island 54
Deemer, Adrian 141, 143
Deloitte Access Economics 210
Denham, Henry 5–6
diversity of Reef life xii, 9, 14, 180, 183,
  195, 205
dugongs 15, 24, 200
Dunk Island see Coonanglebah (Dunk Island)

economic development of Reef 26–7, 61
  1960s 73–6, 76–7, 78–9
  Ladd report, government use of 107
  nineteenth and early twentieth centuries xii,
    6, 14–16, 31–2
  post-war period xii
  underutilisation, belief in 1930s 39
Eden, Charles 11–12, 15
Ellison Reef 86
  application to mine lime xiii, 86–7
  conservationists, responses to 86, 87–8
  decision 105
  hearing of application 86
  lessons conservationists learnt 92
  media articles 90–1
  objections 89
  personal attendance required for
    submissions 90
  QLS surveys 90–1, 111
  scientific expertise, use of 93
  tourism, seen as main loser 89
  warden's recommendation 91–2
Embury, Monty 31, 32
  Hayman Island, development 29
  Reef expeditions 29–30
Endean, Robert
  crown-of-thorns and 71, 95–6, 98–9, 125–6
  Ellison Reef and 89, 90, 100, 101, 105

Endean, Robert *continued*
  perceptions of 99–100
  publicity 96–9, 125–6
Endeavour 1, 2, 3
Endeavour Reef 1
Endeavour River 11
environmentalism xiv–xv
  see also Reef conservation; 'Save the Reef'
    campaign
  1950s and 1960s global emergence of 65
  Australian organisations, emergence 65–7
  broad membership 67

Family Islands 11–12, 15, 24, 54
farmers
  land management practices 81–2, 85
  regulatory oversight 83, 84
  water-quality improvement, poor results
    83, 84
Fauna Protection Act 1952 56
Fenton, Arthur 89, 101, 105
ferry services 54, 208
fertiliser run-off 81
First Nation peoples
  care and attention of environment 45
  cultural continuity 48
  dance of the rising ocean 42
  dispossession of Country 43
  exploitation for labour 43, 44
  forcible relocation 43
  formation of the Reef story 42
  interactions with the Reef xiii
  management of Reef 47, 48
  massacres 44
  Reef as traditional Country xii, 48
  scientific expeditions, labour in 47
  tourism 46–7
Fish and Oyster Act 36, 52, 56
  green turtles, taking 63
Fisheries Act 1952–1966
  extension of sovereignty over fisheries 94
fisheries rangers 73
fishing industry 74
  fish stocks 200
  yellow-fin tuna 74
Fitzroy Island *see* Koba (Fitzroy Island)
Flinders, Matthew 3–4
  charting 80
  descriptions of Reef 7
  naming the Reef 4
Fly 4, 6, 8
Forbes, Donald 86–7, 88
Forestry Amendment Act 1971 196
fossil fuel use 164, 204, 205
Frankland Group 10
Fraser, Malcolm 199
Fraser Island *see* K'gari (Fraser Island)

geological origins of the Reef 8
  glacial event 42
  subsidence theory 8, 14, 58
  volcanic upheaval 14
geological resources of the Reef 59–61, 64
geological surveys 58
Georges, George 131, 141
Gimuy-walubarra Yidi people 42
glass-bottomed boats 37, 71, 97
Goold Island 54
Gorton, John 107, 110, 111, 119, 121, 132–3,
  142, 150, 153, 155, 159, 160
    GBRRAC conference 136–9
  royal commission into oil drilling 152, 157
Grassle, J. Fred 108, 182–3
Great Barrier Reef
  beauty of, interest in 6–8, 9, 12–13
  charting *see* charting the Reef
  conservation *see* Reef conservation
  destroyers of 33
  economic function 1, 2
  economic value 210
  human disturbances, impacts xvi, 78, 81–2
  Indo-Pacific oceanic system, as part of 85
  inner route 3, 4, 5, 6
  length xix
  loss of, measuring 210–11
  naming 4
  outer route 4–5
  outer wall 2, 3, 32
  politicisation of 163, 166–7
  Reef catchment area 80
  scientific interest in 8–9, 14, 21, 26–9
  sovereignty of, legal position 117
  stakeholders, diversity of xx, 84
  The Great Barrier Reef film 50
  threats to 200–1
Great Barrier Reef Committee (GBRC)
  change of position on geological exploitation
    105, 114, 145–6
  'controlled exploitation', positions on 101–2,
    112, 174, 185
  disbanding of, calls for 105
  economic resources, discovery 28
  economic value of Reef 29
  Ellison lime mining application 89–90, 92,
    100, 185
  establishment 27
  geological exploitation, position on 49, 59,
    89–90, 101, 112
  geology v biology 56–7, 146
  Heron Island research station 57, 58
  management authority for Reef, proposal
    147, 184
  marine biology 57
  moratorium on oil drilling, call for 107,
    109
  NPA, relationship with 40

oil companies and 49, 101, 116
oil drilling and 185, 186
proposed agreement for inquiry into oil
    drilling 144–5
Reef research body, as 27, 31
Great Barrier Reef Foundation (GBRF) 161–2
    government grants to 162, 163, 164, 201
Great Barrier Reef Marine Park Act 1974 190,
    197
Great Barrier Reef Marine Park Authority
    (GBRMPA) 162, 207
    depoliticise the Reef, as attempt to 167
    establishment xiii, xviii, 189, 190, 199
    management area 80
    Mather's proposal to royal commission
        186–8, 200
    members 194
    outlook reports 163
    Queensland government and 194–5, 198–9
    role in the future xix
    Senate assent 198
Great Barrier Reef Resources Advisory
    Committee (GBRRAC) 186
    1970 Canberra conference 136–40
    Commonwealth inaction as to 133
    establishment 102–3
Great Keppel Island *see* Woppaburra
    (Great Keppel Island)
Green Island *see* Dabuukji (Green Island)
guano mining 12, 14, 33

Hawkesworth, John 3
Hayles Magnetic Islands Pty Ltd 70
Hayman Island
    Ansett ownership 54
    Embury development 29
    sanctuary, declaration as 31
Herald 5
Heron Island 35, 40, 51, 52, 72, 171
    flying boat link to Brisbane 53
    marine park, declaration as 195
Heron Island research station 57, 64
    funding 58
    work to be conducted 58
Hewitt, Bill 93
Hiley, Thomas 73
Hill, Dorothy 118, 145
    *The Geology of the Great Barrier Reef in
    Relation to Oil Potential* 59
Hinchinbrook Island *see* Pouandai
    (Hinchinbrook Island)
Hixson Cay 59
Holt, Harold 66, 110
Hook Island 52
Housewives Concerning the Protection of the
    Barrier Reef 119
Houston, John 93, 141
Hughes, Terry 124, 125, 203, 204

Humanist Society of Queensland 120
hydrography 5, 6

industrial waste 78
Innisfail xiii, 90
    WPSQ branch 65, 92, 105, 116
International Union for Conservation of Nature
    (IUCN) 125, 163, 164

James Cook University (JCU) 89, 124, 165–6
JAPEX
    black ban xiii, 131–2, 135, 141
    compensation from Queensland government,
        request 137, 148–51
    Repulse Bay drilling proposal 118–19,
        120–22
Jeffrey, P.J., QC 158, 175–6
Jiigurru (Lizard Island) xix
    marine park, declaration as 195
    peak 3, 10
John Brewer Reef 129
Johnstone Chamber of Commerce 89
Johnstone Shire Council 89
Jones, Owen Arthur 72, 73, 77, 174
Jukes, Joseph Beete 8–9, 12, 14
    Cook, comments about 11

Keppel Bay Shell Club 95–6
K'gari (Fraser Island) 4, 99
Kikkawa, Jiro 112
King, Phillip Parker 4, 6, 10
Koba (Fitzroy Island) 6, 52
Kumboola Island 24

Ladd, Harry 104, 118
    survey 106–7
Ladd report
    conservationists response 108
    'controlled exploitation' 108
    government adoption of 107, 108
    oil drilling, support for 108, 109
land-clearing practices 82
Langford Reef 129
lime deposits, abundance 14, 15
limestone mining 88
    1922, Dabuukji (Green Island) 33–4
    Ellison Reef, on *see* Ellison Reef
    fertiliser, for 33, 88
Lindeman Island *see* Yara-kimba (Lindeman
    Island)
Lippiatt & Co. 156, 157
Lizard Island *see* Jiigurru (Lizard Island)
Lockhart River 3
Long Island 59
Low Isles
    1928–29 scientific expedition to 31, 47, 76
    research facility, closure during Depression 56

McCalman, Iain xiii, 6, 112, 116, 190
MacGillivray, John 6, 10
MacGillivray, William 22, 31
Mackay 7, 64, 75
McKenzie, Col 124, 125
McMahon, William 155
McMichael, Donald 90, 91, 199
   'The Future of the Reef' 77, 78
McNeill, Frank
   turtle preservation campaign 63
   'Wealth in Coral Gravels' 60, 61
Magnetic Island *see* Yunbenun
   (Magnetic Island)
management authority for Reef
   ACF call for 185
   GBRC proposal 147, 184, 186–8
   Mather proposition 186–8
marine biologists 31, 146
   marine geologists and, schism between 146
marine debris, threats from 201
marine parks
   see also Great Barrier Reef Marine Park
      Authority (GBRMPA)
   oil drilling not prohibited 196
   Queensland government declarations as
      to 196
marine research
   government funding, reliance on 57
   stations *see* research stations
   vessels xix
marine scientists *see also* Reef science
   Australian-educated, 1920s and 1930s 57
   climate change, limitations imposed by xx
   conservationists, divide with 112
   expeditions *see* research expeditions
   interference from employers 166
   'Save the Reef' campaign, contribution xv
marine sculptures 129
Mather, Dr Patricia 99, 114, 144, 175, 185–6,
   200, 207
   management authority and legislation,
      proposal 186–8, 200, 207
Maxwell, William 118
Mission Beach 82, 88
Molle Islands 31
Monkman, Kitty 68
Monkman, Noel 68
Moorhouse, Frank 31, 37
Moreton Bay 5, 15, 61, 106
Moroney, V.J. 151, 152, 155, 191, 192
Morrill, James 44
Mound Island *see* Purtaboi (Mound Island) 24
Musgrave Island 35
muttonbirds 35

Napier, Sydney Elliott 32, 35, 37, 39
Nathan, Sir Matthew 28, 29
national parks 25, 53, 56

National Parks Act 55–6
National Parks Association of Queensland
   (NPAQ) 40, 51
   calls for a single Reef National Park 55–6
   proposal for three marine parks 104
National Tertiary Education Union 166
Native Bird Protection Act 1905 24
Navigator 119, 131, 150
Nicklin, Frank 59–60, 100, 101
North Queensland Naturalists Club 64
   guided tours 39
North West Island 29, 35, 52, 59
nutmeg pigeon 12, 22–3
   protection of 23, 24
   sanctuaries, creation 24
   shooting 12, 22, 45
   vulnerable, identification as 22

Obama, Barack xvii
Ocean Siren sculpture 123, 124, 129, 130
ocean temperatures
   coral bleaching 124, 203
   coral reefs, vulnerability to higher xix
   expected continued rise to 2050 201
   increased xvii, 72, 82
   lower 33
Oceanic Grandeur oil leak 153–4, 176
oil companies 49, 77, 89, 101, 116, 121,
   137–9, 142, 156–7, 171
oil exploration
   Commonwealth government subsidy
      system 59
   exploratory borings 59
   moratorium on drilling, calls for 109–14
   permits xiii
   Petroleum (Submerged Lands) Bill 1967
      93–4
   pollution risks from 78, 110, 132, 171,
      175–6, 179, 182, 191
   Queensland land under prospecting titles
      59–60
oil reserves, offshore
   Commonwealth sovereignty over 190, 193,
      198
   High Court challenges to Commonwealth
      claim 190, 193, 199
One Tree Island xix, 173
ornithologists 21, 22, 23, 24
Oyster Cay mining lease 33, 35

Pabaju (Albany Island) 15
Pacific Ocean 3
'Pacificise' Reef, attempts to 48
Palm Islands 12
   Bwgcolman Aboriginal reserve 43, 46
Pan-Pacific Science Congress 1923 28
passive habitat protection 202, 204
pastoral industry 2, 26, 75

Patterson, Rex 75–6
Pearl Shell and Bêche-de-Mer Fishery Act 1881
  18, 19
pearl shell fishery 1, 17–18, 27, 28
  cultivation, encouragement of 18–19
  debates about 20
  depletion of 18, 38
  Indigenous labour 38
  innovation of techniques 18
  Japanese and Chinese labour 21
  Japanese divers 21
  post–World War I 38
  royal commissions about 20–1
  size limits 18–19
  value of industry, decrease 18
Pearson, Robert 71, 98
Peel Island *see* Teerk Roo Ra (Peel Island)
Pelletier, Narcisse 44
People the North Committee 109
Percy Islands 7
pesticide run-off 78, 95
petroleum
  exploration permits 60, 114
  offshore concessions 74–5
  pollution risks from 78
  prospect permits 60
  reserves xiii
  royal commission into petroleum
    drilling 104
Petroleum (Submerged Lands) Act 1967 110,
  114, 115
  validity of 118, 121, 190
Petroleum (Submerged Lands) Bill 1967 93–4
Piesse, Dick 115, 170, 184–5
Pizzey, Jack 55, 101, 102
plastic drinking straws 204, 205
Plymouth Marine Biological Laboratory 31
Pocock, Celmara 37, 46
Pollock, E.F. 29, 30, 31
pollution 78, 189
  marine debris 84, 202
  oil drilling, risk of 78, 110, 132, 171, 175–6,
    179, 182, 191
  tourism operators, created by 82
Port Douglas 31
port expansion xi, 82
Potts, Donald 99
Pouandai (Hinchinbrook Island) 12, 25, 52, 54
Providential Channel 3
Purtaboi (Mound Island) 24

Queensland Conservation Council 196
Queensland Department of Harbours and
  Marine 71, 89, 92, 102, 105
Queensland Department of Mines 89, 92, 102,
  105, 108
  royal commission into oil drilling 158,
    170, 184

Queensland Department of Primary Industries,
  Fishery Branch
  crown-of-thorns starfish 70
Queensland Geographical Journal 26
Queensland government
  1928 scientific expedition funding 31
  1950 prohibition on taking green turtles and
    their eggs 63
  1958 recession of ban on taking green
    turtles 63–4
  area controlled by after Commonwealth
    sovereignty assertion 194
  catchment management policies 82–4
  deferral of granting future mining
    permits 115
  economic benefits of Reef, interest in 14–15
  GBRMPA creation and 194–5, 198–9
  marine parks other than GBRMPA, creation
    of 195
  offshore petroleum concessions, granting 74–5
  oil exploration permits, approval xiii, 60
  petroleum exploration permits, approval 60
  report of royal commission, response to
    197–8
  Repulse Bay drilling 118–19, 120–22, 133–6
  royal commission *see* royal commission into
    oil drilling in the Reef
Queensland Government Mining Journal 170
Queensland Government Tourist Bureau
  (QGTB) 25–6
  advertising 39
  establishment 25
  promotion of 26
Queensland Littoral Society (QLS) 66, 96, 106
  Ellison Reef 89, 90–1, 92
  moratorium on oil drilling movement
    109–14
  petition against Reef geological
    exploitation 111
  WPSQ, unity with 112
Queensland-Papuan continental shelf 59
Queensland Rail service 30
Queensland Tourist Development Board
  (QTDB)
  1947 report 52
  identification of islands for further
    development 52
  land tenure, recommendations as to 52
  shell and coral collection 52, 53

railway
  Charters Towers-Townsville link 14
  coastal rail link, 1927 25
Raine Island 5
  oil exploratory bore 59
  turtles, nesting 63
rainforests 66
Ratcliffe, Francis 67, 113

Rattlesnake 5, 6, 10
Reclus, Élisée 12
Reef catchment area 80
  fertiliser run-off 81
  government catchment management
    policies 82–4
  land clearing 82
  land management practices by farmers 81–2
  management area, included in 80
  sediment run-off 33, 81, 82
  urban land use 81
  water-quality improvement, poor results
    83, 84
Reef conservation
  ACF symposium, rifts caused by 116
  bird preservation 24
  Commonwealth government, proposal it
    take control of Reef 110–11
  coral IVF 203, 205–6
  early forms xv, 50
  honorary protectors 53
  localised xv, 64
  mineral and petroleum industries, forming
    of 64
  moratorium on oil drilling movement
    109–14
  no single way 207
  passive habitat protection 202, 204
  pre–World War II, no sustained
    movement 41
  report of royal commission 192
  Repulse Bay drilling proposal 119–22
  restoration and rehabilitation projects 201–4
  scientific community, divide with 112
  shell and coral collection, prohibition 52,
    54–5, 56
  tourism development, impacts 64
  WPSQ 65–6, 87
Reef ecosystem
  imbalance in 72, 77, 96, 187, 204
Reef environmentalism xviii
  see also Reef conservation; 'Save the Reef'
    campaign
  Australian organisations, emergence 65–7
  broad membership 67
'Reef language' xvi–xvii
Reef Restoration and Adaption Program
  (RRAP) 201–2
Reef restoration/rehabilitation projects
  critics of 201–4
  proponents of 204–6
  temporal bridge, as 205
Reef science
  1928–29 Low Isles expedition 31, 47
  advocates for the environment, as 167–8
  'climate conspiracy', accusations of xvi
  coral reef biology 202
  coral reef geology 201–2

politicisation of xvi, 164, 165
quality assurances, criticism of 165
restoration scientists 204–5
Repulse Bay drilling proposal 118–19, 120–22
  black ban xiii, 131–3, 135, 136
  JAPEX request for compensation 149–51
research expeditions
  1928 29, 30, 31, 32, 47
  economic potential, into 32
  First Nations peoples, labour used in 47
research stations xix
  biology research station, call for 27, 28
  calls for permanent 25, 56
  Heron Island 57, 58
  makeshift 30
  Richard Island 54
Richards, Henry Caselli 27–8, 40
  biology research station, call for 27, 28
Ridd, Peter 165–6
Rockingham Bay 12
Romano, Jack 88
Roughley, Theodore 32, 35, 36
  US lecture tour 1945–46 50
  Wonders of the Great Barrier Reef 32, 39
Royal Australian Ornithological Union
  (RAOU) 22
  Emu 24
  nutmeg pigeon, efforts to protect 23, 24
royal commission into oil drilling in the Reef
  adversarial nature of 169–72
  agreement for 138–40
  animosity between pro- and anti-drilling
    parties 169
  benefits of drilling, possible 177
  candidates for 151–3
  commissioners 155
  commissioners, differing conclusions 191,
    192
  Commonwealth funding of conservationists
    159–60
  conservationists, divisions among 145, 157
  conservationists financing witnesses 142,
    143, 157
  conservationists lobbying for funds 158
  controlled exploitation *see* 'controlled
    exploitation of the Reef'
  disadvantages of drilling, potential 177–8,
    181–2
  findings, overshadowing 190
  lack of knowledge, acknowledgement of
    174–5, 188–9
  management authority proposal 186–8
  oil industry practice, evidence as to 176
  Queensland government, position 173, 182
  report 191–4
  resilience of Reef, government assertions as
    to 182
  terms of reference 155–6

tourism industry, evidence about 179–81
uniqueness of Reef, government questioning 182–4
witnesses, aggressive questioning of 169–72
Royal Geographical Society of Australia (Queensland) 26, 28, 29, 33
    Great Barrier Reef Committee (GBRC) 27
Royal Zoological Society of New South Wales 29

sanctuaries
    1905 declaration 24
    1932 declaration 31
    animals and birds, for 24, 31
    high-tide mark, protection to 56
Santa Barbara oil leak 114, 151, 153, 176, 179
Sapp, Jan 99
'Save the Reef' campaign xiii, xviii, 49, 65
    see also royal commission into oil drilling in the Great Barrier Reef
    beginning of Reef conservation, as xiv–xv
    broad membership 67
    car stickers 111
    Ellison Reef lime mining application see Ellison Reef
    marine scientists' contribution xv
    moratorium on oil drilling movement 109–14
    petition against Reef geological exploitation 111
    Repulse Bay drilling proposal 119–22
Save the Reef Committee (STRC) 119
Saville-Kent, William 27, 31, 167
    commissioner of fisheries role 18, 19
    The Great Barrier Reef: Its Products and Potentialities 20, 26
scuba diving xv, 37, 69, 202
sea routes
    inner route 3, 4, 5, 6
    outer route 4–5
    secure 3
    South-East Asian markets, to 4, 5
Seas and Submerged Lands Act 1973 193
Seas and Submerged Lands Bill 1973 193
Seas and Submerged Lands case 190, 193, 198
    High Court decision 199
sediment run-off 33, 81, 82
Senate Select Committee on Off-shore Petroleum Resources 114
Serventy, Vincent 69
shark fishing industry 1, 20, 39
shells
    giant triton shell, removal 95, 97
    licence required to collect 73
    over-collection of shells and coral 50, 51, 52, 68, 72–3
    prohibition on collection 52, 54–5, 56, 78–9
    sale of collected shells 53

Sherrington, Doug 93–4, 131
shipwrecks 2–5, 44
'silencing of science' 166
Sinclair, John 98
Smith, Dr Eric H. 151, 155, 191, 192
    Torrey Canyon disaster 156
'snorkel diplomacy' 164
snorkelling 37
Society for the Prevention of Cruelty to Animals 33
Somerset 15
Spender, Percy 117, 155
sponges 27–8
Stanley, Owen 5
steam ships 5, 11, 13, 14
Steer, Molly 204
Stirling Castle 2
Stoddart, David 175
Stokes, John Lort 7–8, 10
Strachan, John
    'A Cruise along the Great Barrier Reef' 12, 13
Straw No More project 204
sugar industry 75
sunscreen and coral bleaching 203, 204, 205
Swain Reefs 59, 104, 106

Talbot, Frank 116, 173–4
Teerk Roo Ra (Peel Island) 195
Thompson, Barbara 44
Thursday Island see Waiben (Thursday Island) 17
Torres Strait 2, 4, 106
    sea route to South-East Asian markets, as 4, 5
Torres Strait passage 3
tourism xii, 25
    1930–1939 advertising, increases in 39
    1939, lack of infrastructure 40
    1955, lack of infrastructure 55
    1967 expansion plans 78
    1967, lack of infrastructure 75–6
    big game fishing 29
    Bureau see Queensland Government Tourist Bureau (QGTB)
    destruction caused by 40
    early operators 14
    economic importance of 179–80
    employment in 123
    First Nations peoples, role in development 46–7
    international tourists 128–9
    interstate and Queensland tourists 50
    late 1800s, recreational visits 11–13, 16
    marine sculptures 129
    oil spill, potential impacts on industry 179–80
    over-collection of shells and coral 50, 51, 52
    post–World War II 49

tourism *continued*
  Reef rehabilitation, work in 129
  responsible users of the Reef 128
  size and value of Reef tourism 123
  tourist expeditions, 1920s and 1930s 29–31
  United States servicemen, marketing aimed
    at 50–1
Townsville 7, 11, 22, 40, 44
  Charters Towers rail link 14
  ferries from 54
  Ocean Siren sculpture 123, 124, 129, 130
  port expansion 82
  The Strand 123
Townsville and District Natural History
  Society 64
trade unions
  Ampol-JAPEX drilling, response to 120
  black ban xiii, 131–3, 147
  conservations response to black ban 141–2
Transport Workers Union
  black ban xiii, 131–3, 147
trochus fishery 1, 21, 27, 28, 31, 38, 69
  Japanese and Chinese labour 21
turtles 6, 12, 35–7, 200
  1932 protection measures 36–7, 63
  1950 prohibition on taking green turtles and
    their eggs 63
  1958 recession of prohibition on taking
    turtles 63–4
  export of green turtles to Britain 62
  killing 35, 36
  late 1950s revival of turtle industry 64
  preservation efforts 36–7, 62–3
  protests about slaughter of 50, 62
  turtle canning 29, 35, 37
  turtle riding 37
  turtle shell as resource 27, 28

UN climate change report 2016 163
University College of Townsville 87, 89, 106,
  108
University of Queensland (UQ) 31, 57, 66, 71,
  89, 103, 105, 112
Upolu Reef mining lease 33, 35
US National Oceanic and Atmospheric
  Administration (NOAA) 210

Veron, Charlie
  *A Reef in Time: The Great Barrier Reef from
    Beginning to End* xiv
Vlasoff, Vince 69–70, 97

Waiben (Thursday Island) 17
Wain, Barry 90–1, 111
Walkabout magazine 37, 39, 72
Wallace, Sir Gordon 151, 155, 159, 176,
  187, 191
water contamination 33

water quality decline
  impacts on Reef 80, 81, 85, 201
Webb, Len 66
whaling 6
Whitlam, Gough 111, 190, 194, 195, 197,
  198, 199
Whitlam government
  Great Barrier Reef Marine Park Act 1974 190
  sovereignty over offshore oil, claim 190, 193
Whitsunday Islands 52
  flying boat link to Brisbane 53
Whitsunday Passage 13–14
  cruise, 1915 promotion of 25–6
Wide Bay 15
Wildlife Preservation Society of Queensland
  (WPSQ) 65
  Dabuukji (Green Island), damage to 68
  Ellison lime mining application 87, 90, 92
  geological exploitation, formal rejection of
    any form 143
  Innisfail branch 65, 105
  marine park, call for 68
  moratorium on oil drilling movement
    110–14
  petition against Reef geological
    exploitation 111
  'preservationist' 144
  QLS, unity with 112
  report of royal commission 192
Wildlife Protection Society of Australia 157
Wistari Reefs 195
Woodhead, Peter 171
Woods, J.T. 170–1
Woodward, A.E. 152, 169, 176, 183
Woppaburra (Great Keppel Island) 125
World Heritage Listing xix, 163
World Life Research Institute 187
World Wildlife Preservation Fund 89
Wreck Island
  deep oil prospect wells 60, 77
Wreck Reef 4
Wright, Judith 65, 179, 181
  Ampol-JAPEX drilling proposal 122
  black ban 132, 141
  Ellison lime mining application 87, 90–1
  GBRC, scepticism of 145
  moratorium on oil drilling movement
    113–14, 116
  royal commission into oil drilling 144, 145,
    156, 157, 158–9
  The Coral Battleground xiv, 67, 68, 78, 100,
    142, 144, 190
Wulgurukaba people 44, 123

Yara-kimba (Lindeman Island) 29
Yarrabah mission 46, 47
Yeppoon 59
Yongala 84

Yonge, Charles Maurice 31, 32, 36, 38, 167
  Low Isles expedition 47
Yunbenun (Magnetic Island) 7, 25, 44, 82,
  123, 208
    1870s, holiday/picnic visits 11
    hotels, roads and jetties 14, 40
    post–World War II tourism 54

9 780702 265754